What Your Colleagues Are Sayii

Reading is language, on the same plane as talking and writing. Yet in our pursuit of improving students' comprehension, we sometimes neglect to include enough "talk" and "write" in our instructional plans, fearing we don't have the minutes in the day or the magic to ensure productive discourse about texts. But we actually lose progress with this omission, for when students write and talk about what they read we are asking them to dig and think even more deeply about the text than what would happen with reading alone. Laura Robb understands just what teachers need to get the read-talk-write synergy going in their classrooms, and has done a masterful job of providing us with insight and guidance into making these important connections work for all texts. The result of *Read, Talk, Write* will be more highly engaged students and deeper levels of comprehension.

—TIMOTHY RASINSKI
Literacy Consultant and Author of *The Fluent Reader*
Kent State University

In *Read, Talk, Write*, Laura Robb helps both novice and experienced teachers create a curriculum of rich conversations that can enhance any reading instructional model. She includes practical resources such as model lessons, checklists, planning guides, and supports for English learners. Reading this book felt like I was at a common planning meeting with Laura and we were mapping out student conversation lessons together. What is especially helpful are her clear explanations of not just what to teach students, but how the different types of student conversations benefit readers, allowing teachers to choose talk structures that match the students right now.

—GRAVITY GOLDBERG
Literacy Consultant and Author of
Mindsets and Moves: Strategies That Help Readers Take Charge

Noticing and naming are crux moves of literacy. Talk and the words we use matter. Talk makes a big difference to reading, composing and learning, as well as to human agency. How talk develops strategic reading and comprehension, and how it supports composing of all kinds, has been a somewhat neglected topic in both the research realm and in the realm of practical pedagogies. To fill the gap, here comes Laura Robb with *Read, Talk, Write*. Laura Robb is a great-hearted teacher and person, and in this book she carefully guides all of us who teach how to use specific kinds of procedures and language to develop student engagement, literacies, agency and independent capacity more robustly.

—JEFFREY D. WILHELM
Author of *Diving Deep Into Nonfiction:
Transferable Tools for Reading ANY Nonfiction Text*
Distinguished Professor of English Education
Boise State University

Read, Talk, Write offers teachers and students a magical tapestry of collaborative thinking and learning around texts. Laura Robb gently, and with great expertise, weaves reading, writing, listening, and speaking into thought-provoking routines. Teachers are going to love the easy-to-follow suggestions for prompts, lessons, and beautiful mentor texts. This highly practical resource brings the famous "easy button" to the world of text response!

—LINDA HOYT
Literacy Consultant and Author of the *Crafting Nonfiction* Series
and the *Explorations in Nonfiction Writing* Series

Read

TALK

WRITE

In memory of Patrick Daley, a creative and innovative force in education

Read TALK WRITE

35 Lessons That Teach Students to Analyze Fiction and Nonfiction

LAURA ROBB

Foreword by Harvey "Smokey" Daniels

http://resources.corwin.com/readtalkwrite

CORWIN LITERACY

FOR INFORMATION:

Corwin

A SAGE Company

2455 Teller Road

Thousand Oaks, California 91320

(800) 233-9936

www.corwin.com

SAGE Publications Ltd.

1 Oliver's Yard

55 City Road

London EC1Y 1SP

United Kingdom

SAGE Publications India Pvt. Ltd.

B 1/I 1 Mohan Cooperative Industrial Area

Mathura Road, New Delhi 110 044

India

SAGE Publications Asia-Pacific Pte. Ltd.

3 Church Street

#10-04 Samsung Hub

Singapore 049483

Publisher: Lisa Luedeke

Editor: Wendy Murray

Editorial Development Manager: Julie Nemer

Editorial Assistant: Nicole Shade

Production Editor: Melanie Birdsall

Copy Editor: Sarah J. Duffy

Typesetter: C&M Digitals (P) Ltd.

Proofreader: Caryne Brown

Indexer: Sue Nedrow

Cover Designer: Scott Van Atta

Marketing Manager: Rebecca Eaton

Printed in Great Britain by Bell & Bain Ltd, Glasgow

Library of Congress Cataloging-in-Publication Data

Names: Robb, Laura, author.

Title: Read, talk, write : 35 lessons that teach students to analyze fiction and nonfiction / Laura Robb ; foreword by Harvey "Smokey" Daniels.

Description: Thousand Oaks, California : Corwin, 2017. | Includes bibliographical references and index.

Identifiers: LCCN 2016021878 | ISBN 9781506339573 (pbk. : alk. paper)

Subjects: LCSH: Reading comprehension—Study and teaching (Elementary) | Discussion—Study and teaching (Elementary) | English language—Composition and exercises—Study and teaching (Elementary) | Language arts (Elementary)

Classification: LCC LB1573.7 .R62 2017 | DDC 372.47—dc23 LC record available at https://lccn.loc.gov/2016021878

This book is printed on acid-free paper.

18 19 20 10 9 8 7 6 5 4 3

Contents

Chapter 3. Lessons That Build Comprehension Skills in Any Genre   62

Reproducible Fiction and Nonfiction Texts

Aim 2. Teach Students to Read, Talk, and Write About Fiction   121

Chapter 4. Taking the Plunge: How to Talk and Write About Fiction   122

Chapter 5. Going Deeper: How to Analyze Literary Elements

Aim 3. Teach Students to Read, Talk, and Write About Nonfiction

Chapter 6. Taking the Plunge: How to Talk and Write About Nonfiction

Visit the companion website at
http://resources.corwin.com/readtalkwrite
for downloadable resources.

Reproducibles for Teachers and Students

 Reproducibles are available for download at
http://resources.corwin.com/readtalkwrite

Chapter 4

Chapter 5

Chapter 6

Chapter 7

Foreword

Laura Robb is a national treasure, and this book is the latest gift from her seemingly infinite trove of instructional innovations.

For decades, we have understood *in principle* that kids need to talk about their reading. But *in practice,* we have been slower to develop a broad repertoire of classroom structures that stimulate, facilitate, guide, and assess that kind of abundant, intelligent talk. Laura Robb to the rescue once more!

Read, Talk, Write: 35 Lessons That Teach Students to Analyze Fiction and Nonfiction begins as Laura classifies literate student talk into six sensible categories (and opportunities).

- Turn-and-Talk
- Whole-Class Discussions
- Partner Talk
- Small-Group Discussions
- In-the-Head Conversations
- Teacher–Student Discussions

Clearly, kid conversation is not confined to literature circles anymore! Laura gives each talk type a detailed definition, clearly delineating one from the next and offering highly practical tips and materials for teaching each. Then, she launches us into a gold mine of 35 lessons that make all six kinds of conversations doable—and delightful.

Laura understands that vigorous conversations can occur only in a classroom (indeed, a school) culture of safety, trust, empathy, and respect. In other words, before we can expect students to engage deeply in challenging literary conversations, we must explicitly teach them the discussion (and social) skills they need all along the way. (And Laura's not shy about giving us specific solutions for kids who don't do the reading, don't speak up, interrupt others, or hog the airtime in groups.) Step 1, as Laura consistently points out, is *teachers modeling* how they think, read, discuss, and write before expecting kids to do so. We can't leave students to guess what we mean when we send them off to "have a debate" about two challenging poems or three opposing articles.

Laura is all over the reading-writing connection; no surprise, given her previous work. As she reminds us, "The research on the importance of writing and its correlation to reading comprehension suggests that the request for more writing time at school is a clarion call. However, the kinds and amounts of authentic writing about reading that students do at school needs to be reevaluated and revised." Too much of students' current writing practice remains in the genre "tell the teacher the right answer." This duty writing, a small step above filling in blanks, does not offer students enough responsibility and ownership to work hard and take risks. Steering clear of such drone work, Laura shows us how to move kids from out-loud conversations with peers to written conversations with themselves, building their capacity to go metacognitive with their textual analyses.

All the lessons in the book are fleshed out and enlivened by reading selections that already are—or will soon become—student favorites. Laura draws on classic novels we all have in our schools: *The Giver, Shiloh, Bud, Not Buddy, Finding Freedom,* and others. Specially written shorter pieces by Seymour Simon, Kathleen Krull, Sandra Athans, Priscilla Cummings, and Anina Robb fill out the roster of engaging text. Keep your eye peeled for the especially endearing short story "Hoops Tryouts."

As Laura closes this special book, we are reminded why she continues to be such an important voice in our field: She looks through kids' eyes and sees into their futures. Literary conversations don't just enrich kids' days with us; they offer young people gifts that keep on giving: the ability to take risks, exercise creativity, build empathy, and develop the ability to negotiate.

And Laura Robb trusts teachers. "You are the key to developing highly literate students," she says. "By bringing rich and meaningful talk into your classroom, you give students daily opportunities to clarify what they do and don't understand about a lesson or text. Equally important is the energy and intensity for exchanging ideas that occur during literary conversations as, together, students journey toward deeper understandings of texts they read and view."

Laura, thanks again!

Harvey "Smokey" Daniels
Santa Fe, NM

Acknowledgments

Deepest thanks to Paul Green, fourth-grade teacher at Powhatan School. Both Paul and his students helped me test ideas for student-led literary conversations. My sincere thanks to Louise Jaffe, sixth-grade teacher at Powhatan School, and Katy Schain, seventh-grade teacher at Daniel Morgan Middle School, for letting me learn with their students. I truly appreciate the support of Deb DePalma, curriculum coordinator, as well as fourth-grade teachers Jean Hoyt and Sarah Amesbury, who teach at Discovery Charter School, in Rochester, New York. All three spent several telephone calls conferring with me about in-the-head conversations and bookmarks.

My sincere thanks to Gretchen Bernabei, who championed the idea for this book and pointed me in the right direction for designing short, focused lessons so that teachers of every experience level could engage in the read, talk, write process.

To my editor, Joanna Davis-Swing, my heartfelt thanks for always supporting and encouraging me, for all of her exceptional suggestions, and for enjoying the project as much as I did. To Wendy Murray, my appreciation for her vision of what this book could become and for her unflagging faith in my work.

To the Corwin Literacy team: I predict that educators everywhere will become more and more grateful for the work they do on behalf of children.

Aim 1

Introduce Students to Six Types of Comprehension-Building Conversations

CHAPTER 1

Talking About Texts

Getting Started

When I teach or coach in classrooms in various parts of the United States, I have noticed that talk and collaboration among students has decreased in the last few years, while the use of workbooks and skill-and-drill activities seems on the rise. The pressure schools are under to do well on high-stakes tests may be largely to blame, because the worksheets I see on kids' desks and going home as homework often fall under the umbrella of test prep activities. Alas, we are spinning our wheels and wasting precious time bowing down to the tests, for a recent study of 66 urban schools found no correlation between the time students spend taking tests and improved reading scores (Superville, 2015). In fact, the results of the 2015 National Assessment of Educational Progress (NAEP), the nation's report card, show that scores in reading have dropped in Grades 4 and 8 (Heitin, 2015).

To me, lower scores in reading are the canary in the coal mine, warning us of a more pervasive issue: More students are disengaged with reading.

So how do we turn things around? Well, there are about hundred answers I could give, but for this book I've chosen one, just one, because right now I think it's the easiest and most powerful platform on which to rebuild our students' relationship with reading.

Talk.

Really? You might be thinking that there can be nothing new to say about instructional conversations. After all, two types of talk, literature circles and book clubs, thankfully have a placehold in many schools (Daniels, 2002)—but not in enough schools, and in this digital age and test prep craze, it's critical that we make sure our students know how to talk to learn, and do so every day. Some research has shown that teachers talk a full 80% of the school day; our goal has to be to reach a 50–50 split and then work to make it so that student talk predominates.

Lessons and Texts to Take Students From Talk to Literary Conversation

I remember the time as a young teacher I told a group of my fifth graders to "talk about Chapter 4" in a novel they were reading and thought that was sufficient direction. I *heard* the folly of my ways within 5 minutes, in the form of animated chatter about sports, lunch, and a favorite new game! Learning-rich conversation about books has to be modeled and practiced—a lot. So in this book, we begin with ready-made lessons that provide students with models of six different types of literary talk. What they have in common is that they allow you to step out of the conversation so that students can get good at guiding it. Tech-savvy students who "talk" continually on social media want to be in charge of their literary conversations online and at school. And that's just what these lessons help you accomplish.

I've also included original pieces and excerpts by authors whose work students know and admire, including Kathleen Krull, Seymour Simon, and Priscilla Cummings. You can use them repeatedly for your own instructional purposes, beyond this book.

A section called "Reflect and Intervene" equips you with on-the-spot scaffolding tools. And you don't have to design assessments; they're in every lesson and include reproducibles for students and checklists that are reminders of what you heard and observed.

Yes, talk matters, especially when student talk becomes a literary conversation. With time and practice, these conversations develop and improve analytical and critical thinking and ultimately ramp up students' reading comprehension, helping them become the critical readers and thinkers they need to be.

Five Benefits of Student-Centered Talk

Our students love to talk, and they arrive at school with talking experience and expertise. A powerful form of thinking and communicating, talk also brings social interactions to learning. The kind of talk I'm proposing for students to engage in is literary conversations. Conversations are literary when the talk is about high-quality fiction or nonfiction and powerful movie and video clips. Such texts draw students into familiar and unfamiliar worlds that can spark emotional reactions and prompt them to think about themselves and others. Such texts have multiple interpretations, and the literary and personal experiences a reader brings to a text start an original conversation between the reader and the text. These conversations initiate deep thinking about characters, people, plot, conflicts, and information (Rosenblatt, 1978).

My hope is to build on these literary conversations between readers and texts by inviting students to have similar conversations with a partner, a small group, and the entire class. To illustrate the benefits of bringing literary conversations to your classroom, I have identified five key reasons for integrating this student-centered approach into daily lessons.

Benefit 1: Talk Supports Recall and Comprehension

As a reading or content teacher, you know that students' ability to recall plot and text details is the key to using this information to infer and identify main ideas and themes—in other words, to engage in analytical and critical thinking. If your students are like mine, then you also know that this kind of thinking poses a challenge to many students. The good news is that during literary conversations, students must organize and present their ideas in ways that listeners can understand and follow. You can teach listeners how to ask questions that prompt speakers to clarify and extend ideas and provide evidence from the text. In this way, students support one another as they apply strategies, analyze texts, and think through an idea or position. In addition, talk about text builds vocabulary, enlarges listening capacity, and exposes students to peers' divergent ideas and the stories peers use to think about and discuss texts (Newkirk, 2014)—all skills that facilitate comprehension of complex texts.

Benefit 2: Talk Engages and Motivates

We've all heard our students say things like "Yeah, that's what I was thinking" or "Man, I never thought about that person like you're doing" or "I gotta reread that part—I missed that idea." Such comments are indicators that students are engaged in the literary conversation, listening closely and comparing their ideas with peers' ideas. Participating in whole-class, small-group, and partner discussions gives students opportunities to interpret texts independently and explore questions they're interested in.

When students are in charge of *leading* discussions, when they use questions that *they* composed, and when you encourage them to explore a range of interpretations the text supports, the motivation to engage in these discussions is off the charts. Harvey "Smokey" Daniels (2002), in his book on literature circles, put it this way: "Working with our kids over weeks, and months, and years, I feel grounded in a new way. Now I will never underestimate what kids can do in peer-led groups, because I've seen what our students can accomplish" (p. 15).

Benefit 3: Interactive Talk Becomes a Model for In-the-Head Conversations

What does it mean to engage with a story? What does deep engagement really feel like? It's important to drill down into these often-used terms, because that's how we know exactly the kind of emotional state we want our students to achieve. Yes, emotional state. I want students to feel angry about a character's poor decisions and silently yell at the character. I want students to fall in and out of love, feel grief, frustration, fright, acute loneliness, profound joy—to be so involved with the characters' journey they can't stop reading. This happens when students can step into a character's or person's shoes, experience his or her life, and have conversations with themselves while reading. Robert Coles (1990) calls this being in "cahoots" with a character. The irony of the concept of getting lost in a novel is that the truth is, through narrative, we find ourselves. Someone once said, with informational texts we know how to live, but with fiction we know how to be.

Such a deep level of involvement can happen with nonfiction texts, too, as long as these texts use stories to present information (Newkirk, 2014). An important and reachable goal of teaching reading is to develop students' ability to have dialogues with themselves about a text they are reading. I call these "in-the-head" conversations.

As students participate in literary conversations in different settings, they cultivate the modes of thinking and the language needed to engage in internal conversations while reading, listening to, and viewing texts. Having conversations with oneself while reading is the heart of metacognition, which can improve visualization, recall, understanding, and critical analysis.

Benefit 4: Talk Activates Ideas for Writing About Reading

Throughout this book you will find guiding questions. These questions are like lighter fluid for student conversations, and the goal is to have them ignite students' *own* questions (see How to Craft Guiding Questions, page 9) and responses that delve into layers of meaning. View these discussions as a rehearsal for deeper independent thinking and writing about texts. We want our students to explore interpretations in a situation where peers support them as they test the validity of their ideas (Rosenblatt, 1978).

This rehearsal is like trying on five pairs of jeans until you find the right pair—no one criticizes the jeans that don't fit. You are in charge of deciding which to purchase. It's like this for students trying to find valid interpretations of texts. It works best in an environment that encourages students to try on interpretations without worrying if they're right or wrong. It encourages divergent thinking about a text and then invites students to further explore ideas that the text can support. Rehearsal—trying on ideas during discussions—can scaffold writing about a text and support students as they develop their ability to move from thinking through talk to thinking on paper.

Benefit 5: Talk Changes How Students Think and Feel About Fiction and Nonfiction

As students become more skilled at conversations, they move beyond recall of plot and information to critical analysis, making inferences, finding themes, and, most important, arriving at an interpretation of a text that "works" for them, and in a sense is tailor-made for them. In a very real sense, four students sitting at a table talking about the same novel will negotiate a shared understanding (almost like lawyers in an amicable negotiation!), but each person will stand up from that table with a take on the novel that is uniquely her or his own—and that's what we want. Writing in the By Heart series in *The Atlantic*, novelist Ethan Canin asserts, "At the end of a story or novel, you do not want the reader thinking. Endings are about emotion, and logic is emotion's enemy" (Fassler, 2016, para. 14).

Having multiple opportunities to develop their ideas helps students independently apply reading and thinking strategies as they work toward using stories to build knowledge that matters to them (Newkirk, 2014). To accomplish this, students can draw on other texts, personal experiences and stories, and their knowledge of genre to construct their understanding of a specific text or an issue raised by a guiding or essential question.

The Research Support

One of the most important thinkers and researchers on classroom talk is Peter H. Johnston, perhaps best known for his book *Choice Words* (2004). As you start the journey of integrating a range of talk into your classes, it's helpful to become familiar with Johnston's research because he shows how teacher talk affects students' learning. I highly recommend that you discuss Johnston's ideas and suggestions with colleagues so that as you make teaching and learning decisions, you can articulate how they relate to best practices.

By studying the language of accomplished literacy teachers, Johnston demonstrates how the words we speak to our students can affect them in positive and negative ways. Effective oral language can guide students to become strategic, analytical thinkers who use talk to solve problems.

As Johnston notes, the words that teachers speak in the classroom can position their students as competitors or collaborators. If our goal is to build a community of collaborators who can work together, supporting one another as they develop into expert readers, writers, speakers, and thinkers, then we need to pay attention to how our language fosters this type of culture in our classroom. In his book, Johnston provides myriad language prompts that teachers can use in diverse situations to create a healthy, positive environment while promoting rigorous learning. For example, a statement such as *I liked the way you figured that out* lets a student know that she did the thinking and work. Or pointing out what a child can do and building on it, with a statement such as *I see you know how to spell the beginning of that word,* confirms what the student can do but also sends the message that there's still work to be done. Many of the routines, prompts, and scaffolds in the lessons in this book are designed to encourage a classroom culture that supports risk-taking and collaboration and that puts students in charge of their talk to construct knowledge.

Johnston (2004) devotes a chapter to "Noticing and Naming," pointing out that "pattern recognition is very powerful. Once we start noticing certain things, it is difficult not to notice them again; the knowledge actually influences our perceptual systems (Harre & Gillet, 1994)" (p. 11). For students to become proficient at analyzing literary elements, they must first learn to recognize them. The lessons in Chapter 5 include prompts that guide students to notice and name various literary elements in the texts they read and discuss. With practice, identifying literary elements becomes second nature, which deepens readers' comprehension of narrative. Similarly, as students identify various text features and structures, they become more adept at analyzing informational texts.

The lessons, student pages, and intervention strategies in this book embed language that encourages students to notice and name what they see as they read.

Johnston also discusses the idea of agency, the belief that what we do affects our environment. For students to become independent readers, they must believe that they are capable of making meaning from text. Student talk, and especially literary conversations, can help foster this sense of agency by inviting students to work together to uncover an author's meaning.

As a means of encouraging students to dig into text, prompts in the lessons and student pages ask students to choose questions to explore, to apply reading strategies, to provide evidence for their thinking, to ask questions, and to consider the author's purpose.

Finally, Johnston highlights the importance of using language to facilitate transfer, the ability to generalize learning from one specific situation to a new one. To foster transfer, Johnston offers teachers phrases that encourage students to consider different contexts. Ask *How else . . .* to nudge students to think of diverse ways to solve a problem, or say *That's like . . .* to observe similarities in texts, words, or figurative language. Teaching for transfer means that students view learning as more than the set of information that makes up a specific lesson. Instead, they're keenly aware of the benefits of transferring strategies and processes practiced and learned in one context to different contexts. See http://resources.corwin.com/readtalkwrite for specific ideas on how to teach students to transfer their learning.

Coming Full Circle With Literature Circles

In 1994, with the first edition of his book *Literature Circles,* Harvey "Smokey" Daniels transformed the nature of student talk in the classroom by moving it from teacher-directed and teacher-controlled to peer-directed and peer-controlled. According to Daniels (2006), it all started in the 1980s, when "a number of teachers and students around the country simultaneously and independently invented the idea of literature circles. Pioneers like Becky Abraham Searle in Chicago and Karen Smith in Arizona began organizing their students into small, peer-led book discussion groups" (p. 10). Almost 20 years later, Daniels wrote a second edition of *Literature Circles,* and book clubs and literature circles have become a positive classroom experience for students in the United States as well as in Finland, Australia, and Canada.

Teaching Tip: Transfer

To foster students' growth into independent learners, teach them specifically about the idea of transfer.

- Introduce the idea of transfer in a mini-lesson, explaining why it's important to students' progress. To illustrate the concept, first review what students have practiced that you want them to transfer. Then demonstrate how the skill or knowledge works in different situations and subjects. Here's what I say to help students transfer the skill of comparing and contrasting, which they've practiced with literature, to other contexts.

   You've been comparing and contrasting settings, characters, and conflicts using my read-aloud text, Through My Eyes *by Ruby Bridges, and your instructional reading materials. The skill you've developed—finding how specific literary elements are alike and how they differ in a text—can be used in other situations. You can use compare and contrast to show how two different informational texts treat the same topic. You can also use it to evaluate two or more websites or two ways to solve the same math problem. Comparing and contrasting can also help you with life decisions that you make. For example, you can evaluate two summer camps this way to decide which one you'd rather attend. You can also use it when buying clothes to compare brands and/or styles before choosing one. It's a useful and practical strategy because it's helpful beyond school tasks.*

- Be explicit when showing students how they can transfer a skill discussed from your read-aloud text to a new situation. For example, if you point out and explain flashback in reading, show students how they could use that technique when writing a memoir or story. Help them see more generally that what they notice while reading can be used in their own writing.
- Have students share or debrief, and ask them to link what they are presently doing to a skill or strategy they previously learned. For example, one group of sixth-grade students pointed out that learning to evaluate websites in English class enabled them to choose websites that their teacher found acceptable for a research project in history.
- Provide time during guided practice with instructional materials and independent reading using self-selected books for students to practice a new skill so they have a depth of understanding that can result in transfer.
- Have conversations with students where they can showcase and explain transfers they've made first to you and then to classmates.

In today's data-driven climate, it's important to have research that proves the efficacy of peer-led literature circles. According to Daniels (2006), we can assess students' discussion skills through "teacher observations; forms that record kids' preparation, participation, specific comments, and levels of thinking" (p. 14). A study in 2001 by Davis, Resta, Davis, and Camacho, concluded that literature circles increased students' motivation to read, improved their performance on tests, and raised their reading levels.

In 2003, Applebee, Langer, Nystrand, and Gamoran published a study conducted in 64 middle and high school English classrooms. The results suggest that when students engaged in discussion-based approaches with high academic demands, students developed the skills to participate in and complete challenging literacy tasks independently.

Sixth grader Rick summed up some of the benefits perfectly: "If my group and I decide the guiding question, and use a book we chose and loved, then I can't wait to talk about it and see what friends think."

Types of Talk and How They Fit Into the Lessons

As you incorporate more purposeful talk into your classroom, think about the varying contexts in which it can occur:

- Turn-and-talk
- Whole-class discussions
- Partner talk
- Small-group discussions
- In-the-head discussions
- Teacher–student discussions

In the next chapter, I include detailed lessons for these six kinds of talk. They are in the order I recommend you try them, and they follow a framework that can deepen your knowledge of a specific kind of talk. I also offer guidelines for integrating student talk during the following:

- **Interactive mini-lessons:** Pause during your mini-lesson and ask students to turn-and-talk to discuss part of the lesson or respond to a question you pose.

- **Daily read-alouds:** As you read, pause once or twice and have students turn-and-talk to respond to a focused prompt.

- **Guided practice:** Students can use partner talk and turn-and-talk as they practice applying the lesson you've modeled using a focused prompt, a literary element, text features, or a comprehension strategy. Including talk during guided practice helps students clarify their thinking and analyze texts. You can wrap up guided practice with a short whole-class discussion and spark the conversations with a prompt or guiding question.

- **Independent practice:** Reserve time for students to partner talk or participate in a small-group discussion after independently completing books in the same genre. Students can use their books to discuss a guiding question the teacher provides (see How to Craft Guiding Questions below) or questions students have composed. These discussions provide opportunities for students to share and support interpretations as well as discuss how they transferred a skill they internalized during guided practice.

▶ **Teacher–student discussions:** As you meet with students in conferences, encourage them to discuss parts of a text that confuse and challenge them. By working with their teacher, students can move from dependence to independence with a task.

Initiating Talk With Questions and Prompts

Asking questions is a key part of any literary conversation and often serves to launch such a discussion. Teachers can pose a guiding question to focus inquiry for a unit of study. But students should also be taught how to ask thoughtful, open-ended questions to extend thinking about an idea, issue, or text as well as to clarify or respectfully challenge a classmate's thinking.

How to Craft Guiding Questions

A guiding question goes beyond text-specific questions and leads students into a discussion by inviting them to consider an issue that is enticing and complex enough to explore. Guiding questions go beyond one specific book and help students explore diverse materials to learn about a topic such as *What is survival?* (McTighe & Wiggins, 2013; Wilhelm, 2012). Here are tips for developing and determining the effectiveness of guiding questions:

▶ **Develop questions before a unit of study starts**, as the guiding question drives the thinking and talk during the unit and can be used as a springboard for inquiry, where students develop a series of questions related to the guiding question. For students to develop a guiding question for a unit, they'll need background knowledge of the topic. Whether the teacher or students develop the guiding question, it's helpful to ask students to use inquiry to generate additional queries. Students can start inquiring before the unit starts, and then throughout the unit questions will arise as students read and talk. For example, the theme of a unit of study for a sixth-grade class I worked with was *trust*. Students agreed on this guiding question: *What is trust?* Then inquiry enabled them to develop additional questions to investigate before and during reading, such as these: *Why is trust important to friendship? How does trust affect confidence? Explain why trust creates feelings of safety.*

▶ **Decide on the theme or concept you want students to explore**, such as survival, obstacles, or stereotyping. Use your theme to compose a question that can't be answered in a sentence or two. Instead, a guiding question has a variety of interpretations and can be supported by several different texts. For example, one class I worked with was reading different biographies, and the teacher chose the theme of obstacles. Her guiding question was *How do obstacles affect the course of a person's life?*

▶ **Avoid editorializing in your questions**. For example, *Why is it stupid to stereotype groups?* limits student thinking about the topic. Instead, make questions short, clear, and open-ended. For example, *Why is stereotyping unjust?*

Lessons at a Glance

TALK STRUCTURE	GROUP FORMAT	TIME	GREAT FOR	CHECK OUT THESE LESSONS
Turn-and-Talk	Partners	2–4 minutes	• Building background knowledge • Applying a strategy during read-alouds • Thinking about a literary element or technique during read-alouds • Processing mini-lesson topics • Analyzing a text feature or structure	• Chapter 2, Lesson 2.1: Turn-and-Talk, page 27 • Chapter 2, Lesson in Action: Turn-and-Talk, page 29 • Chapter 3, Lesson 3.1: Inferring With Informational Text, page 72 • Chapter 4, Model Lesson: The Importance of Inferring: "Snow Day" by Priscilla Cummings, page 133 • Chapter 5, Lesson 5.5: Compare and Contrast Notes, page 174 • Chapter 5, Model Lesson 5.5: Teaching Compare and Contrast Notes: "How Athens Got Its Name" Retelling by Joanna Davis-Swing, page 176
Whole-Class Discussions	Whole class	5–30 minutes	• Exploring guiding or interpretive questions • Analyzing text(s) • Comparing and contrasting multiple texts • Sharing ideas after partner talk	• Chapter 2, Lesson 2.2: Whole-Class Discussions, page 32 • Chapter 2, Lesson in Action: Whole-Class Discussions, page 34 • Chapter 3, Lesson 3.2: Exploring Interpretative Questions: Biography, page 74 • Chapter 5, Lesson 5.2: Conflict, Plot, and Setting, page 154 • Chapter 5, Model Lesson 5.2: Teaching Conflict, Plot, and Setting: "Coming Clean" by Anina Robb, page 156 • Chapter 7, Lesson 7.2: Thinking About Issues: Obstacles, page 205 • Chapter 7, Model Lesson 7.2: Teaching About Obstacles: "How Ada Lovelace Leaped Into History" by Kathleen Krull, page 210 • Chapter 7, Lesson 7.3: Teaching the Problem-Solution Text Structure, page 212 • Chapter 7, Model Lesson 7.3: Teaching Problem-Solution: "New Horizons in Space" by Seymour Simon, page 216 • Chapter 7, Lesson 7.5: Identifying Main Ideas, page 224 • Chapter 7, Model Lesson 7.5a: Teaching Explicitly Stated Main Ideas: "Who Climbs Everest?" (Excerpt From *Tales From the Top of the World*) by Sandra Athans, page 229 • Chapter 7, Model Lesson 7.5b: Teaching How to Infer Main Ideas: "Defying Gravity: Mae Jemison" by Anina Robb, page 231
Partner Talk	Partners	5–20 minutes	• Applying mini-lesson topics • Developing guiding questions • Developing interpretive questions • Exploring guided or interpretive questions • Applying reading strategies • Analyzing literary elements and techniques • Analyzing text features and structures • Discussing the gist • Summarizing texts	• Chapter 1, How to Teach Students to Compose Interpretive Questions, page 12 • Chapter 2, Lesson 2.3: Partner Talk, page 38 • Chapter 2, Lesson in Action: Partner Talk, page 40 • Chapter 3, Lesson 3.1: Inferring With Informational Text, page 72 • Chapter 3, Lesson 3.2: Exploring Interpretative Questions: Biography, page 74 • Chapter 3, Lesson 3.3: Determining the Author's Purpose: Informational Text, page 76 • Chapter 4, Model Lesson: The Importance of Inferring: "Snow Day" by Priscilla Cummings, page 133 • Chapter 5, Lesson 5.2: Conflict, Plot, and Setting, page 154 • Chapter 5, Model Lesson 5.2: Teaching Conflict, Plot, and Setting: "Coming Clean" by Anina Robb, page 156 • Chapter 5, Lesson 5.3: Identifying Themes, page 161 • Chapter 5, Model Lesson 5.3: Teaching Theme: "Snow Day" by Priscilla Cummings, page 163 • Chapter 5, Lesson 5.4: Planning and Writing a Summary: Fiction, page 166 • Chapter 5, Model Lesson 5.4: Teaching Summary: Fiction: "Hoops Tryouts" by Anina Robb, page 168 • Chapter 5, Lesson 5.5: Compare and Contrast Notes, page 174

TALK STRUCTURE	GROUP FORMAT	TIME	GREAT FOR	CHECK OUT THESE LESSONS
Partner Talk (cont.)	Partners	5–20 minutes	• Applying mini-lesson topics • Developing guiding questions • Developing interpretive questions • Exploring guided or interpretive questions • Applying reading strategies • Analyzing literary elements and techniques • Analyzing text features and structures • Discussing the gist • Summarizing texts	• Chapter 5, Model Lesson 5.5: Teaching Compare and Contrast Notes: "How Athens Got Its Name" Retelling by Joanna Davis-Swing, page 176 • Chapter 6, Lesson 6.1: Mining Text Features for Information, page 186 • Chapter 6, Lesson 6.2: Teaching Text Structures, page 189 • Chapter 7, Lesson 7.1: Taking Heading Notes and Finding a Main Idea, page 198 • Chapter 7, Model Lesson 7.1: Taking Heading Notes and Finding a Main Idea: "Who Climbs Everest?" (Excerpt From *Tales From the Top of the World*) by Sandra Athans, page 203 • Chapter 7, Lesson 7.3: Teaching the Problem-Solution Text Structure, page 212 • Chapter 7, Model Lesson 7.3: Teaching Problem-Solution: "New Horizons in Space" by Seymour Simon, page 216 • Chapter 7, Lesson 7.4: Personality Traits and a Person's Achievements: Biography, page 218 • Chapter 7, Model Lesson 7.4: Teaching Personality Traits: "Defying Gravity: Mae Jemison" by Anina Robb and "Isaac Newton and the Day He Discovered the Rainbow" by Kathleen Krull, page 222 • Chapter 7, Lesson 7.5: Identifying Main Ideas, page 224 • Chapter 7, Model Lesson 7.5a: Teaching Explicitly Stated Main Ideas: "Who Climbs Everest?" (Excerpt From *Tales From the Top of the World*) by Sandra Athans, page 229 • Chapter 7, Model Lesson 7.5b: Teaching How to Infer Main Ideas: "Defying Gravity: Mae Jemison" by Anina Robb, page 231
Small-Group Discussions	3–8 students	10–30 minutes	• Exploring guiding or interpretive questions • Writing interpretive questions • Applying reading strategies • Analyzing literary elements and techniques • Analyzing text features and structures	• Chapter 1, How to Use the Fishbowl Technique, page 18 • Chapter 2, Lesson 2.4: Small-Group Discussions, page 45 • Chapter 2, Lesson in Action: Small-Group Discussions, page 47 • Chapter 3, Lesson 3.4: Why Characters Change: Small-Group Discussion Using a Short Story, page 78 • Chapter 5, Lesson 5.1: Protagonist and Antagonists, page 142 • Chapter 5, Model Lesson 5.1: Teaching Protagonist and Antagonists: "Hoops Tryouts" by Anina Robb, page 144 • Chapter 5, Lesson 5.3: Identifying Themes, page 161 • Chapter 5, Model Lesson 5.3: Teaching Theme: "Snow Day" by Priscilla Cummings, page 163
In-the-Head Conversations	Individual	5–15 minutes	• Monitoring comprehension • Applying reading strategies • Analyzing literary elements and techniques • Analyzing text structure and text features • Thinking about the gist	• Chapter 2, Lesson 2.5: In-the-Head Conversations, page 51 • Chapter 2, Lesson in Action: In-the-Head Conversations, page 53 • Chapter 3, Lesson 3.5: Prompting In-the-Head Conversations: Biography, page 80
Teacher–Student Discussions	Teacher and student	2–3 minutes for desk side conversations 5 minutes for a conference	• Scaffolding reading strategies, summarizing skills, literary elements and techniques, text structures and features • Modeling strategies and skills • Setting goals • Discussing assessments	• Chapter 2, Lesson 2.6: Teacher–Student Discussions, page 58 • Chapter 2, Lesson in Action: Teacher–Student Discussions, page 60 • Chapter 3, Lesson 3.6: Teacher–Student Talk: Conferring, page 82

> ❏ **Test your questions to make sure that each one has more than one valid answer** to ensure that it requires students to do high-level analytical thinking. Once you develop a knack for composing guiding questions, teach students the process so groups can devise and investigate their own. Here are research-based criteria to share with your students (Wilhelm, 2012). The question should

> ○ Compel students to think and talk right now

> ○ Cause students to talk, debate, agree, and disagree as they use the guiding questions to build understanding and a knowledge base

> ○ Ask students to study, learn, research, and talk about print and e-books, as well as the Internet, and conduct interviews that enable them to engage in a rich exploration of the guiding question

How to Teach Students to Compose Interpretive Questions

In addition to guided questions, students should raise and explore interpretive questions of their own during literary conversations. Research shows that students who are taught to generate their own questions after reading can develop a deeper understanding of the text than students who receive no training and practice (Pearson, Roehler, Dole, & Duffy, 1992; Robb, 2010; Rothstein & Santana, 2011; Zimmerman & Keene, 2007). The reason for enhanced comprehension is that to write text-specific interpretive questions, students must have a thorough knowledge of the reading material. Moreover, when students compose their questions, they are motivated to talk about them, leading to greater independence with reading and discussion.

Explain that there are two kinds of questions: open-ended, interpretative questions that have more than one answer and closed questions that have one correct answer. For example, an interpretative question for *The Giver* by Lois Lowry is *Why does the Giver encourage and help Jonas to escape the community?* A closed question is *Who does Jonas take with him when he leaves the community?*

Encourage students to write open-ended, high-level, interpretive questions after they've read a chunk of a novel or informational text or a complete short text. An interpretive question has more than one valid answer that can be supported with text evidence. I tell students that as soon as they can find two valid answers, they can think about composing another question.

Questions can be about literary elements, text features, themes, important information, and the author's point of view. Here are some verbs that usually signal open-ended questions: *analyze, examine, compare and contrast, evaluate, show, classify*. Once students can write open-ended questions with these verbs, have them read and discuss the verbs on the revised Bloom's taxonomy. You can use a search engine to access the taxonomy.

Making Student Talk Productive

In the coming chapters, you will notice that the teacher's role in student discussions is flexible, and while the teacher always is there to ensure that talk deepens comprehension, the goal is for students to be independent. For example, at first the teacher supports and respects students' thinking by jump-starting a discussion and then steps aside to observe and listen. While the teacher can become a co-participant in discussions, the students should take the lead (Adler & Rougle, 2005; Johnston, 2004; Wilhelm, 2007). When teachers embrace students leading discussions and see it as transformative for their student readers, it becomes a self-fulfilling prophecy as students are transformed by what they read as they understand it on a deep level (Coles, 1990; Paterson, 1989; Tyler, 2013; Wiggins, 2012).

Students will feel comfortable using questioning techniques before, during, and after reading if you have created a positive learning community where students trust you and their peers (Baca & Lent, 2010; Lent, 2007; Robb, 2010). Trust permits students to risk talking to a partner, a small group, or the entire class about ideas they've just begun to probe.

How to Build Trust

Building a community of learners starts the first day of school and continues throughout the year. Listening to and interacting with students sends the message that you're interested in what they like and dislike.

- Get to know each one of your students while they read or write independently by asking them to complete an interest inventory (see pages 14–15).

- Hold short, 4- to 5-minute conferences with students and use the survey as a conversation starter. Offer positive feedback and avoid being judgmental in order to let students know you value what they wrote.

- Provide opportunities for groups of 4 to talk about their interests, what they love to do during their spare time, and what they like and dislike.

- Recognize and celebrate cultural diversity and diverse learning styles. To create a safe community, adapt your lessons and curriculum to the wide range of needs in your class. Honor and respect the cultures in your class, and use this diversity as an opportunity to share ideas and life experiences. Often, engaging in literary discussions enables students to share family stories and life experiences. You can invite students to bring in a photograph that reveals something about their culture and discuss it with a partner or small group. You can also include in your units books and stories about diverse cultures.

- Abandon a one-size-fits-all curriculum and find materials for students reading below grade level that they can learn from and enjoy.

- Organize desks into groups of 4 to 6, and as units change, change where students sit so they can learn from and with different students.

- Encourage students to take risks with developing interpretations of texts. However, doing this will definitely raise the need for adjusting and refining ideas, and that's okay, because this is part of the analytical thinking process.

- Support the developing literacy skills of English language learners (see suggestions in each lesson).

For an in-depth look at creating a community of motivated learners, read *Building a Community of Self-Motivated Learners: Strategies to Help Students Thrive in Schools and Beyond,* by Larry Ferlazzo, Routledge, 2015.

Interest Inventory

Name _____ Date _____

Directions: Respond to the prompts on this handout.

What are your favorite . . . ?

Books

_____

_____

Comics

_____

_____

Magazines

_____

_____

Authors

_____

_____

School Subjects

_____

_____

Movies

_____

_____

Television Programs

_____

_____

Music

_____

_____

(Continued)

(Continued)

Sports

_____

_____

Hobbies

_____

_____

Afterschool Activities

_____

_____

Weekend Activities

_____

_____

Social Media

_____

_____

Foods

_____

_____

Electronic Games

_____

_____

If you could travel anywhere, where would you go? Explain why.

_____

_____

 Available for download at **http://resources.corwin.com/readtalkwrite**

How to Help Students Initiate Discussion

If students have little to no past experiences with leading and sustaining a literary conversation, you'll have to scaffold the process so they can talk independent of your orchestrating the discussion. I've provided a handout you can use as a starting point for preparing students for literary conversations: Guidelines for Discussion (see page 17). Before your first discussion, give each student a copy and walk through it, highlighting what students should do:

> ◗ Come to the discussion prepared. Complete the reading assignment, and bring the text, reader's notebook, and a pencil.
>
> ◗ Collaborate with peers to compose open-ended questions about the text (if not using a teacher-assigned guiding question).
>
> ◗ Choose a moderator, whose job is to keep the discussion moving forward. (There is a list of prompts the moderator can use on Prompts That Keep a Discussion Moving Forward, page 25.)
>
> ◗ Participate in the discussion, being respectful of others, listening carefully, asking questions to help a speaker clarify an idea, and citing text evidence to support points.

Here are some suggestions for gradually moving students to independent literary conversations:

> ◗ Start with the turn-and-talk strategy (see Lesson 2.1 in Chapter 2 on pages 27–28) so students have brief talking encounters and can experience sharing, questioning, and listening. Use the prompts in the lessons or your own.
>
> ◗ Move to a whole-class discussion and motivate talk with a guiding question or an open-ended question; encourage a student to volunteer to start the discussion. Tell students that they don't have to raise their hands, but they can participate by adding thoughts or asking questions once the student speaking has finished.
>
> ◗ Debrief after the first whole-class discussion and ask students to reflect on what worked and what could be improved.
>
> ◗ Invite students to design guidelines for productive discussions. Revisit the guidelines after 2 to 3 months so students can make adjustments based on experience. Here are the guidelines fifth-grade students developed early in the school year:

   Come prepared; do the reading; bring your notebook.

Continue using turn-and-talk to give students the experience of sharing ideas with and listening carefully to a partner. If students have difficulty maintaining a conversation, you can provide the Ways to Contribute to a Discussion section of the Guidelines for Discussion handout (also available at http://resources.corwin.com/readtalkwrite).

How to Teach Students to Listen Actively

In order to become active listeners during discussions, students benefit from having multiple opportunities each week to talk with a partner, a small group, and the whole class. All participants should listen actively during discussions, but this doesn't come

Guidelines for Discussion

Name _____ Date _____

- Come to the discussion prepared. Complete the reading assignment, and bring the text, your smart notebook, and a pencil.

- Collaborate with peers to compose open-ended questions about the text (if not using a teacher-assigned guiding question).

- Choose a moderator, whose job is to keep the discussion moving forward.

- Participate in the discussion, being respectful of others, listening carefully, asking questions to help a speaker clarify an idea, and citing text evidence to support your points and inferences.

Ways to Contribute to a Discussion

- **Restate the speaker's idea.** If you would like to clarify an idea a classmate suggested, restate it in your own words and ask if that was the intended meaning. You can use phrases such as I heard you say < >. Does that sound about right?

- **Ask a question.** If you would like the speaker to elaborate on or clarify his or her thinking, or if you're curious about a speaker's take on a related issue, ask a question. Can you say more about < >? / I'm not sure what you meant when you said < >. Can you help me understand? / What do you think about < >?

- **Connect to the speaker's idea.** You can build on a speaker's idea by first connecting to it. I like the point you made about < >, and I have this to add. / I had a similar idea.

- **Offer a different view.** You can honor a speaker's contribution and then share your own perspective in a respectful way. I hear what you're saying about < >. I had a different thought when I read that part. / I have a different perspective on that scene.

- **Disagree respectfully.** Sometimes you will disagree with classmates, and that's fine as long as you can state your disagreement respectfully. Here are some prompts that can help you respectfully disagree: I didn't see it that way. Instead, I think < >. / I don't agree; I think it means < > because < >.

- **Refer to the text.** Always refer to the text to support your ideas and thinking during discussions. You can use these prompts to show you will be providing text evidence: When it says < >, I infer < > because < >. / Let's take a look at this description; it says a lot about the protagonist.

··

naturally to most students. Take some time to define active listening, discuss why it's important, and model it for students. Tell them that when someone else is talking, listeners should

> Keep focused on what the speaker is saying

> Set aside any distracting thoughts that arise

> Not think about what to say in response

Listeners may jot notes to help them remember what the speaker said, but the focus should be on understanding the ideas the speaker is conveying first, rather than formulating their own ideas.

How to Use the Fishbowl Technique

The fishbowl permits students to observe a partner or small-group literary conversation (Fisher, Brozo, Frey, & Ivey, 2007). The students who will discuss sit in a circle while the rest of the class forms a circle of observers and listeners around them. Set aside about 15 minutes for the discussion and about 10 minutes for debriefing.

Guidelines for Implementing the Fishbowl Technique

> Use a prompt or guiding question that has more than one possible answer and relates to a text all students have heard or read. I suggest using a read-aloud that you completed.

> Set up the room with an inner circle of four to six chairs, or two chairs if it's a discussion between partners. Chairs are for the students who will discuss the text.

> Establish a purpose or goal for students in the outer circle to observe. Choose from these options: considering the role of moderator, asking high-level questions, listening carefully, or responding positively to the remarks of others.

> Review discussion guidelines. Remind students that one person talks while others listen and that all participants should respond respectfully and use text evidence to support a point.

> Hold the discussion.

> Debrief the fishbowl discussion by asking students what they learned about the purpose or goal of the literary conversation. Require that students not refer to peers by name, but focus on the discussion. These reflections can support students' progress with meaningful discussions and provide you with topics for whole-class mini-lessons.

> Have students write their goals for the next small-group or whole-group discussion in their readers' notebooks. A reader's notebook is also an excellent place for students to document what they discussed and/or learned from a discussion.

How to Use Smart Notebooks

Smart notebooks are a spin-off of readers' notebooks and are indispensable for literary conversations. Students can use partner talk to generate ideas for small-group and whole-class discussions and then jot notes about the text to prepare for the discussion. Such preparation makes for "smarter" discussions as students clarify their thinking and pose questions they want the group to address. Smokey Daniels (2002) aptly explains: "This kind of writing is open-ended and personal; it invites kids to generate extended, original language, not to jot 'correct' phrases in response to workbook blanks" (p. 22).

After discussions, students can write a summary, a list of key points discussed, or a reflection of the discussion when it's finished. In this way, the smart notebook becomes a record of students' responses and reactions to their reading throughout the school year and can illustrate progress in thinking and writing fluency.

Of course, smart notebooks can be used for many other purposes as well. Writing in them regularly encourages students to construct their reading identities by recording hunches, theories, interpretations, and questions about texts they listen to and read as well as model lessons that you present. Smart notebooks can also include lists of books students have read and loved along with books they want to read.

Smart notebooks are safe places for readers to try out ideas, adjust or change the course of their thinking, or express anger toward a character or event. Fourth grader Jamal wrote this about Judd (a character in *Shiloh* by Phyllis Reynolds Naylor): "I hate you Judd. You're mean to Marty. You beat and kick and starve your dogs. Your heart is steel." At the end of the book, Jamal had an epiphany about Judd and his notebook entry reflected it: "I see why Judd was mean. He was treated mean and beaten and punished by his dad." Try to view notebook writing as an opportunity for students to discover what they think and know about a text. It's a place to try on and try out ideas that can and often do change as the story unfolds. It's not a place to look for correct responses or responses the teacher expects.

Use a marble-covered composition book as a notebook because the pages are sewn. If students tear out pages, the notebook falls apart, and I want students to keep every entry. Saving all notebook writing permits students to review entries and reflect on their progress. You can also make notebooks by stapling composition paper between two colored pieces of construction paper.

Additional Prompts for Documenting Discussions

Students can document their discussions in notebooks after groups experience a few practice discussions. This is especially helpful as during a class you can listen to one, at the most two, group discussions. If students have difficulty writing about their discussions, ask them to choose an open-ended query from this list:

- How did the discussion change your thinking?
- What new ideas did you learn from the discussion?
- Did you disagree with an interpretation? Explain.
- How did the discussion change or reinforce your feelings about a character, person, event, or information?
- Did students offer enough text evidence to convince you of an interpretation? Explain.
- Did the discussion raise questions? If so, what are they? Why are the questions important to deeper comprehension?

What's Ahead

In the next chapter, we turn to lessons for teaching six types of talk: turn-and-talk, whole-class discussions, partner talk, small-group discussions, in-the-head conversations, and teacher–student discussions.

Reflect on Your Teaching

▶ How much student talk are you including in your lessons?

▶ What kinds of talk will you integrate first? I suggest that you start with turn-and-talk and whole-class discussions as these prepare students for partner and small-group discussions. Once you're comfortable with these, you can introduce small-group discussions and partner talk.

▶ Why is it important to help students see the benefits of in-the-head conversations and have conversations with themselves when they read, watch videos and movies, and listen to texts?

Don't Miss Reading and Learning From: *Choice Words* by Peter Johnston, Stenhouse, 2004.

CHAPTER 2

Lessons for Teaching Six Types of Talk

In this chapter, I present lessons that demonstrate how to facilitate literary conversations. The first five lessons are in the order I recommend you introduce them to students. The sixth, which addresses teacher–student talk during conferences, can be scheduled as soon as you notice students need scaffolding. It's helpful if most of your students feel comfortable with one type of talk before introducing a new type. Note that turn-and-talk is the first type of talk introduced; it builds the basic skills students need to participate in literary conversations and can be woven into many lessons and activities.

How Literary Conversations Help Students

Longer discussions—as opposed to teachers posing questions to the whole class—help to show students that there isn't one correct interpretation of a text. Students learn to appreciate and become tolerant of the diverse ideas classmates present. In addition, students also learn to

- Agree or disagree with a partner in a respectful manner
- Refine and improve their use of academic language
- Be a contributing participant in the discussion
- Develop their own open-ended discussion questions
- Move from literal interpretations to critical analysis
- Value the interpretation of a partner even when disagreeing
- Use recall of details to support their thinking
- Learn how a peer processes and interprets information

Texts for Talk-Based Reading Lessons

Longer texts: In the lessons that follow, you will notice that I base them on six outstanding fiction and nonfiction books. The snapshots of student talk also make use of these works. Happily, the world abounds with excellent books, so if you don't use these titles in particular, no worries.

Short texts: Some lessons are built around short texts; I provide summaries of them to make it easier for you to know when to use them.

Fiction:

> **Grades 4–5:** *Riding Freedom* by Pam Munoz Ryan; *Shiloh* by Phyllis Reynolds Naylor
>
> **Grade 6:** *Bud, Not Buddy* by Christopher Paul Curtis
>
> **Grades 7–8:** *The Giver* by Lois Lowry

Nonfiction:

> **Grades 4–5:** *Through My Eyes* by Ruby Bridges
>
> **Grade 6:** *Drowned City: Hurricane Katrina and New Orleans*, a graphic informational book by Don Brown
>
> **Grades 7–8:** *Terrible Typhoid Mary* by Susan Campbell Bartoletti

These books provide concrete examples for talk, guiding questions, and a wide range of strategies, literary elements, and informational text features that this book addresses.

When to Use the Six Types

You can engage students in literary conversations in many ways throughout the day. Here are a few ideas to get you started.

During daily read-alouds: As you read aloud, you can pause to think aloud to model key discussion skills, such as asking a question or making an inference and providing text evidence to support it. You can also think aloud to model reading strategies and then invite students to turn-and-talk to evaluate your strategy use or practice it on another portion of text. Students can use a read-aloud text to participate in a whole-class discussion using a guiding question or a quote from the text.

To practice a strategy within a lesson: As you present lessons on reading strategies, literary elements and techniques, text features and structures, readers' notebooks, or writing conventions, incorporate talk to help students process your meaning and clarify their understanding. Turn-and-talk is ideal for this, but you can also use partner talk for longer conversations.

During instructional reading time: As students read texts at their instructional reading level, either for guided reading or during readers' workshop, engaging in partner talk with someone at their level can support their comprehension and expand their thinking. In addition, students reading the same text may participate in small-group discussions about their texts, perhaps in guided reading groups, literature circles, or book clubs.

To augment independent reading: Students can engage in partner talk and small-group discussions about their independent reading materials. Students can be reading the same book or different books within the same genre to have productive discussions.

In the midst of viewing videos: After students view these types of text, invite them to talk using turn-and-talk, partner talk, or small-group or whole-group discussions. Literary conversations allow students to analyze these visual texts and view them as literary experiences.

Tips for Managing Literary Conversations

The lessons on talk that are in this chapter can support students' learning in reading, English, and content classes. In addition, review the student handout that follows; it provides students with prompts they can use to maintain the flow of a discussion.

Offer Prompts That Keep a Discussion Moving Forward

I have provided a student handout that offers prompts students can use to maintain the flow of a discussion (page 25). These prompts can support students' ability to lead and participate in literary conversations independent of their teacher.

Be sure to review the handout with students first, giving each student a copy and explaining its purpose. Then refer to it as necessary during literary conversations.

Provide a Timeframe

Let students know how long they will have for their literary conversation. Turn-and-talk discussions last just a few minutes, while partner talk and small-group discussion may extend over several class periods. Establish a timeline that provides a deadline date for wrapping up extended discussions and specify what, if any, documentation they should complete, such as a journal entry or reproducible. On the chalkboard, list the due date, and each day partners or group members meet to discuss, remind them to use their class time well. Let students know that they need to tell you in advance if they can't meet a deadline. Negotiate extra time for students if they have been working hard every class.

Reflect and Intervene

As students talk, circulate among them and listen to and observe their conversations. Provide desk-side scaffolding for students who can benefit from a 2- to 3-minute intervention. Note the names of students who require more time to move to independence, and support them in 5-minute conferences and document these on the conference form (see page 26). You might need to schedule a few conferences for a student; do this over several classes. In addition, when planning a conference, have two to three scaffolds ready, so if one doesn't work, you have another at your fingertips to try. You'll find assessment and scaffolding ideas for each lesson in this book.

Set a Signal for Closing a Discussion

Once it's time to end a discussion, it's helpful to have a signal that informs students when the discussion will end, as this can help them bring closure that is satisfying. You can flick the classroom lights to get students' attention and say, "You have about 20 seconds to finish." Let students know how you plan to close the conversation and consistently use the same method. The last thing that you do is to share positive statements with students based on your observations of their talking. You can say something like *I noticed that everyone participated; I liked that careful listening; I noticed that you kept the discussions going; I heard different interpretations;* and so on.

Prompts That Keep a Discussion Moving Forward

- So we're supposed to [restate prompt].

- Does anyone have a different idea?

- Can you find evidence in the text that supports that?

- Is there more than one way to think about that?

- Can you explain that term?

- What points in the text support that claim?

- I'm unsure of your point. Can you clarify it?

- What made you say that? Can you give text evidence?

- Tell me more about that idea.

- Here's how I see that idea.

- Let's check the directions (or rubric).

- I agree with _____ but disagree with _____.

- Let's check that idea against the question we're discussing.

5-Minute Intervention Conference Form

Name _____ Date _____

Title and author of text used or topic:

_____

_____

_____

Scaffolds students used:

_____

_____

_____

Teacher's observations:

_____

_____

_____

Negotiated goal:

_____

_____

_____

Check one:

____ Next conference on _____

____ Work with a peer _____

____ Work independently

Turn-and-Talk

What It Is

Turn-and-talk is a 2- to 4-minute conversation between partners that the teacher initiates to engage students in exchanging ideas about a text or lesson.

How It Helps

- Engages every student in the lesson.
- Allows students to practice strategies, express ideas, and rehearse thinking prior to sharing with the whole class or writing in a notebook.
- Develops the ability to think quickly and generate ideas and hunches, hone their listening skills, and value other interpretations.

Introducing Turn-and Talk

▶ Tell students that turn-and-talk asks them to quickly share ideas with a partner.

▶ Help students understand that partners will alternate being the speaker and the listener and that both students should have equal talking time.

▶ Explain that sometimes you will assign partners, and sometimes students will simply turn to the student on the right.

▶ Teach students to use Prompts That Keep a Discussion Moving Forward (page 25, and available for download at http://resources.corwin.com/readtalkwrite) if they have difficulty getting started or continuing the conversation.

Prompts

▶ Say something about [a literary element, reading strategy, genre, etc.].

▶ Share an emotion [word, warning, theme, etc.] that the text raised.

▶ Explain why that information is a key idea or detail.

▶ Show how a detail connects to earlier (or later) parts of the text.

▶ Give evidence from the text that shows the motivation for a decision.

▶ Discuss x number of important ideas or details.

Variations

▶ To prepare students for in-the-head conversations, have them practice the turn-and-talk strategy with themselves alone using a book at their instructional reading level or an independent reading book (see Turn-and-Talk About Reading to Yourself, page 30).

Reflect and Intervene

If you notice students who aren't participating, try these scaffolds:

▶ Point students to the list of prompts on the reproducible on page 25, and ask partners to use them to get the conversation going.

▶ Jump-start a pair's discussion by repeating the prompt and starting the conversation. Stay with the pair until you observe both are participating.

(Continued)

(Continued)

> ❱ Plan short interventions, such as a 5-minute conference. If students need more than one conference, set up a series and hold one each day with the pair. The chart below can help you pinpoint a behavior and offers scaffolds to try.

STUDENT BEHAVIORS	POSSIBLE SCAFFOLDS
Little to no recall of lesson or read-aloud passage	• Students might need you to reteach the lesson. While teaching, ask questions that will help you determine the level of understanding. • Some students will need to hear the read-aloud passage twice in order to have recall.
Partners aren't comfortable working together	• Reassign partners before the next turn-and-talk.
Students feel their ideas aren't good enough to share	• Help everyone understand that you're not looking for correct answers, but for students to explore a range of ideas.

Assessing Turn-and-Talk

1. Have students summarize some of their conversations in readers' notebooks.

2. Use the reproducible Turn-and-Talk About Reading to Yourself (page 30).

3. Use the reproducible Self-Evaluation of the Turn-and-Talk Strategy (page 31).

Supporting English Language Learners

> ❱ Give clear and precise directions, and model what you want students to do.

> ❱ Explain that it's okay to make mistakes with word choices because you'll support them.

> ❱ Pair an English language learner (ELL) student with a fluent English-speaking student when the ELL student can comfortably use English to express ideas.

> ❱ Give lots of praise and additional practice.

Reproducibles

Turn-and-Talk About Reading to Yourself (page 30)

Self-Evaluation of the Turn-and-Talk Strategy (page 31)

Notes to Yourself About Teaching the Lesson

_____

_____

_____

_____

_____

Turn-and-Talk

LESSON IN ACTION

Preparing the Lesson

A primary purpose of this lesson is to help students understand that science fiction often warns readers about a shortcoming of our society by projecting that element far into the future. Understanding that science fiction can be a cautionary tale is important.

In "Eyes That Do More Than See," a short, short story by Isaac Asimov, my goal is for my eighth graders to understand Asimov's warning about people's desire for eternal life. Before reading the story out loud, I invite partners to turn-and-talk about the positives and pitfalls of eternal life. After students share ideas, I ask partners to set a purpose for reading. Here are three purposes that students suggested:

1. What does the title have to do with eternal life?

2. What are the pitfalls of having eternal life?

3. How did the idea of eternal life affect the characters?

I invite them to choose a purpose; then I read the story aloud.

Story Summary

It's hundreds of billions of years into the future, and men and women have given up their human forms in exchange for eternal life as energy beings. Two of these beings are Ames, who was once a man, and Brock, who was once a woman. Bored with the ongoing and seemingly endless attempts to find new ways to manipulate energy, Ames re-creates a human head by scraping matter from the universe. This ignites Brock's memories of her physical form and past life, with painful and powerful results.

My Turn-and-Talk Prompt

Share a warning about people's desire for eternal life.

Student Turn-and-Talk Exchange

Marina: A mind without a body and feelings isn't enough.

Michael: I agree. They're [the energy beings] bored. There's nothing new and it's forever. So what's the warming? [*Michael moves right to the prompt. But only after he and Marina have pinpointed an important theme.*]

Marina: I think the warning is don't ask to live forever. [*Notice how the conversation flows and each partner adds more details.*]

Michael: And think of what you give up.

Marina: Yeah. What you lose. Brock and Ames feel the pain. They lost eyes that see and show feelings and their bodies and senses.

Michael: I agree. They didn't see how great what they had was and gave it up. [*Michael points out the importance of thinking beyond what you wish for.*]

Marina: And they could never get it back. That's the big warning. [*Notice how each student's statement leads to a deeper and related idea by their partner.*]

These quick collaborations build fluency with reflecting and connecting details to figure out the warning.

Turn-and-Talk About Reading to Yourself

Name _____ Date _____

Purpose: To practice having an in-the-head conversation with yourself so you can use the strategy as you read any text and figure out how much you recall and understand.

Directions:

1. Write the title and author of your text. Choose a stopping point halfway through the text and note it below.

2. Read the text. At the stopping point, choose a prompt from the box. Take a few minutes to think about the prompt, much as you would when you turn-and-talk with a partner.

3. Repeat Step 2 at the end of the text.

4. Jot a list of the key details and ideas that resulted from your turn-and-talk.

Title: _____

Author: _____ Page: _____

Choose a prompt. If you create your own, write it in below and run it by your teacher for approval.

- Say something about a character, setting, or set of details.
- Connect the title to the text.
- Discuss a word the text raised in your mind and explain why.
- Show how a key detail connects to earlier parts of the text.
- Discuss x number of important ideas or details.

Write your ideas here.

_____

_____

_____

_____

_____

_____

Self-Evaluation of the Turn-and-Talk Strategy

Name _____ Date _____

Directions:

1. Turn-and-talk to your partner about how this strategy has helped you.

2. Read each prompt or question below, and answer each one by making a list.

How has turn-and-talk improved your thinking about a text, video, or read-aloud?

_____

_____

_____

_____

Has your ability to immediately talk about an idea improved? Explain.

_____

_____

_____

_____

Do you talk in your head while you read to develop and improve understanding? Explain with a specific example.

_____

_____

_____

_____

Write any additional thoughts you have about the turn-and-talk strategy.

_____

_____

_____

_____

Whole-Class Discussions

What It Is

Student-led talks about a lesson, text, or topic that invite all students to participate and take 5–20 minutes.

How It Helps

Students learn to

- Participate in discussions using questions that have more than one answer.
- Risk discussing a hunch as well as justifying a response with text details.
- Manage the discussion without raising their hands.

Introducing Whole-Class Discussions and Tips for Participation

▶ Establish a learning goal for the discussion. For example,

Today, we're going to discuss main ideas and themes.

▶ Review Polite Ways to Disagree With a Classmate (page 36).

▶ Tell students they don't have to raise their hands. Instead, students wait until a classmate finishes before sharing a comment.

▶ Remind students to use text evidence to support their ideas and that you are looking for diverse interpretations.

▶ Initiate the discussion with a guiding question and then serve as a catalyst, asking a question only to fuel the discussion and periodically summarizing points students make.

▶ Project onto a whiteboard Prompts That Keep a Discussion Moving Forward (page 25) that students can use.

Prompts

▶ Select a quote from the text and write it on the board.

▶ Ask students to complete a fast write. For example, fast write about a theme or main idea or about the protagonist and problems or conflicts. Have three to four students share theirs to ignite the discussion.

▶ Pose a guiding question such as

How did Ruby Bridges help desegregation?

Variations

▶ Have students turn-and-talk and develop the goal for the discussion.

▶ Invite a student to volunteer and wrap up the discussion's key points.

Reflect and Intervene

▶ If you feel they need you to guide the discussions at first, ask students to raise their hands and you can call on them. The goal is to turn the conversation over to students.

▶ Help students who aren't participating by letting them prepare for a whole-class discussion in advance. Give them the quote or guiding question, discuss it with them, and explain that you will expect them to participate.

▶ Listen to the questions students ask. If questions are factual and have only one answer, review or reteach posing open-ended, interpretive questions (see How to Teach Students to Compose Interpretive Questions, page 12).

▶ Help students who don't offer text evidence by thinking aloud using your read-aloud text to remind them how to skim to locate details.

▶ Invite the class to debrief after students have experienced two to three discussions. Have students turn-and-talk to discuss what worked and what they could improve. Possible improvements could be along these lines:

  ○ Let a classmate finish before jumping in.

  ○ Provide more evidence from the text.

  ○ Make sure you disagree politely.

▶ Ask students to set a goal for the next discussion based on their debriefing.

Assessing Whole-Class Discussions

1. Ask students to complete the Self-Evaluation of Whole-Class Discussions reproducible (page 35).

2. Have students complete the List of Key Points Discussed: Whole-Class Discussions reproducible (page 37).

Supporting English Language Learners

▶ Stop to summarize points more frequently to help these students better understand a fast-paced discussion.

▶ Encourage students to comment on the quote you provided or on their fast writes.

▶ Praise students for offering thoughtful points.

Reproducibles

Self-Evaluation of Whole-Class Discussions (page 35)

Polite Ways to Disagree With a Classmate (page 36)

List of Key Points Discussed: Whole-Class Discussions (page 37)

Whole-Class Discussions

Preparing the Lesson

Sixth-grade students have listened to me read aloud "Harrison Bergeron," a short story by Kurt Vonnegut about a dystopian society that makes all citizens equal in beauty, grace, and intelligence by using handicaps that mask above-average traits. After this read-aloud, students read the short story "Examination Day" by Henry Slesar twice, first to get the gist and second to deepen their understanding of family.

Story Summary

"Examination Day" is a story about a boy named Dickie Jordan. The family celebrates Dickie's 12th birthday, but the celebration has a tense and worried tone because all 12-year-olds must take a government exam that evaluates their intelligence. Dickie's parents know that he is smart, so they give their son incorrect information because the government doesn't value intelligence. However, Dickie fails the test because his intelligence is above regulations; his parents receive a call that informs them of their son's death.

> You can access "Examination Day" by Henry Seslar by putting the title and author into a search engine.

The Goal and Guiding Question

Students created the goal: to explain what "all men are created equal" means. Students used the same guiding question posed for "Harrison Bergeron": *How does this society interpret "all men are created equal"?* What follows is an excerpt of this discussion:

Jamal: Well, they kill off people who are intelligent.

Tony: That means only average or below-average people live.

Lucien: It's plain murder. Parents have no say. That's how they control people. No one's smart enough to question the government.

Latisha: Yeah. But why do they want to control people? [*Excellent question that moves the group to finding reasons.*]

Michael: The government wants to keep its power.

Lucien: It felt like the Jordans could never get a better place to live in or the dad a different job.

Latisha: They didn't have choices.

Emily: Maybe equality means you have choices. It's not having the same intelligence. [*Synthesizes reasons offered and tries to define equality.*]

Robb: Can you turn-and-talk and come up with an explanation of equality as stated in the Declaration of Independence?

With the input from pairs, the class constructed this explanation of "all men are created equal." Here are points students made: *It's equality before the laws of our country. Equal opportunity for jobs and education. Choice of who to marry and where to live. Our choices in life can limit this equality. Like if you murder someone, you lose opportunities.*

Michael and a few other students said that all these ideas don't work because poor people and African Americans and immigrants often don't have equality before the law.

Open-ended discussions trust students' thinking and allow them to explore and understand a concept. Rick said the Declaration of Independence was idealistic, but reality isn't always the same.

Self-Evaluation of Whole-Class Discussions

Name _____ Date _____

Directions:

1. Reflect on the whole-class discussions you've participated in, and think about how they supported your learning and understanding of a text.

2. Read each statement or question below, and answer in your reader's notebook.

   - How do you feel about participating in whole-class discussions? Explain.

   - Have you become a better listener? Explain.

   - List three examples that show how whole-class discussions supported your thinking.

   - How much of the discussion do students control? Is this okay? Explain.

   - How has your analytical thinking improved through these discussions?

   - How do you think the quality of these discussions can be improved?

Polite Ways to Disagree With a Classmate

Here are prompts to help you disagree with statements and ideas classmates present.

- I understand your idea, but I have a different interpretation.

- That's an interesting point that I did not think of, but here's my idea.

- I find that idea interesting, but I'm not sure you can support it with text evidence.

- Even though our positions seem different, I believe they have common points. Let me explain.

- You proved your idea with text evidence. Let me share my idea, which differs from yours.

- It's okay to have more than one interpretation. Here's what I think.

- Your idea intrigues me and I'm thinking my idea grows out of it. Let me explain.

List of Key Points Discussed: Whole-Class Discussions

Name _____ Date _____

Directions:

1. Reflect on the key points made during this whole-class discussion.

2. Choose five to six important points and list them below.

_____

_____

_____

_____

_____

_____

_____

_____

3. Reread your key points and connect them to state a theme or inference.

_____

_____

_____

_____

_____

_____

_____

_____

Partner Talk

What It Is

Two students reading the same text, different texts in the same genre, or texts on the same topic have an in-depth discussion about a guiding question, an issue, themes, or student-generated questions. Partner talk can focus on a small chunk of text (quote or chapter) or the whole text; the conversations can take 5–30 minutes and may extend over multiple class periods.

How It Helps

- Enables students to apply strategies, discuss student-generated, open-ended questions, and observe each other's thinking process.
- Helps students move deeply into a lesson, a text, or an issue.

Introducing Partner Talk

- ❱ Organize students in pairs whose instructional reading levels are no more than a year apart.
- ❱ Ask pairs to find a comfortable place in the classroom to discuss.
- ❱ Change partners after they've completed discussing a book or worked together throughout a unit.
- ❱ Give partners clear directions for their discussions that include the amount of time they have, what they will discuss, and the writing they'll do.
- ❱ Give students a copy of Prompts That Keep a Discussion Moving Forward (page 25) and ask them to refer to it when necessary.

Prompts

Have students use open-ended questions they created (see Initiating Talk With Questions and Prompts, pages 9–12).

- ❱ Start the discussion with a guiding question. For example, here is a guiding question for *Riding Freedom* by Pam Munoz Ryan:

  Explain how Riding Freedom *refers to more than riding a horse called Freedom. When Charlotte changes her identity, is she always riding freedom? Explain.*

Variations

- ❱ Ask students who have read the same independent reading book to develop their discussion questions about literary elements or information.
- ❱ Invite students reading different books to complete the reproducible Partner Book Conference: Independent Reading (page 43).

Reflect and Intervene

Here are some scaffolds to try.

STUDENT BEHAVIORS	POSSIBLE SCAFFOLDS
One student does most of the work.	• Find out why the student isn't doing his or her share of the work. A couple possibilities are that the text might be too difficult or the student has little prior knowledge. If there's time, change the text or switch partners so that the match between student and text works for everyone. • Restart the discussion by posting a question, and invite each student to respond.
Both or one of the partners can't recall details from the text.	• Have students reread a section of the text and assess their recall. Explain that rereading sections can support recall. • Encourage students to stop and assess their recall at the end of a page and/or a short chapter. • Consider changing a text so students can read a text they can learn from.
Neither student completed the required reading.	• Ask the students why they didn't complete the assignment as their reason might not have to do with text difficulty. • Students might need extra time or they might need to complete the reading at home if class time doesn't suffice. • Consider offering students an easier text if the one they have is too difficult.

Assessing Partner Talk

1. Read students' writing about their discussions in their notebooks.

2. Grade the reproducible Partners Discuss a Book: Fiction (page 41) or Partners Discuss a Book: Informational Text (page 42).

3. Give students the reproducible Partner Book Conference: Independent Reading (pages 43–44).

Supporting English Language Learners

▶ Help partners find reading materials they can learn from.

▶ Review directions with students to check for understanding.

▶ Complete frequent check-ins with pairs, and support them as needed.

Reproducibles

Partners Discuss a Book: Fiction (page 41)

Partners Discuss a Book: Informational Text (page 42)

Partner Book Conference: Independent Reading (pages 43–44)

Partner Talk

Preparing the Lesson

Since *The Giver* (Lowry, 1993) is a dystopian novel, I wanted students to have a clear understanding of the term so they could better understand the society Lowry created. After organizing students into partners, I invited the pairs to read articles about the characteristics of dystopian societies on their computers, then write a list of these characteristics in their notebooks. My intention was to have students periodically return to and use their lists to discuss the book. Here are some characteristics students shared: *The society limits the information people receive. The society prevents freedom and independent thinking. There's a leader who people don't interact with. The leader has rights and can do things that the people can't do. The people fear the outside world—the world beyond where they live.*

Giving Directions for Partner Talk

Using Chapters 1 and 2 of *The Giver*, here are two questions you can discuss:

1. What do you learn about the term *release*? Cite examples that help you understand this term.

2. What evidence of a dystopian society do you find in these chapters?

These questions are on the whiteboard, but you should jot them in your notebook on a page headed "Chapters 1 and 2, *The Giver*." You have about 20 minutes for your discussion. Here's part of a discussion by two eighth-grade students:

Leila: When I read *release* the first time, I thought people were sent outside. But now I think they were killed.

Maria: Maybe the definition of release can help. It says: release means to set free from restraint. [*Great idea to clarify meaning of* release *by using the dictionary.*]

Leila: Hmm. I still think they kill them, and I guess death is sort of a release from a situation the community thinks is bad.

Maria: Let's get examples and see. [*Students cite these and discuss.*] [*Smart move. Examples can help students figure out release the way Lowry uses it.*]

Leila: I still think it's plain murder. [*Leila stays firm.*]

Maria: But I think going outside might be worse 'cause who'd help them? What's there? It feels scary.

Leila: Yeah. But when it says that new children—babies—can be released, it would have to be death 'cause they'd die outside. [*Leila uses newborns to rebut Maria's idea of "going outside."*]

Maria: That helps. I agree. It's death.

It's important to capitalize on a teachable moment, so after partners shared, I introduced the term *euphemism*. A euphemism, I explain, is substituting a milder word for one that could inspire fear and unpleasant feelings. The community didn't want to use a harsh word, like death, so they called it release.

Partners Discuss a Book: Fiction

Name _____ Date _____

Purpose: To use literary elements in a text to dive deeply into the book's layers of meaning.

Directions:

1. Use the same or different fictional texts. Different texts should be in the same genre.

2. Choose two or three prompts from the box below and discuss your book.

3. In your notebook, write the highlights of your partner discussion and what you better understood about your book.

Discussion Prompts

- Name your book's genre and share some characteristics of the genre.

- Explain how two antagonists worked against the protagonist. How did the antagonists affect the protagonist? Any changes? What caused these changes?

- Show how a person or main character changed from the beginning to the end of the book.
  - Use adjectives to describe two personality traits observed in the first three to four chapters.
  - Next, use adjectives to show how the traits observed at the start of the book changed by the end.
  - Choose one key event and a person, character, or problem that caused one of the changes, and explain why.

- Why do you enjoy this genre? Be specific.

Reminder: In your notebook, write the important parts of your discussion about your book.

Partners Discuss a Book: Informational Text

Name _____ Date _____

Purpose: To use key details and important information in a text to dive deeply into the book's layers of meaning.

Directions:

1. Use the same informational text.

2. Choose one to two prompts from the box below and discuss your book.

3. In your notebook, write the highlights of your partner discussion and how the discussion helped you better understand the book.

Discussion Prompts

- Discuss four to five key details from two chapters you choose. Reread these details and make an inference that the details suggest or imply.

- State a point that a section of your book argued for. Then, discuss the ideas the author used to support the point.

- Discuss a part of the book that explained an idea, a device, or a machine. In your own words, summarize the author's explanation.

- Discuss the title of your text and link it to specific information in the book.

Reminder: In your notebook, write the important parts of your discussion about your book.

Partner Book Conference: Independent Reading

Name _____ Date _____

Purpose: To complete a book conference with a partner, take notes, and use the notes to write up the conference.

Directions:

1. Use the prompts in italics for getting discussion going.

2. Jot notes based on the conversation between you and your partner.

3. On a separate sheet of paper, write up your notes under each question, and organize the write-up into paragraphs.

Why did you select this book?

- *Is it a topic and/or author you love? Did someone recommend it? Who? Why did they recommend it?*

- *What about the book made you enjoy or dislike it?*

_____

_____

_____

_____

_____

What kept you interested in this book?

- *Can you find a favorite part, read it, and explain why you liked it?*

- *What new information did you learn?*

- *Was there an interesting photograph or illustration? Share and discuss it by showing how it connects to the book.*

- *What did you learn about characters or people and how they cope with problems? Discuss an event and person or character that changed the protagonist.*

_____

_____

_____

_____

_____

(Continued)

Can you link the title to a theme or a problem?

- *Connect the title to a specific event, setting, person, or set of details.*

- *Does the title connect to a theme or big idea? Explain.*

_____

_____

_____

_____

_____

Would you recommend this book to classmates?

- *What about the book made it a great read? Suspense, a cliffhanger at the end of chapters, the characters or persons, the problems and conflicts? Explain.*

- *Would you read a different book by this author? Explain why or why not.*

- *Use a search engine to find the author's website or information related to the author. Discuss what you learned and share the website with your partner.*

_____

_____

_____

_____

_____

Small-Group Discussions

What It Is

Three to six students read and discuss a common text. These student-led discussions can take 10–30 minutes and might need more than one class.

How It Helps

- Provides opportunities for students to create and discuss open-ended questions.
- Sharpens students' listening skills and refines the language needed to express ideas.
- Helps students value diverse interpretations.

Introducing Small-Group Discussions

- ❯ Give students a copy of Prompts That Keep a Discussion Moving Forward (page 25) and ask them to refer to it when necessary.
- ❯ Use the fishbowl technique to build students' mental model of small-group discussions if this is a new experience (see How to Use the Fishbowl Technique, page 18).
- ❯ Provide groups with clear directions that include the assigned reading, materials to bring, the discussion's focus, and the time allotted.
- ❯ Tell students they will ask questions, share ideas, and offer text evidence as they talk together.
- ❯ Invite a student volunteer to be a moderator, noting that the role will change for each meeting.

Prompts

Display the prompt(s) on a whiteboard.

- ❯ Create and discuss open-ended questions and/or a guiding question.
- ❯ Select a short passage, read it to the group, and discuss its meaning and connection to the text.
- ❯ Discuss specific literary elements and give text examples.
- ❯ Discuss text features and explain how these connect to big ideas.
- ❯ Make logical inferences using information, dialogue, photographs, or a character's or person's decisions.

Variations

- ❯ Invite students to choose a book and decide how much they'll read before meeting.
- ❯ Have students use a guiding question or text-dependent questions they wrote.
- ❯ Negotiate how much time students need to complete the discussion; provide extra time if necessary.

(Continued)

(Continued)

Reflect and Intervene

Use the Teacher's Checklist for Assessing Small-Group Discussions (page 48) or your observations to plan, or try scaffolds from the chart.

GROUP/STUDENT BEHAVIORS	POSSIBLE SCAFFOLDS
Members don't use text evidence to support ideas.	• Model, when the group meets, how to cite text evidence: Recall and paraphrase details or find the place in the text that supports the thinking, skim it, and paraphrase.
Some students don't participate.	• Speak to each student one on one to find out why there is no participation. • Encourage students to reread the section of text before the group meets to improve recall of information. • Explain that you will join the group and expect a student to risk sharing. Offer positive feedback.
Group is frequently off task.	• Have students review the directions prior to the discussion. • Encourage the group leader to keep members on task and ask questions that keep a discussion moving forward.
Some students come without materials.	• Send students to their cubby or locker to retrieve materials. • Try to have a few extra texts in case a student can't find his or her own. • Confer with the students to find out why the materials aren't in the classroom; help them store materials in a safe place.
Some students have not read the material.	• Have a conversation with the students about the importance of preparation. • Ask the students to set a goal for the next group discussion.

Assessing Small-Group Discussions

1. Complete the Teacher's Checklist for Assessing Small-Group Discussions (page 48) to assess participation, listening, and questioning.

2. Use the reproducible My Role in a Small-Group Discussion (page 49).

3. Evaluate discussion content with the reproducible Listing Discussion Highlights (page 50).

Supporting English Language Learners

❱ Make sure students understand the directions.

❱ Monitor progress and provide support and positive feedback.

❱ Model for the small group how prompts can keep a discussion going.

Reproducibles

Teacher's Checklist for Assessing Small-Group Discussions (page 48)

My Role in a Small-Group Discussion (page 49)

Listing Discussion Highlights (page 50)

Small-Group Discussions

LESSON IN ACTION

Background Information

I chunked the book *Shiloh* by Phyllis Reynolds Naylor into five sections for fourth-grade students. While students read and discussed pages 11–36, each one had a copy of the book. However, not one student used text details to support an idea or opened the book to refer to a passage or page that supported a position.

Discussion Follow-Up

To help students increase their use of text evidence, I continued modeling with daily read-alouds, reminded students to use text evidence in their student-led discussions, listened to discussions, and debriefed with students to see what was working and what scaffolding was needed. Here is a snapshot of the final discussion of *Shiloh*, from page 120 to the end, that reflects the progress students made with citing text evidence.

Discussion Snapshot

Students' Guiding Question: *Was there a pivotal event that changed the course of the story and the main character's thoughts and personality? Explain.*

Before the discussion started, I reminded students to give specific text evidence and point to the page they found it on. Anton reads aloud the guiding question the group selected.

Ann: The pivotal event was Marty standing up to Judd and blackmailing him so he could keep Shiloh. On page 121 Marty says that he "feels taller than I really am," when he sees Judd. [*Sends group to a page in book that shows Marty will stand up to Judd.*]

Jamal: But Marty is smart. He uses the fact that Judd killed a deer out of season to get Shiloh. Marty saw Judd kill the deer. Marty threatens to tell the warden [what Judd did] if Judd doesn't work out a way to let Marty keep Shiloh. [*Gives evidence using recall of details.*]

Ebony: When Judd says that he found the deer eating up his garden, on page 121 Marty tells Judd, "That's a lie." Marty has lots of courage. I think his need to keep Shiloh gives him courage. [*Cites page and makes an inference about Marty.*]

Keisha: That's the pivotal event—really like a flash. When Marty stands up to Judd, like Ebony said, it's his [Marty's] love for Shiloh that gives Marty strength to give it to Judd. [*Notices Ebony's comment on the pivotal event; Keisha supports it by saying "when Marty stands up to Judd."*]

Anton: On page 123, Marty tells Judd you don't shoot deer out of season, "especially a doe." I think Marty dares Judd when he says, "Going to shoot me like that dog I found up here six months back with a bullet in its head." [*Quoting text evidence strengthens the point.*]

What great progress this shows in students' ability to cite specific text evidence. Repeatedly, they turned to details in the text and showed peers what sparked their ideas and inferences. Reminders to use text evidence prior to a discussions, offering positive feedback when students cited text details, and lots of practice all affected students' growth in leading literary discussions.

Teacher's Checklist for Assessing Small-Group Discussions

Group members _____

_____

Date observed _____

Key: P = Prepared   U = Unprepared

PREPARATION	COMMENTS
_____ Brings the book and materials.	
_____ Completes the assigned reading.	
_____ Helps to develop discussion questions.	
PARTICIPATION	**COMMENTS**
_____ Contributes to the discussion.	
_____ Listens without interrupting.	
_____ Respects different ideas.	
_____ Uses recall of details to support ideas.	
_____ Rereads a passage to point to details.	
_____ Comments on ideas presented by peers.	
_____ Asks meaningful questions.	
_____ Keeps the discussion moving forward.	
INTERPRETS TEXT	**COMMENTS**
_____ Uses pictures and photos to explore meanings.	
_____ Discusses literary elements using text examples.	
_____ Uses text features to discover meaning.	
_____ Uses structural elements in discussion.	
_____ Can identify themes and big ideas.	
_____ Can explain the author's purpose and point of view.	
_____ Makes logical inferences.	

My Role in a Small-Group Discussion

Name _____ Date _____

Directions: Evaluate your role in the discussions by using the key to mark the space at the left of each statement. Under "Comments," jot notes that offer extra details.

Key: R = Rarely   S = Sometimes   A = Always

PREPARATION	COMMENTS
_____ Brings the book and materials.	
_____ Completes the assigned reading.	
_____ Helps to develop discussion questions.	

PARTICIPATION	COMMENTS
_____ Contributes to the discussion.	
_____ Listens without interrupting.	
_____ Respects different ideas.	
_____ Uses recall of details to support ideas.	
_____ Rereads a passage to point to details.	
_____ Comments on ideas presented by peers.	
_____ Asks meaningful questions.	
_____ Keeps the discussion moving forward.	

INTERPRETS TEXT	COMMENTS
_____ Uses pictures and photos to explore meanings.	
_____ Discusses literary elements using text examples.	
_____ Uses text features to discover meaning.	
_____ Uses structural elements in discussion.	
_____ Can identify themes and big ideas.	
_____ Can explain the author's purpose and point of view.	
_____ Makes logical inferences.	

Available for download at **http://resources.corwin.com/readtalkwrite**

Listing Discussion Highlights

Name _____ Date _____

Directions: Use the prompts to create lists of key points in your group's discussion. Answer those prompts that apply to your discussion. If you need more room, use the back of this sheet or a piece of notebook paper.

List three to four important ideas your group discussed.

_____

_____

_____

Write two questions you discussed, and under each one, list the points the group discussed.

_____

_____

_____

Write two inferences your group made, and give the evidence that supports each one.

_____

_____

_____

Note one to two questions the group discussed that enabled you to figure out themes and big ideas. Now, write one theme.

_____

_____

_____

What did you learn about your book's genre from this discussion?

_____

_____

_____

In-the-Head Conversations

What It Is

In-the-head conversations are discussions readers have with themselves while reading, looking at photographs, attending a play, or watching a video or movie.

How It Helps

- Engages students with a written, oral, or visual text.
- Helps students experience and feel a range of emotions and reactions.
- Informs students when to reread or close read to recall or understand information.

Introducing In-the-Head Conversations

- ❯ Explain that good readers have these conversations all the time.
- ❯ Stop when reading aloud and share your in-the-head-conversations.
- ❯ Give students short texts of no more than two pages to respond to on a bookmark (page 56).
- ❯ Model how you complete a written bookmark on your read-aloud text by projecting your thoughts onto a whiteboard.
- ❯ Have students complete a bookmark using My Bookmark (page 56).
- ❯ Avoid overusing bookmarks; have students complete one every 4–6 weeks.

Prompts

You can ask students to write, on a bookmark, what comes into their heads while reading, or you can focus students' thinking with prompts.

- ❯ Infer about a character's personality traits and decisions, and to find themes and main ideas.
- ❯ Compare and contrast two characters or two settings.
- ❯ Note important details in informational texts.
- ❯ Predict, give text support, and adjust when necessary.
- ❯ Raise questions and read on to explore answers.
- ❯ Think about specific literary elements.
- ❯ Think about specific text features.

Variations

- ❯ Use bookmark responses to pair up students who can help one another practice a strategy.
- ❯ Challenge students to continually use in-the-head conversations.

Reflect and Intervene

Disengaged and unmotivated readers rarely have in-the-head conversations. Here are suggestions for helping students who aren't having in-the-head conversations.

(Continued)

(Continued)

▶ Ask a student why there was little writing on the bookmark. Based on what the student says, provide support.

▶ Enlarge students' mental model of the process by continuing to share your in-the-head conversations.

▶ Ask students to tell you how the notes of an in-the-head conversation on a bookmark helped them improve comprehension and recall.

Assessing In-the-Head Conversations

1. Have a 5-minute conversation with each student to clarify ideas on his or her bookmark.

2. Use the reproducible Self-Evaluation of In-the-Head Conversations (page 57).

Supporting English Language Learners

▶ Have students with limited language draw their in-the-head conversations and explain the drawings to you.

▶ Ask a student to dictate to you what's going on in his or her head.

Reproducibles

My Bookmark (page 56)

Self-Evaluation of In-the-Head Conversations (page 57)

Notes to Yourself About Teaching the Lesson

_____

_____

_____

_____

_____

_____

_____

_____

_____

In-the-Head Conversations

The bookmarks on the following pages are by fourth- and fifth-grade students attending the Discovery Charter School in Rochester, New York. The school's curriculum coordinator, Debbi DePalma, worked with fifth graders; teachers Jean Hoyt and Sarah Amesbury worked with fourth graders. Teachers modeled in-the-head conversations and the bookmark process with a read-aloud text, and students practiced using self-selected books. Frequent teacher–student conferences helped move students like Amir (see below) beyond retelling. Jean Hoyt put it this way: "The bookmark format is a simple and easy tool to help students interact with the text."

> Name _____
>
> Date 2/11/16
>
> Book: Amulet #3
>
> Author: Kazu Kubuishi
>
> Pages for this bookmark: Page# 29
>
> The story is about Emilly and navin and their freinds are looking for Ceilis and they found him in this old bontay house and they are trying to feed him and take care of him.

Fourth grader Amir, like others, retells at first.

53

Name

Date 1-8-16

Book: Smile

Author: Riana Telgimer

Pages for this bookmark: 9-145

Riana fell on her tooth Running home from girl scouts Pg. 9

Riana is laughing because she is missing two front teeth Pg. 11

Riania has to wear a tooth for cast. pg 21

She can't eat Normal food like

Pizza, ora Apple. pg 36

When she touches her new braces they hurt. Pg. 44

What does a orthodonist do? Pg. 59

The first time Armara prayed around Riaha was when they had a dangerous earthkacke. Pg. 66

All of the power went out. Pg 69

Everyone camped down stairs in the living

Koou pg 76

Riana body is very hurt beause she got braces her ears peirced and her tooth Fell out pg. 80

Riana loved the little mermaid movie pg. 89

Riana feel very normal with her new Retainer Pg 107

When Riana told her girl scout friends about her Retainer

it fell out and she felt embarr. pg. 109

She figures out that all of her friend have Retain. pg. 121

Riana dicided to ask a boy named sammy to the valentines Dance Pg. 142 why Did Raina get hit on the head with a rubber bande. Pg. 145 Riana wanted to sign up for girls basketball Pg. 149

Fourth grader Carmen started bookmarks by retelling.

Name _____

Date 2/11/16

Book: The magicians nephew

Author: C.S. lewis

Pages for this bookmark: p.1 I think the author Chose the Setting at the mantion because thats also where Lucy, Susan, Edmauind, and peter found the door to narnia. p.2 I know that polly and Digory are french because of how the speak. p.3 I perdict the Ring will take Digory and polly to narnia. p.4 Digory doesn't care about the Ring p.5 Digory's uncle is a magicia

Fourth grader Aiden explains setting and makes a prediction.

Name

Date: 2/8/16

Book: Matilda

Author: Roald Dahl

Pages for this bookmark: 128,
135

Matilda freand laverder got a note and pored it into the glass of water. Miss truchbull is mean to small kids. I wonder why Miss truchbull is so mean to little kids. Some people are like that at same schools. 164 Miss truchbull is blaming Matilda for something laverder did. That is just.

messed up. I wonder why she blamed Matilda 174, Matilda was walking with Miss honey. And I wonded what they are next. I think miss honey is going to tack her to her house and stay in. 182, miss Honey ivited matilda to her small cated and matilda went to the viel and got Miss Honey Scric watercolo miss Honey is teeling matilda that how her life went when she was a kid 200, so matilda just found out who miss

Honey anut is. And from th staret I knew it was miss trucbull, I wonder what is going to happen next. 204, matilda is now practing her trick and with a suger. I wond why that it might hert her. 214, Miss trucbull now got a letter from matilda, I wonder what it says. And they lived happly ever after

The end

Fourth grader Aisha was a reluctant reader who had no recall from books she chose. Bookmarks and conferences about what she was thinking while reading turned her into a reader.

Name

Date 1/22/15

Book: The power of poppy pendle

Author: Natasha Lowe

Pages for this bookmark: p.1-93

Poppy probley loved baking because she was born on a bakery floor. Why did her parents act so surprised when poppy was doing magic when it ran in their family. I was pretty surprising when the author states that she could carry grocies bags at three months. I dont think poppy likes mrs. Roach. I notice and wonder how can she control it when she is a baby and the she shows her feelings with magic. Did poppy know what she was doing or did

It dust come to her mind? people students call poppy a witch how awful. Is matiase mspoodle neibr of a lost freind because she knows about poppy being a witch I wonder if poppy is going to make any freinds at school? Why did mrs.Roach look at poppy when she said we expect great things. I wonder if poppy will end up in prison. What does the motto "Kibet Pallew da" means? I read it means how you treat other people in the school. Poppy studied a wich that used to be a good which but turned into a evil one. poppy wonders If the evil witch was evil because she wanted sing and not be a witch what if poppy goes

How did poppy get good grades if she doesn't even like going to Ruthersfield School for girls?. Every time poppy gets she either bake or thinks and look for new recipies in a oftrad than the nelush and visit the evil witch When poppy walks home she sees a girl that goes to elamation school and she help her.how she helped is poppy can dump really far and high so she knocked darte (wich is her new best and only freind) shoes down. Chat lie flot was swollen when the girls that but the shoes up in a tree pushed her. I wonder if some one from Ruthersfield put her shoes up there because no one mortal can through

shoes and let it land me a branch perfectly. Charlie asked if they can fly on poppy bfam stick but poppy said that she could carry her home. I think that mabey charlie might be playing poppy because she keeps on teling to ride her broom. The pplk say charlie and poppy Meet at the same place and charlie enteled her to her house. poppy tricked her mom into taking her to take her to charlie.

Fifth grader Janna writes what she's thinking while reading without a directed prompt.

My Bookmark

Name _____

Date _____

Title _____

Pages _____

Directions:

1. Read and stop to record your in-the-head conversations _____ times.

2. Use a strategy your teacher selects from the box or one you choose.

- ❐ Infer about a character's personality traits and decisions, and to find themes and main ideas.

- ❐ Compare and contrast two characters or two settings.

- ❐ Note important details in informational texts.

- ❐ Predict, give text support, and adjust when necessary.

- ❐ Raise questions and read on to explore answers.

- ❐ Think about specific literary elements.

- ❐ Think about specific text features.

My Bookmark

Name _____

Date _____

Title _____

Pages _____

Directions:

1. Read and stop to record your in-the-head conversations _____ times.

2. Use a strategy your teacher selects from the box or one you choose.

- ❐ Infer about a character's personality traits and decisions, and to find themes and main ideas.

- ❐ Compare and contrast two characters or two settings.

- ❐ Note important details in informational texts.

- ❐ Predict, give text support, and adjust when necessary.

- ❐ Raise questions and read on to explore answers.

- ❐ Think about specific literary elements.

- ❐ Think about specific text features.

Self-Evaluation of In-the-Head Conversations

Name _____ Date _____

Directions: Answer each question or prompt that follows.

What did you learn about your understanding of _____ strategy from completing bookmarks?

_____

_____

_____

_____

Why are bookmarks helpful?

_____

_____

_____

_____

Do you have in-the-head conversations when you read, listen, or watch a video or movie? Give some examples.

_____

_____

_____

_____

Do you enjoy in-the-head conversations? Explain why or why not.

_____

_____

_____

_____

Teacher–Student Discussions

What It Is

Discussions between the teacher and a student can occur while the teacher circulates among students and pauses to offer a student support. More formal discussions are scheduled 5-minute conferences.

How It Helps

- Helps students who struggle with completing a task on their own develop the expertise that allows them to work independently.

Introducing Teacher–Student Discussions

Prepare two or more scaffolds, so if one doesn't work, you have others to try.

▶ Schedule one to three conferences per class period. Confer while students work independently on reading or writing.

▶ Set up a conference area away from the rest of the class to have privacy.

▶ Plan each conference by completing the "Before Conferring" section of the reproducible 5-Minute Teacher–Student Conference Form (page 61).

▶ Put the student at ease by chatting about his or her interests, strengths you observed.

▶ Explain the reason for or focus of the conference.

▶ Share your observations and ask the student to comment on them.

▶ Record on the conference form notes under specific headings, and store it in the student's literacy folder along with selected written work.

▶ Reread filed conference forms and reflect on the student's progress with the intervention lessons he or she has completed. These can help you decide whether the student requires additional help.

Prompts

▶ How can I help you?

▶ I notice that you do _____ well but need some help with _____.

▶ Tell me how you feel about [sharing ideas, discussing books, etc.].

▶ Let me start helping you by _____.

▶ Here's the progress you made today: _____. This is what we'll work on tomorrow: _____.

▶ Working hard and asking questions has helped you become independent with _____.

Variations

▶ Pair up the student with a peer expert, and have them practice until you notice that the student feels confident with a task.

▶ Complete a brief checkup conference in about 2 weeks to ensure the student has the confidence to participate in different kinds of talk.

Reflect and Intervene

▶ Reread all 5-Minute Teacher–Student Conference Forms you completed for a student.

▶ Ask yourself thoughtful questions:

　○ Is the student making progress? Why or why not?

　○ What progress do you notice? How can you build on this?

　○ Is it time to pair up the student with a classmate? Give reasons.

▶ Continue to observe and interact with students you have conferred with or are conferring with now. Watch for any new challenges that arise.

▶ Save conference forms in the student's folder and use them to inform the focus of future conferences and teaching decisions.

Assessing Teacher–Student Discussions

1. Use your notes on the conference forms to assess each student's progress.

2. Continue to circulate among students to provide support as needed.

Supporting English Language Learners

▶ Make sure the student understands the directions.

▶ Point out progress throughout a conference and praise the student when the practice has gone well.

Reproducible

5-Minute Teacher–Student Conference Form (page 61)

Notes to Yourself About Teaching the Lesson

_____

_____

_____

_____

_____

_____

_____

LESSON IN ACTION

Teacher–Student Discussions

Preparing the Lesson

A fifth-grade student is having difficulty making inferences using details from *Through My Eyes* by Ruby Bridges (1999). I decide to use some of the photographs (on pages 17 and 19) to help him understand that an inference is unstated. Next, I list the points I hope to make during the conference:

▶ Study the photograph and figure out what's happening.

▶ Ask, What are the people feeling and thinking? Make sure you can explain how you drew these conclusions.

Here's a snapshot of our conversation:

Student: I don't think I can infer with a photo if I can't from the writing. [*You can feel the student's lack of self-confidence.*]

Robb: I understand how you feel. Let's work together and see what happens. [*Notice that I sympathize with the student but also present a photograph that he can "read" with ease.*]

[*I have the student look at the photograph of Ruby on the title page and ask*] Can you infer her feelings?

Student: Yeah. She's real happy.

Robb: What made you say that?

Student: She's smiling and her eyes smile and are happy. [*Good use of nonverbal cues.*]

Robb: I noticed how you used her facial expressions to make an inference. You supplied the caption for that photo! Next, take a look at the photograph on page 17. What do you notice?

Student: People are shouting. The signs show they don't want blacks in their school. Two policemen are in front of the crowd. [*He reads the details of the photograph well.*]

Robb: Can you make an inference and give support from the photo?

Student: Well, there's hatred in the crowd. The signs show they hate blacks. [*I wait and say nothing. This is key, as I am giving him time to process. By not jumping in to save him, I send the message that he can do this.*] The police are there 'cause maybe all these people can hurt someone. The way they hold the signs makes me think they're proud of the hatred. [*Great work! I would have been satisfied with two inferences, but he gave three.*]

Robb: You made three inferences and supported each one with specific details. When we meet tomorrow, I'll give you details from the written text and then you can infer using them. [*I always like to tell students what comes next.*]

Having students infer using photographs is an excellent way to create a situation that allows the students to succeed. Then, the transition to text becomes easier.

5-Minute Teacher–Student Conference Form

Name _____ Date _____

Directions: Complete this conference form and file in a folder that contains other conference forms and samples of the student's written work.

Before Conferring

Focus the conference topic:

_____

_____

Points to discuss with the student:

_____

_____

The kind of scaffolding I'll try:

_____

_____

After Conferring

Note important comments the student made:

_____

_____

My observations of the student:

_____

_____

Negotiated goal for the next conference:

_____

_____

Date of the next conference: _____

CHAPTER 3

Lessons That Build Comprehension Skills in Any Genre

In this chapter, as well as Chapters 5 and 7, you'll find sample lessons that integrate the types of talk discussed in Chapter 2 to teach students how to think deeply about a text by making inferences, identifying main ideas and themes, discussing conflicts, and so on. The literature that I use for each lesson is included with this book; you can find the complete texts starting on page 86 and available for download at http://resources.corwin .com/readtalkwrite. You can invite students to read each text if it's at their instructional reading level, or you can read the text out loud. Presenting the lessons in this chapter will give you a feel for a student-centered approach that incorporates talk and writing; you will also get a sense of how I pace lessons, dividing them over two or more days.

Before trying the lessons, let me share some highlights of my planning process in selecting texts so you can adapt it to prepare your own lessons.

Step 1. Mine texts for teaching topics

Step 2. Plan lessons

Step 3. Develop effective assessments

Step 1: Mine Texts for Teaching Topics

If you have to teach genre, refer to the genre chart for fiction in Chapter 4 (pages 128–129) and the chart for nonfiction in Chapter 6 (pages 193–195) for teaching ideas and questions. You can find suggestions for composing guiding questions and interpretive questions in Chapter 1 (page 9). I've included a key issue with each genre as this can support creating a guiding question.

When I read short or long texts to decide whether to use them in my classes, I read with my teacher's eye. If a piece grabs me and makes me think *I wonder what will happen. I must finish before I fix dinner!* or *My students will love this!* I reread or skim it and list possible teaching points, guiding questions, and background knowledge students might need on a chart like the one that follows. Over the years, I've built a treasure trove of reading materials that I can draw upon for read-alouds, guided practice, and instruction.

Generally, I use a short selection to teach one or two topics to students, and then it's time to move on to a different piece. A chapter book, on the other hand, can be used for several topics over a longer period of time. Consider the notes I took for Priscilla Cummings's story "Snow Day," shown on the next page; you can find the lesson using this story on pages 163–164.

Mine Texts for Teaching Topics: Planning Chart

Example of Planning Chart for a Short Story

Title: "Snow Day"

Author: Priscilla Cummings

Genre: Realistic short story

Reading level: Fifth grade

BACKGROUND KNOWLEDGE	THEME/ISSUE	LITERARY ELEMENTS	LITERARY TECHNIQUES/ STRUCTURE	READING STRATEGIES
Have students discuss what they'd do on a day off from school.	Friendship and empathy	Protagonist and problems Antagonists Settings Themes	Figurative language Flashback	Inferring characters' personality traits. Compare/contrast

Potential Guiding Questions Related to Theme/Issue:

How does friendship affect our decisions?

What motivates people to act heroically?

The chart shown above, which I store in my binder, helps me clearly see teaching possibilities for this text. When I see students are ready for a new text, I find one that offers different challenges. For example, if I want to teach conflict or events and people that change characters, then I would use a story like "Coming Clean" (page 86), which deals with a character's internal and external conflicts that cause him to change, or "Hoops Tryouts" (page 93), which shows how a character's actions change him.

Organizing my notes this way makes it easy to locate texts with similar themes or teaching points that I can use for reteaching, and it allows me to quickly find texts in the same genre at different reading levels. Next, let's examine my notes on Seymour Simon's "New Horizons in Space"; the lesson using this text is on pages 216–217.

Mine Texts for Teaching Topics: Planning Chart

Example of Planning Chart for Informational Text

Title: "New Horizons in Space" **Author:** Seymour Simon

Genre: Informational text **Reading Level:** Ninth/tenth grade

BACKGROUND KNOWLEDGE	THEME/ISSUE	LITERARY ELEMENTS	LITERARY TECHNIQUES/ STRUCTURE	READING STRATEGIES
On asteroids, asteroid belt, and mining for minerals	Dwindling rare and important metals Space is the next mining frontier	Point of view Purposes Themes	Problem/ solution	Determining importance Drawing conclusions Main ideas

Potential Guiding Questions Related to Genre/Theme/Issue:

How do dwindling resources affect our world?

What are new horizons in space?

This is an excellent article for helping students draw conclusions, identify the author's purpose and point of view, and study the text structure of problem/solution. However, this piece would not help me teach making inferences using text details. To prepare a lesson on inferring, I could use either excerpt by Sandra Athans: *Tales From the Top of the World* or *Secrets of the Sky Caves*. On pages 72–73 is a lesson on inferring using *Tales From the Top of the World*. Finally, review my notes on Kathleen Krull's "How Ada Lovelace Leaped Into History"; the lesson based on this text is on pages 210–211.

Mine Texts for Teaching Topics: Planning Chart

Example Planning Chart for Biography

Title: "How Ada Lovelace Leaped Into History"

Author: Kathleen Krull

Genre: Biography

Reading level: Seventh grade

BACKGROUND KNOWLEDGE	THEME/ISSUE	LITERARY ELEMENTS	LITERARY TECHNIQUES/ STRUCTURE	READING STRATEGIES
On the poet Lord Byron	Obstacles Domineering parents	Protagonist Antagonists Point of view, purposes Themes Conflict	Flashback	Inferring character's personality traits Compare/ contrast

Potential Guiding Questions Related to Theme/Issue:

What kinds of obstacles affect our decisions and lives?

How do other people influence our lives?

This biography offers several teaching choices; however, I would only use it for two topics. Choice of topics depends on what your students need to learn and practice. You might return to a text later in the year to review a topic or to teach a new topic.

Texts for Teaching Topics: Planning Chart

_____ Author _____

_____ Reading Level _____

BACKGROUND KNOWLEDGE	THEME/ISSUE	LITERARY ELEMENTS	LITERARY TECHNIQUES/ STRUCTURE	READING STRATEGIES

Potential Guiding Questions Related to Genre/Theme/Issue:

_____

_____

_____

_____

_____

Available for download at **http://resources.corwin.com/readtalkwrite**

Step 2: Plan Lessons

As I plan lessons, I like to think about them in three phases: preparation, the lesson, and reflect and intervene. To help you plan your own, I've listed beneath each of these phases some activities that typically occur. You do not have to do everything listed for every lesson! The topic, the content, and the needs of your students will determine what you include in a lesson.

Preparation

- Activate background knowledge
- Preteach vocabulary
- Introduce topic and guiding question
- Read text

The Lesson

- Think aloud
- Interactive read-aloud
- Student talk
- Writing about reading
- Guided and independent practice

Reflect and Intervene

- Assess the learning
- Provide scaffolds
- Set up 5-minute conferences if needed

Setting priorities when planning is a must; otherwise you will feel overwhelmed and frustrated. Decide on the focus of a lesson—let's say internal antagonists—and then plug in the givens: activate background knowledge, assessments, types of talk, writing about reading, guided practice, and independent work. Work through these, and you can determine the amount of time needed, what kinds of modeling you'll do, and how to meet the needs of groups or individuals that require more support. In addition, as you teach lessons, you will gain the experience that makes planning easier and fun! You can use the Lesson Planning Think Sheet (see pages 68–69) to map out lesson ideas.

Lesson Planning Think Sheet

Topic: The topic can be a literary element or technique, genre, text structure, or reading strategy.

Literature Selection: Every student should be able to read the text. If not, read it aloud or offer a similar selection at students' instructional reading level.

Background Knowledge: Consider the background knowledge students need to comprehend the text and how much time you will devote to building it.

Vocabulary: Evaluate the vocabulary in the text. Are there three to five words you should preteach?

 Guiding Question: Craft a guiding question that prompts students to think deeply about the text and your topic.

Text-Dependent Questions: Teach students to work with a partner or in groups of 3 to 4 to write these (see Lesson 3.2, pages 74–75). Writing questions deepens students' knowledge of a text; discussing questions that students made engages them in the discussion. If this is new or too difficult for your students, then develop these questions yourself, thinking aloud to model the process for students.

Assessment: Use the reproducibles in lessons as examples of what to develop.

Adjustments: Make adjustments for English language learners and special education students. These can include easier texts, creating text-dependent questions they discuss and showing them how to locate information in a text that answers questions.

Lesson Planning Think Sheet

Topic

_____

_____

Literature Selection

_____

_____

Background Knowledge

_____

_____

Vocabulary

_____

_____

Guiding Question

_____

_____

Text-Dependent Questions

_____

_____

Assessment

_____

_____

Adjustments

_____

_____

Additional Comments

_____

_____

Step 3: Develop Effective Assessments

Here is where we address the "write" in the Read, Talk, Write process! When you think about assessing students, looking at their writing about reading should be high on your list. Writing in response to texts and conversation can take many forms, from sticky note jots to more developed entries in reading journals. In this book, I share reproducibles that make it easy for you to get started with writing about reading and self-evaluation as well as checklists for teachers and students; you can use these as models for developing your own student sheets. If you design student response sheets, make sure they reflect what students have learned and practiced.

You can also monitor students' progress by conferring and documenting the conference on the form I've included on page 61, and by asking students to apply an aspect of the lesson to their independent reading. In addition, you'll want to observe literary discussions and use checklists and/or jot some notes that document what you notice and use these for on-the-spot conferences and/or 5-minute conferences.

To simplify lesson planning and assessment, store completed plans in a three-ring binder so you can add lessons, insert comments about completed lessons, note adjustments, and record questions on a lesson you've presented.

Ten Top-Notch Short Texts and Lessons

I know what a boon it is to have short, powerful fiction and nonfiction texts right in the professional book, so here they are! You can photocopy them for students beginning on page 86 or download them at http://resources.corwin.com/readtalkwrite.

Texts

"Coming Clean" by Anina Robb

"Defying Gravity: Mae Jemison" by Anina Robb

"Hoops Tryouts" by Anina Robb

"How Ada Lovelace Leaped Into History" by Kathleen Krull

"How Athens Got Its Name" Retelling by Joanna Davis-Swing

"Isaac Newton and the Day He Discovered the Rainbow" by Kathleen Krull

"Making Scientists Into Climbers" (Excerpt From *Secrets of the Sky Caves: Danger and Discovery on Nepal's Mustang Cliffs*) by Sandra Athans

"New Horizons in Space" by Seymour Simon

"Snow Day" by Priscilla Cummings

"Who Climbs Everest?" (Excerpt From *Tales From the Top of the World: Climbing Mount Everest With Pete Athans*) by Sandra Athans

---

 Available for download at **http://resources.corwin.com/readtalkwrite**

Getting-Ready Tips

▶ As you prepare to teach the lessons that begin on page 72, make class sets of the texts and handouts for each lesson. Students should always have available:

  ○ Guidelines for Discussion (Chapter 1, page 17)

  ○ Prompts That Keep a Discussion Moving Forward (Chapter 2, page 25)

▶ If the text that goes with a lesson works for all students in your class, then students can read it independently. If not, you can read the text aloud.

▶ Most of the lessons use two types of talk. I often start with turn-and-talk to warm up students' thinking and then move to another kind of talk.

▶ Remember, it's not always necessary to share after a turn-and-talk when you hear and observe that all students "get it."

▶ As students discuss, accept any response as long as students paraphrase the text to support their position with specific details or with inferences that use details. Use the same partners throughout a lesson, and make sure every student has a copy of the materials for the lesson.

Circulate and listen carefully as students talk; share suggested time limits in each lesson. However, know that your students might need more or less time, so adjust accordingly.

Inferring With Informational Text

The goal of this lesson is to help students experience how a literary discussion can help them infer while listening to you read aloud an excerpt from *Tales From the Top of the World* (page 119). As I read aloud each section of text, I invite students to turn-and-talk to warm up their thinking, but I also add partner talk for longer conversations of 8–15 minutes. Extending the talk offers students opportunities to explore ideas in the text and share their inferences.

Materials

Excerpt from *Tales From the Top of the World: Climbing Mount Everest With Pete Athans* by Sandra Athans (page 119, or download at http://resources.corwin.com/readtalkwrite)

Lesson Guidelines

Day 1

Help Students Prepare to Read *(15 minutes)*

▶ Post a map of Nepal on a whiteboard and locate Kathmandu, where climbers start, and then locate Mount Everest.

▶ Organize students into partners or invite them to talk to the person sitting at their right or left.

▶ Ask students to turn-and-talk about:

What is the height of Everest?

Why is this climb dangerous?

▶ Have students share with the class.

▶ Invite partners to turn-and-talk for 2–3 minutes saying something like:

What do you know about mountain climbing?

▶ Have two to three pairs share different responses.

Day 2

Read Aloud Part 1 *(15–20 minutes)*

▶ Read aloud the section headed "Who Climbs Everest?" and stop at the end of the first paragraph.

▶ Invite students to turn-and-talk by saying something like:

What conclusions can you make about climbing Mount Everest? Why must you have previous climbing experiences and be in terrific physical shape to reach the top?

▶ End the conversations, then read aloud the second paragraph.

▶ Have students partner talk (8 minutes) by saying something like:

Why do expeditions up Everest always include Sherpas?

Read Aloud Part 2 *(15–20 minutes)*   **Day 3**

▶ Read aloud the first paragraph of "Adjusting to Thin Air."

▶ Have partners turn-and-talk for 2 minutes using a prompt such as:

  What do you think "thin air" means?

▶ Read aloud the next two paragraphs.

▶ Invite students to partner talk (8 minutes) by saying something like:

  How does thin air affect people who climb Everest?

▶ Invite a pair to share. If you want more details after they share, ask:

  Does anyone have more information to add?

▶ Ask students to turn-and-talk for 2–3 minutes by saying something like:

  What can you infer about why people want to climb Everest?

Read Aloud Part 3 *(15–20 minutes)*   **Day 4**

▶ Read aloud "Climbers Be Wary."

▶ Have students partner talk (10 minutes) by saying something like:

  Discuss the text and make two inferences and/or connections among ideas about climbing Mount Everest. Include text evidence that supports each inference.

▶ Ask students to share their inferences and then jot two to three in their notebooks.

Notes to Yourself About Teaching the Lesson

_____

_____

_____

_____

_____

_____

_____

Exploring Interpretive Questions: Biography

Interpretive questions have more than one answer and add energy to a discussion, as students' analyses result in diverse responses. Use three kinds of talk to engage students in discussions of the biography for this lesson. Start with the turn-and-talk strategy to build students' background knowledge about the person. Move to partner talk for creating two interpretive questions that focus the discussion on key points. Finally, hold a whole-class discussion to discuss the questions students generated. If a whole-class discussion derails, restart it by asking a question or making a thought-provoking statement.

Materials

"Isaac Newton and the Day He Discovered the Rainbow" by Kathleen Krull; smart notebooks

Lesson Guidelines

Day 1

Build Background Knowledge and Read for the Gist *(30–35 minutes)*

▶ Ask students to turn-and-talk for about 2 minutes and discuss:

  What do you know about Isaac Newton?

▶ If students know little, show a video from YouTube or TeacherTube, or read selected passages from a biography.

▶ Read aloud or have students read "Isaac Newton and the Day He Discovered the Rainbow" to get the gist or the general ideas.

Day 2

Teach Students to Create Interpretive Questions *(15–20 minutes)*

▶ Reread aloud or ask students to reread the biography in order to recall details to create interpretive questions (see guidelines on pages 9–12).

▶ Think aloud and show how you test a question to ensure that it's interpretive. Say something like:

  If I can find two different answers for a question, then it's an interpretive question. I'm going to test this question: Why did Newton purchase two prisms? First, he bought the prism as a toy. But I'm inferring that since Krull says Newton was brilliant and later refers to the prism as a science toy, he saw it as a way to learn. Second, he thought the prism was cool and, though he had little money, bought another.

▶ Explain that words like *why, how, evaluate, compare,* and *contrast* can generate questions with more than one answer. Post these words.

▶ Organize partner talk and have students write two interpretive questions for paragraphs 1–10.

▶ Circulate and support students as they test a question to see if it has more than one answer. Here are the two questions seventh-grade students agreed to discuss:

How did Newton differ from other college students? What does this say about his personality?

How did Newton use the prism to prove that Aristotle and Hooke were wrong?

▶ Record questions.

Whole-Class Discussion Using Interpretive Questions *(15–20 minutes)*

Day 3

▶ Ask students to skim "Isaac Newton and the Day He Discovered the Rainbow" to the end of paragraph 10 to refresh their memories.

▶ Give students a copy of the interpretive questions related to the first half of the text that were generated the previous day, or project them onto a whiteboard. Invite students to discuss the questions as a whole class.

▶ Summarize the key points halfway through the discussion and at the end.

▶ Have students write key points for each question in their notebooks.

Whole-Class Discussion Using Interpretive Questions *(30 minutes)*

Day 4

▶ Give students about 5–6 minutes to skim "Isaac Newton and the Day He Discovered the Rainbow" from paragraph 11 to the end.

▶ Use partner talk to have students compose two interpretive questions for paragraph 11 to the end (10–15 minutes). Here are the two questions seventh-grade students used:

How did Newton conclude that white light wasn't white?

Why did the author include the sidebar "Newton Not Always Right"?

▶ Invite students to discuss as a whole class.

▶ Summarize the key points halfway through the discussion and again at the end.

▶ Ask students to list key points discussed in their notebooks.

Notes to Yourself About Teaching the Lesson

_____

_____

_____

_____

Determining the Author's Purpose: Informational Text

The author's purpose for writing a text can be to explain, argue for, persuade, describe, create suspense, or entertain. By studying the author's words, students can identify the purpose. This lesson has students turn-and-talk to build background knowledge, then partner talk to discuss the gist and text details before discussing the author's purpose.

Each time you schedule partner talk, plan on listening to two pairs—three at the most. To gain insight into partner talks not observed, have students list in their notebooks several key points they discussed.

Materials

Excerpt from *Secrets of the Sky Caves: Danger and Discovery on Nepal's Mustang Cliffs* by Sandra Athans; smart notebooks

Lesson Guidelines

Day 1

Build Background Knowledge *(20 minutes)*

▶ Project a map of Nepal. Locate the Mustang District of Nepal on the map.

▶ Find photographs of the Mustang District of Nepal on the Internet and project these. Have students turn-and-talk:

Why are the caves called "cities in the sky"?

▶ Offer students some background information on the Sky Caves of the Mustang Cliffs. You can use Sandra Athans's book or gather information from an Internet search. This website has a *National Geographic* article about the Mustang Caves and a photo gallery: http://ngm.nationalgeographic.com/2012/10/mustang-caves/finkel-text.

Day 2

Read and Use Partner Talk to Get the Gist and Key Points *(30–35 minutes)*

▶ Read aloud or have students read the excerpt from *Secrets of the Sky Caves: Danger and Discovery on Nepal's Mustang Cliffs*.

▶ Invite students to partner talk to discuss the gist or general points the text makes (3–4 minutes).

▶ Ask partners to share (5 minutes).

▶ Reread aloud or have students reread the text.

▶ Have students partner talk to discuss key details in each section before determining the author's purpose (10–15 minutes).

Teach How to Determine the Author's Purpose *(20–25 minutes)*

▶ Post four prompts to help students determine the author's purpose:

Why did the author write this piece?

Does the structure of the text offer clues?

How does the author's use of language and structure make you feel?

Do you find more than one purpose?

▶ Think aloud and use the prompts to determine the author's purpose for "The Rescue and Recovery Expedition." Say something like:

> *The author explains why the 2008 expedition occurred. It was to find the papers in the caves. The author creates a feeling of mystery by using "mysterious" to describe the papers and by concluding that the papers have to be valuable because they had been stored in a high, remote place.*

▶ Invite students to partner talk to determine the author's purpose for paragraphs 3 and 4 (5–7 minutes). Here's what eighth-grade students said:

> *In paragraph 3 the purpose is to explain how the team got permission for the expedition.*

> *In paragraph 4, the purpose is to show the team was nervous and could be cursed; they want the blessing of Buddhist lamas. Three lamas went with them as protection from "danger and troublesome spirits."*

Use Partner Talk to Determine the Author's Purpose *(25–30 minutes)*

▶ Post the four prompts from Day 3 for students to use.

▶ Divide the class into two groups. Partners in one group use "Making Scientists Into Climbers," and partners in the second group use "Library in the Sky" to determine the author's purpose (10–15 minutes).

▶ Invite students to share the author's purposes they uncovered.

  ○ Here's a purpose from group one:

  to explain why the climb is dangerous and why Ramble feared the climb

  ○ Here's a purpose from group two:

  to show the joy in seeing the papers

▶ Ask students to jot a purpose for their section in their notebooks.

3.4

Why Characters Change: Small-Group Discussion Using a Short Story

Books and stories are fictionalized representations of people and their lives. Lived-through events, other people, and personal decisions can change our beliefs, values, and who we are. A satisfying short story or novel—one that mirrors life—helps readers understand why and how plot, conflicts and problems, setting, and decisions can change the protagonist. Moreover, not only does the protagonist change, but the reader comes away with lingering thoughts about these changes that can impact his or her values.

This lesson asks you to organize students into groups of 4 or 6 for a small-group discussion using "Coming Clean" by Anina Robb. Small-group discussions invite students to be in charge of the entire discussion. Students will also engage in turn-and-talk and partner talk before launching their small-group discussions.

You can listen to one or two small-group discussions during 25–30 minutes. Have all students make a list of key points they discussed in their readers' notebooks.

Materials

"Coming Clean" by Anina Robb; smart notebooks

Lesson Guidelines

Day 1

Preparation and Reading "Coming Clean" *(25–30 minutes)*

▶ Organize students into groups of 4 or 6.

▶ Ask students to turn-and-talk to discuss the meaning of *bodega* (1–2 minutes). Have students share so everyone understands its meaning.

▶ Invite students to think about a time they made a decision based on peer pressure and its consequences; have them write about this decision in their notebooks (4–5 minutes).

▶ Have students read "Coming Clean" to get the gist or general idea (10 minutes).

▶ Ask students to partner talk (10 minutes) by saying something like:

> *Discuss the gist of the story and identify the decision Jasper made in order to be part of the skate park regulars.*

Day 2

Small-Group Discussions of a Guiding Question *(20–25 minutes)*

▶ Have students reread "Coming Clean" to recall plot details.

▶ Make sure each group has a discussion facilitator who understands the role and can use the Prompts That Keep a Discussion Moving Forward (page 25).

▶ Have the group facilitator say the guiding question. Here's one I offer:

> *How do decisions change our lives?*

▶ Ask students to discuss the question, clearly showing how peer pressure and Jasper's decision changed him (12–15 minutes).

▶ Ask students to list the key ideas from the discussion in their notebooks.

▶ Invite group leaders to share two key points with the whole class (5–6 minutes). Here's what sixth graders shared. (Their teacher required them to give text evidence, but that's not included here.)

> *Jasper thinks friends are more important than family. He wants to be with Savion instead of helping in the bodega.*

> *Jasper's decision to let the skaters steal from the bodega is selfish—that gets him in the group.*

> *Jasper feels guilt when he passes Savion the note. But he [Jasper] let them steal penny candy. He loses his value of doing right when he decides to cheat his Papi to get in the skateboarder's club.*

> *Guilt after the boys steal for two days changes Jasper. His dad gave him trust by putting him at the cash register. His dad cooks and cares for him; he sees that the bodega is his, too.*

> *Jasper decides to tell Papi the truth. Jasper learns that being honest to Papi and himself is more important than being a skateboard regular.*

> *Making a bad decision changes Jasper. He goes from liar and robber 'cause he lets the boys steal to being honest and respecting Papi and work.*

Notes to Yourself About Teaching the Lesson

_____

_____

_____

_____

_____

_____

_____

_____

_____

_____

_____

Prompting In-the-Head Conversations: Biography

By asking students to use a bookmark to write their thoughts and reactions, teachers can observe the kinds of in-the-head conversations students have while they read. Bookmarks provide helpful insights that enable teachers to improve students' application of strategies through short conferences.

Your prompts can be directive and ask students to monitor how they infer or think about genre, literary elements, or text structure. However, you can also ask students to write what's going on inside their heads as they read in order to observe their thinking process.

Materials

Excerpt from "How Ada Lovelace Leaped Into History" by Kathleen Krull; a bookmark

Directions for Completing a Bookmark for Biography

Have students prepare a bookmark by folding a sheet of notebook paper in half lengthwise. You can direct students to one of the following prompts and have students write on the top of the bookmark their name, date, the prompt, and the title and author. Students can respond using as many sides of the bookmark as needed.

1. Evaluate Annabella's mothering abilities, paraphrasing evidence from the text.

2. Skim the text, thinking about Ada and noting what you learn about her personality. Paraphrase evidence from the text and use details to infer.

3. Write what you think as you read.

4. Note what about the text you found interesting and made you want to continue reading.

Lesson Guidelines

Day 1

Help Students Prepare *(20–30 minutes)*

▶ Give students a copy of the entire text "How Ada Lovelace Leaped Into History," and ask them to read the selection for the gist.

▶ Invite students to turn-and-talk and share what they thought the gist, or general meaning, was.

Day 2

Document In-the-Head Conversations *(15–20 minutes)*

▶ Explain what kind of responses you want students to make by reviewing the directions for the bookmark with them.

▶ Show students how to set up their bookmarks by completing a model on the board. Here are some notes that show my reaction to information in the text, for *Write what you think as you read.*

Wonder what was unusual about her growing up. Weird marriage and Ada didn't know Byron, her dad. Ada's mom seems to love math more than her daughter.

- Have students select a prompt and write it on the bookmark as part of the heading.
- Have students retrieve their copy of the excerpt from "How Ada Lovelace Leaped Into History."
- Ask them to reread the selection carefully and jot responses on the bookmark.
- Suggest that students reread their responses to ensure that they are clear.

Notes to Yourself About Teaching the Lesson

_____

_____

_____

_____

_____

_____

_____

_____

_____

_____

_____

_____

_____

_____

_____

_____

_____

_____

_____

_____

Teacher–Student Talk: Conferring

When students have difficulty applying a reading strategy, linking literary elements to a text they are reading, or showing how text features and structures support understanding of main ideas, themes, and/or a character or person's decisions and motivation, conferring with them and scaffolding the process can move them out of the frustration zone into the learning zone, and ultimately to independence.

5-minute conferences are manageable during a 42- to 50-minute reading class. Conferences occur while students read and/or write independently. Meet with students at a small table or desk that provides some privacy so students feel comfortable discussing challenges with you. Start small, and complete one conference during a class period. Then, once you're comfortable with this, schedule two to four, depending on how much time you have.

In addition to a completed conference form, on page 84 you can explore Ten Tips for Conferring With Students. You'll find a blank conference form on page 85 and available for download at http://resources.corwin.com/readtalkwrite.

See *The Reading Intervention Toolkit*, by Laura Robb (2016) for a detailed discussion of interventions, assessments, and scaffolds.

Notes to Yourself About Teaching the Lesson

_____

_____

_____

_____

_____

_____

_____

_____

_____

_____

_____

_____

_____

_____

_____

_____

5-Minute Intervention Conference Form

Name <u>Seventh-Grade Student</u>   Date _____

Directions: Complete this conference form and use the information it contains to inform your practice. Store in the student's assessment folder to consult later as necessary.

Before the Conference

Focus the conference topic: Finding themes, using "Isaac Newton and the Day He Discovered the Rainbow" by Kathleen Krull

Points to discuss with the student:

- See what the student knows about theme.

- Think aloud using the three steps for identifying theme [see Lesson 5.3, pages 161–162] to model how I find theme using read-aloud or another common text.

- Encourage the student to ask questions.

The kind of scaffolding I'll try:

- I'll identify the protagonist and then I'll ask the student to identify the topic using "Isaac Newton and the Day He Discovered the Rainbow."

- We'll discuss what Newton does, thinks, and says, and I'll see if the student can link this to the topic.

- I'll think aloud and create a theme statement and then ask the student to create one using a different general topic.

After the Conference

Note important comments the student made: "This is hard; can't do it."

My observations of the student: Comments revealed low self-confidence that stopped her from taking risks. By sharing the process, I helped the student be able to write a theme statement. Gave lots of praise and explained how pleased I was that she tried and succeeded.

Negotiated goal and how to reach it for the next conference: Use a different short text to write two different theme statements. Use the three steps and write the thinking for each one. Do this when the class works independently.

Date of the next conference: One week from today

Ten Tips for Conferring With Students

1. **Choose a Single Topic:** Zoom in on one strategy, such as making inferences, linking literary elements to themes, determining important details and ideas, or showing how text features connect to main ideas.

2. **Complete the "Before the Conference" Section:** The prompts in this section help you reflect on what you plan to discuss and think of more than one possible scaffold to try. Having multiple scaffolds helps because if one doesn't work, you have another at your fingertips.

3. **Be Positive:** Start by pointing out what the student has done well. It could be something you recently observed or the effort the student puts into analyzing texts.

4. **Count to 100:** When you ask a question to start the conversation, count to 100 and give the student time to think. The tendency is for teachers to fill the silence with talk and solutions. This doesn't support students. Though your wait time might feel like an eternity, resist the urge to talk.

5. **Listen Carefully:** Avoid interrupting a student. Listen carefully and jot down questions you have; ask these once the student has finished talking. Throughout the conference, use your knowledge of this student to make comments and ask questions that boost the student's confidence and encourage him to talk.

6. **Pose Questions That Prompt the Student to Recall Prior Lessons:** Review a mini-lesson or a think-aloud that relates to the conference's topic. When you point the student to a specific lesson, you shift the focus away from her own thinking, which sometimes frees her up to find the solution from the lesson.

7. **Model and Think Aloud:** Sometimes you'll need to think aloud to show the student how you apply a strategy to reading in order to refresh his memory and build enough confidence so the student risks completing guided practice.

8. **Negotiate Goals:** Start by recapping the conference and then inviting the student to set a goal that she can achieve in 1–2 weeks. If the student struggles with this, suggest two goals and ask her to choose one.

9. **Have the Student Develop a Plan to Achieve Goal:** Having a goal is the first step, but reaching that goal requires a plan. Help the student figure out what he has to do to reach the goal, and write the plan on the conference form. Give a copy of the plan to the student to tape into his reader's notebook.

10. **Close a Conference With Positive Comments:** Say something positive to the student at the end of the conference so she leaves feeling that she improved and deepened her understanding of the conference's topic. Start with *I noticed . . .* or *I like the way. . .*

5-Minute Intervention Conference Form

Name _____ Date _____

Directions: Complete this conference form and use the information it contains to inform your practice. Store in the student's assessment folder to consult later as necessary.

Before the Conference

Focus the conference topic:

_____

_____

Points to discuss with the student:

_____

_____

The kind of scaffolding I'll try:

_____

_____

After the Conference

Note important comments the student made:

_____

_____

My observations of the student:

_____

_____

Negotiated goal and how to reach it for the next conference:

_____

_____

Date of the next conference: _____

COMING CLEAN

by Anina Robb

"Oh, not today, Papi," Jasper shrugged and shrank down into his chair at the breakfast table. "Can't I get a break? I just want to go to the skate park after school with Savion." 1

Jasper's father poured him a bowl of cereal and shook his head. 2

"No, not today. You know that Wednesday is the busiest day at the bodega and I need your help stocking shelves. The park will be there another day. I know you are disappointed. But this is the way that things are right now." 3

Hunh. Right now? Jasper thought. This is the way things have been forever. Jasper had been helping his dad at the store for as long as he could remember. When he was a little kid, he had liked it. It made him feel grown up—especially when the customers got to know him and would slip him a dime or a quarter for helping. But now that he was in middle school, helping at his dad's store was a drag. He wanted to hang out with Savion after school. He wanted to sleep in on the weekends. Instead, he was stocking shelves and mopping floors. 4

"At least will you teach me the register? I am almost 12 you know, Papi." 5

"Okay. It's a big responsibility. But maybe it is time you got a seat at the head of the store. I'll show you this afternoon." 6

"Great. Thanks! I'll see you after school!" And Jasper was gone—heading out the apartment building down the block to his middle school—happy to have something to look forward to. 7

Savion, his best friend since first grade, was waiting by his locker. "So, are you going to come skating after school with all the guys?" 8

"I can't. I have to work." Jasper dug through his locker for his books. 9

"Man, you are always at that store."   *10*

"Well, I'm working up front today."   *11*

"Really? Interesting." And Savion walked away.   *12*

"Hey, Wait up!" Jasper called after him.   *13*

In the lunchroom, a group of boys who were regulars at the   *14*
skate park walked past Jasper and Savion. One of them, the
best skater, nicknamed Spike, spoke up. "Hey, I hear you work
at that bodega? You know, I really like candy." They kept on
walking past.   *15*

"What does that mean?" Jasper asked Savion. "And why do they
all wear tie-dye shirts?"   *16*

"I don't know." Savion's voice wandered off.   *17*

After school, Jasper went straight to the bodega like he
promised his father. He left his book bag behind the counter
and got to work restocking the shelves with all the Wednesday
deliveries until his father was free to show him the register. His
father was helping Ms. Santos with her shopping list in the back of
the store. It was then when everything happened quickly. Savion
came in holding his skateboard and right behind him was Spike.
They both had their heads down and walked quickly down the
penny-candy isle. Spike gave Jasper a look that made Jasper's
blood feel like ice in his veins, and Jasper froze as he watched his
best friend scoop up a handful of penny-candy and shove it in
his jean's pocket and walk right out of the store. Spike did the
same thing. It all happened so fast. Jasper had no time to think
about what he should do or say. He just stood there—frozen like a
snowman. Like an idiot.   *18*

The next day at school, Savion was not waiting at Jasper's locker
for him. Instead, he was a few lockers down standing next to Spike
and wearing a tie-dye shirt. In English class, Jasper passed Savion this
note:

I CAN'T BELIEVE YOU STOLE FROM MY DAD'S STORE.

After class, Savion waited for Jasper. "Hey, Jasper. Listen, I know you   *19*
are bent out of shape, but listen, it was just a little penny-candy.

And if you let the skaters steal from your dad's store then you can be a skater, too. Do you know how cool we will be? Do you know what this will do for our cred?"

Jasper asked with amazement in his voice, "Those guys will let me be a skater? Even though I can't get to the Wednesday practices?" 20

"Yeah, dude, you will be like the cool candy-man." 21

Jasper had never done anything like this before in his life. In fact, he'd always done the right thing. And he knew how hard his father worked to keep the store going and to make sure things were okay for him. It wasn't always easy—especially when his mom had gotten sick. Then it was just Jasper and his dad. But they had done okay, and the bodega had become the most popular one in the neighborhood. 22

But, wow, did Jasper ever want to be one of those skaters—and there was no way he was ever going to get to the Wednesday practices after school. His papi had made that clear. What was a little candy? His papi probably would not even notice. It couldn't matter that much. 23

"All right," he shook hands with Savion. "Let's do this." For the next two days after school, Spike sauntered in with Savion. They cruised the candy aisle, and Jasper turned his eyes down to the register while they pocketed fistfuls of hard candy and chocolates. When Jasper saw them, his heart raced so fast he thought he was going to pass out. Little beads of sweat gathered at his forehead and by his ears. He started to shake. Was this worth it after all, he wondered? 24

He peered out the corner of his eye and could see his father leaning over a mop in the store's back storage room as his friends raced out the front door of the store, laughing, shoving candies in their mouths. His father was in the back—trusting him to watch out for the whole store, for *their* whole store. Jasper decided that he had to tell his father what was going on that evening. 25

The walk with Papi from the bodega to their apartment was torture. Jasper dropped his book bag by the front door. While Jasper did homework, Papi cooked dinner. The smell of the fragrant rice and tortillas made Jasper's stomach grumble. "Wash up. Dinner is ready," Papi called. 26

Jasper turned the water faucets on and let his hands soak under   *27*
the warm stream. He looked up at his reflection in the mirror. How
could he have been so stupid? His father works all day then comes
home and makes him dinner, and he is letting boys steal from his—
no from *their* store, to be cool. What was he thinking? It was time
to come clean. Jasper cupped his hands and splashed his face with
water. He walked out of the bathroom knowing just what he had
to do.

Source: Courtesy of Anina Robb.

DEFYING GRAVITY: MAE JEMISON

by Anina Robb

Have you ever wanted to float above the earth? Or maybe defy gravity? Dr. Mae Jemison did, but she couldn't decide how to best achieve this goal. Perhaps she should study science and become an astronaut? Or maybe she should follow her love of dance and become a professional dancer? At first glance, these two dreams seem like they belong at the opposite ends of a wish list, but Mae Jemison followed both her dreams of dancing and becoming an astronaut. She became the first African American woman astronaut and showed the world how dancing and space travel aren't that different.   1

Born October 17, 1956, in Decatur, Alabama, Mae and her family moved to Chicago when she was only three. Mae always considered Chicago her home. As a young girl, Mae imagined "by now we'd be going into space like you were going to work." Her parents were always very supportive of her dreams of studying science—even if her teachers were not always so open-minded. When Mae was five years old, her kindergarten teacher asked her what she wanted to be when she grew up. Mae replied, "A scientist!"   2

Her teacher was surprised as there weren't many women scientists in 1961. So her teacher said, "You must mean a nurse?"   3

And Mae remembers thinking that there was nothing wrong with being a nurse, but that was not what she wanted to be. So she said, "No, a scientist!"   4

Mae also loved to dance. As a young girl, she took every kind of dance that she could—ballet, tap, jazz, and African. Most people might think that dance is the exact opposite of science. After all, it is an art. What could dance training possibly offer to becoming a scientist or an astronaut? As Mae put it, "In dance class, I grew stronger and gained an appreciation for hard work, physical strength, and grace." The lessons she learned from dance would eventually serve her very well in her astronaut training.   5

Mae graduated from high school early; she was only 16. At the   6
time she did not realize that this was an achievement. It wasn't until
she arrived at the campus of Stanford University in California—far
from her Chicago home—that she realized how young she was.
Throughout Mae's college years, her interests remained wide and
varied—not just science. At Stanford she studied both physical and
social sciences. Mae learned Russian and African languages. Her
college degrees were in chemical engineering and African studies.

After college Mae was trying to figure out what she wanted to   7
do with her life; she was trying to decide whether to continue on
to medical school at Cornell or to become a professional dancer.
Like a lot of young adults, she turned to her mother for advice. Her
mother told her, "You can always dance if you are a doctor, but you
can't doctor if you are a dancer." So Mae put aside her dream of
professional dancing and went on to medical school for four years
and became a doctor.

The next stop on Mae's career path was the Peace Corps. She   8
served as a medical officer in the Peace Corps from 1983 to 1985.
Her main job was to care for Peace Corps volunteers serving in
Liberia and Sierra Leone, Africa. It was during this time that she
applied to the astronaut program at NASA. Mae was inspired to
follow through on her dream of becoming an astronaut by the
African American actress who played Lieutenant Uhura on the
TV show *Star Trek*. She also could tell that the space program was
opening up to women after the historic flight of the first American
woman, Sally Ride, in 1983.

In 1987, NASA accepted Mae into its Astronaut Training Program.   9
Only 15 candidates were chosen that year out of over 2,000
applicants. She was part of a highly select group of trainees being
groomed to fly the next shuttle into space. She
trained at their facilities in Texas and in Florida
and learned all about space exploration—the
hard work and the physical strength needed
to be an astronaut. She worked for NASA and
waited for a chance to go up on one of the
space shuttles.

Fast Fact

In 2015 NASA received over 18,000 application for its astronaut training program!

In 1992 that chance finally came. The space shuttle *Endeavor* 10 launched September 12, 1992, and Mae Jemison became the first African American woman to orbit the Earth. Mae has happy memories of that flight and looking out the window down onto planet Earth. She looked down at the Earth from the space shuttle and saw the city of Chicago—her childhood home. She said, "I felt like I belonged right there in space. I realized I would be comfortable anywhere in the universe because I belonged to and was part of it as much as any star, planet, asteroid, comet, or nebula."

Because of her love of dance and as a salute to creativity, Mae 11 took a poster of the Alvin Ailey American Dance Theater along with her on her historic space flight. Jemison says, "Many people don't see the connection between science and dance, but I consider them both to be expressions of the boundless creativity that people have to share with one another."

What is it that we can take away from Mae Jemison's life 12 experiences? It might be to never stop following your passions and dreams because we never know where they might lead us—maybe right out of this world!

Source: Courtesy of Anina Robb.

HOOPS TRYOUTS

by Anina Robb

"Brian! Breakfast!" Brian's mom was knocking at his locked bedroom door. "Why is this door locked, young man?"   *1*

"I'll be out in a second, Mom." Brian leapt down from the top bar of his bunkbed from where he'd been hanging, stretching, his toes dangling, his white pajama pants flapping like a flag of surrender.   *2*

And, in fact, today that was all that Brian wanted to do—give up. He'd been stretching from his bunk for the last month and he was still the shortest boy in seventh grade. He was shorter than most of the girls.   *3*

Heck, he was shorter than the sixth graders. Basketball tryouts were today, and if he didn't make the team, he'd disgrace his family.   *4*

"Finally," his mom sighed as Brian slid into his chair at the kitchen table. She piled a heaping serving of scrambled eggs on his plate. "Eat up, you have a big day!" His big brother, Jonas, had already finished breakfast.   *5*

"A kiss good-bye for your mama?" Mom joked, and Jonas turned to bend down to kiss her. Then he smacked Brian on the head. Brian thought this could mean one of two things: I love you or you are an idiot.   *6*

Jonas was a sophomore in high school and almost six feet tall. He'd been a starter on the basketball team since junior high. Everyone knew he'd get a basketball college scholarship. Brian shoved the eggs in his mouth.   *7*

"Alex is here. Don't forget your lunch money!" Mom called as Brian slid his plate into the sink and grabbed the coins from the bowl. Alex knocked on the screen door like a trusty alarm at 8:05. The two friends had been walking to school together since the second grade. But Alex only cared about basketball because his friend liked it—he was more interested in computers.   *8*

"Ready for tryouts?"   *9*

"I guess, ready as I'll ever be." Brian shrugged.   *10*

"What you gonna do about Lesh?" Matt Lesh thought he was the 11
best basketball player in seventh grade because he was five feet ten.
He'd been picking on Brian for being short for so long that Brian
couldn't remember a time that he hadn't. In fact, it was Lesh who
had inspired Brian to try to stretch himself out. Of course, Brian
didn't tell anyone he was trying it.

BRRRRING. The first bell was ringing, which meant five minutes 12
to get to class. Brian fumbled at his locker. When he finally opened
it, Matt Lesh darted around the corner and slammed his locker door
shut, "Oops, my bad!" and he was gone. Brian didn't have time to
react or say anything. He had to get his locker open again so he
could get to first block on time.

At lunch things just got worse. In the lunch line Matt was full of 13
put-downs: "How about some shrimp today? No, maybe a small fry?
Would you like some peanuts with that?" Brian was getting hot; he
could feel his face flushing red like the roses in his grandmother's
garden.

"Just ignore him, Brian," Alex elbowed his friend along in line. 14
"He's not worth it.'

After school, the gym was bustling with boys trying out for the 15
basketball team. The coaches lined everyone up in order from tallest
to shortest, and wouldn't you know? Brian was dead last.

"End of the line, huh, Brian?" Coach Peters chuckled. For a 16
moment, Brian thought of splitting, just hightailing it out of there
and not looking back. Geez, even the coaches were making fun of
him. But he'd been practicing for weeks to get on this team, and
he knew that being tall was not the end-all, be-all for junior high
basketball. Besides, he was bound to grow sometime soon, and then
everyone would need someone else to sneer at.

"All right," Coach Peters boomed. "This tryout is made up of four 17
different stations: a dribbling through cones drill, jump shooting,
passing, and an agility drill. Let's pair up and get started! Front of the
line—you are with the back of the line and so on!"

Brian froze. It couldn't be. This was his worst nightmare ever. He 18
was paired with Matt Lesh. Matt jogged over, "You better make me
look good, short stuff."

And in that moment, Brian decided the thing to do was to make himself look good—to take all the work that he had put in over the last few weeks and show it off—not for Matt or his brother or his mom but for himself. He deserved a spot on this team because he was good and he worked hard and he was a team player. Brian took off to the first station, leaving Matt in his shadow. "Hey, wait up!" And that is how each station went—Brian dribbled by Matt, he out-passed him, he threw more jump shots, and his feet were lighter on the basketball court during the agility drills.

19

Sweaty and hot, the boys slumped onto the bleachers when the coaches blew the whistles.

20

"All right, good work out there today. Good hustle. A team roster will be posted tomorrow morning by the gym."

21

As everyone started shuffling out of the double doors, Brian spotted Alex waiting for him across the street. Just as he turned to slip on his jacket, there was Matt Lesh behind him. He braced himself for the coming insult. Instead Matt raised his hand for a high-five. Brian reluctantly raised his, too. "Nice," Matt nodded his head, and jogged away.

22

"What the heck was that?" Alex asked as they fell into step together.

23

Brian shrugged his shoulders. Even if he didn't make the team tomorrow, he was hoping things would be different from here on out.

24

Source: Courtesy of Anina Robb.

HOW ADA LOVELACE LEAPED INTO HISTORY

by Kathleen Krull

Ada Lovelace (1815–1852) grew up in a seriously unusual way. It was more like a science experiment than a childhood: How could her mother, Lady Annabella Byron, raise Ada to be as unlike her notorious father as possible? 1

Ada never knew her dad, who left England when she was still a baby. Annabella refused to tell her daughter anything about him until after he had died in Greece, when Ada was eight. Lord Byron may have been England's most famous poet, but he was also—in the words of a former girlfriend—"mad, bad, and dangerous to know." There was even a term—"Byronic"—for someone who was wild, dark, dramatic, rebellious. Just the opposite of a proper person in the stuffy Victorian era. 2

Annabella's wealthy friends were appalled when she married Byron, and soon so was she. During their brief marriage, he dubbed Annabella the Princess of Parallelograms for her love of geometrical shapes. She was a well-educated woman for her day, especially in math and science, logical to a fault. Not particularly affectionate to her daughter, she was even known to refer her as "it." 3

Annabella kept an iron grip on her daughter's days from the moment Ada awoke at 6 a.m. until bedtime. She hired an army of top-notch scholars to educate Ada at home on every subject—except poetry. The emphasis was on facts, logic, and all branches of math, as well as languages and other subjects useful to know. Anything to squelch flights of fancy and prevent her from becoming a poet. 4

Poor Ada had no siblings or playmates. Instead she was watched over by several close friends of her mother, all unmarried. If she showed any rebelliousness or bad behavior, like talking too much or riding her horse too often, they reported back to her mother. Ada called them "the Furies" and hated them. 5

If she had a moment to herself, she could be found on the lawn outside the family's elegant estate, her cat Puff on her lap, reading a tome like Bingley's *Useful Knowledge*.

6

Even her diet was controlled, chiefly mutton (sheep) oozing grease, with fruits and vegetables served only rarely.

7

Ada decided early on she was a genius. She dabbled in drawing, music, and other fields, including—gasp—poetry. By age eight, she was definitely in love with numbers. Equations and calculations became her focus, as well as the latest news in science.

8

One day when Puff dragged in a bird he had killed, 12-year-old Ada carefully studied its wing. For the next year, she did experiments and research on bird anatomy. She became obsessed with getting humans to fly, even designing wings for herself of paper and wire. She was trying to invent a new branch of science, which she called Flyology.

9

At 13 she completed the drawing of a "Planetarium," a comprehensive map of the stars. At 17 one of her tutors raved that with her math talent Ada could become "an original mathematical investigator." Ada felt she was destined for a brilliant future in science—it was just a matter of focusing.

10

The following year, through another tutor, she met Charles Babbage, professor of mathematics, prolific inventor, and social butterfly. Every Saturday afternoon he invited a glittering crowd to his home to marvel at his amazing machines. Soon Ada, wearing one of her bright-colored dresses, was attending.

11

One of his marvels was the "Silver Dancer," a beautiful metallic figure that performed elegant dance moves according to its clockwork mechanism. Visitors loved the life-like dancing, but Ada was more interested in the coils and cogs inside.

12

Other machines of his were more practical. Babbage was wonderstruck at the gas lamps, the steam engine, the electricity revolutionizing England. He was also inspired by a French weaver who had invented the Jacquard loom. Using a sequence of cards with holes systematically punched in them, looms were being automated, "programmed" to weave beautiful patterns in fabrics. Babbage envisioned machines that would work in a similar fashion

13

to do automatic calculations, with a goal of improving accuracy in British navigation and engineering.

People were calling his creations "thinking machines," but had little idea of what that meant or how they would work. The word computer wouldn't be coined for another hundred years. Indeed, Babbage's ideas were so ahead of his time that hardly anyone knew what he was talking about.

14

Ada was an exception. She asked him for copies of his plans for machines that she could study.

15

Babbage, in turn, was impressed by Ada's brain, and especially her math skills. He called her the "Enchantress of Numbers." They took long walks together, discussing science and math.

16

At 20, Ada married a gentleman approved by her mom, the Earl of Lovelace, a bit of an amateur inventor himself who tinkered on his two country estates. Having three children didn't slow Ada down, and she kept up her math studies and visited Babbage whenever she could.

17

To his dismay, the English government was balking at the amount of money it would cost to fund his latest machine. "A very costly toy . . . worthless," sniffed the prime minister. Babbage's research stalled.

18

Then he was invited to Italy to lecture on the machine. An Italian engineer wrote up Babbage's speech in French—a language that of course Ada knew. Babbage turned to her to translate the paper into English, and then asked her to add her own notes to it.

19

Ada Lovelace's claim to fame rests on the nine months she took to carry out his request.

20

Her notes, published in 1843, were much longer than the original paper. She took it upon herself to explain how Babbage's new machine differed from his others, a challenge that had defeated other scientists.

21

Ada did get frustrated, needing Babbage's help with the algebra, not her strongest suit: "I am in much dismay at having got into so amazing a quagmire & botheration with these Numbers." But she persisted until she understood the new machine—and presented a sample set of rules for it to carry out. It was a method for calculating a complicated set of numbers, and it was also the world's first

22

computer program. It would weave "algebraical patterns just as the Jacquard loom weaves flowers and leaves," she wrote.

Ada is often credited with being the first computer programmer. *23* She didn't really invent programming, but rather the idea of it. A way of testing it didn't exist yet. But she could look at Babbage's plans and see the possibility of something entirely new—a logic machine.

Babbage's Engines

The "Difference Engine" was Babbage's first attempt at a computing machine. It could do one simple task: process numbers in sequences. He succeeded in getting government funding to build one and started showing it off. Ada was fascinated by the way it looked— like the inside of a clock, but on a much bigger scale, with hundreds of interlocking cogs and wheels.

His next attempt was the "Analytical Engine," which he claimed would be able to solve math problems. Powered by steam, it would have required 25,000 parts and been 15 feet high and 20 feet long—the most complex machine ever built. He never did succeed in getting the funding to build one.

Finally, in 1991 the Science Museum of London used his diagrams to build an Analytical Engine—and it worked.

Then she leaped ahead of Babbage. *24* With startling insight, she foresaw the ability of his device to do a lot more than crunch numbers. She envisioned all kinds of general uses, from producing new music to figuring out how much fabric to buy for a gown to determining what proportions were needed to build a flying machine. "It can do whatever we know how to order it to perform," she declared. She was talking about the modern computer in a way no one else was at the time. It was all about information, not just numbers. This was an imaginative leap worthy of her poet father.

She took a moment to congratulate *25* herself. She boasted that she had become her own role model at 28: "a completely professional person."

Alas, plagued by illnesses, her life was short and mostly *26* unhappy. She used her math skills to try to predict the outcome of horse races, got addicted to gambling, and ran up huge debts. She died of cancer at 36 in 1852, still mostly under the thumb of her mother, who lived to be 68. According to Ada's request, she was buried in the Byron family vault next to the father she had never known.

It took almost 100 years for Ada's work to move forward. During *27* World War II, a gigantic machine called the Automatic Sequence Controlled Calculator was used to break enemy codes and help win

the war for the Allied Powers. Another woman, U.S. Navy officer
Grace Murray Hopper, was one of its first programmers.

As computers took over our world, the United States Department   *28*
of Defense created a new computer language in 1980 and called it
Ada—in honor of Countess Ada Lovelace.

Source: Courtesy of Kathleen Krull.

HOW ATHENS GOT ITS NAME

Retelling by Joanna Davis-Swing

In ancient times, when the world was young, Cecrops was born of the earth. Half man, half snake, he roamed rugged mountains, wooded valleys, and rocky shores. He traveled wide before venturing into the region of Attica in Greece. Here lived goat farmers and bee keepers in peaceful tranquility, and Cecrops became their king.

1

He planned a beautiful city, set atop a large rock that rose from the plains. Fertile land spread out below, and the nearby sea boasted two open harbors. The gods on Olympus watched Cecrops and approved of his plans. They could foresee that his city would rise to fame and fortune in the world, and they wanted a share of the glory. Indeed, the gods fought over who was to be the patron of the city. Zeus, who deplored fighting on Mount Olympus, declared a contest between Poseidon, god of the sea, and Athena, goddess of wisdom. Each would give Cecrops a gift, and Cecrops himself would decide who would be patron of his city.

2

On the appointed day, Poseidon and Athena gathered with Cecrops and his people on top of the rock. Poseidon carried his trident and stood proudly surveying the land. Modest Athena wore her golden helmet and carried her spear. Cecrops signaled for the contest to begin, and Poseidon immediately raised his trident high, then struck it mightily into the ground. The rock shook and the earth trembled. A great crack appeared in the rock and spread wide, filling with water. The people gasped at this marvel and rushed forward to taste the water. It was saltwater, fitting for Poseidon, god of the sea, but of limited use to humans and farmers.

3

Athena smiled gently, then bent to the ground. In silence, she dug into the earth and worked in the dirt. Gradually, a small plant emerged; it grew and grew until it was full size, covered in green leaves and laden with yellowish-green berries. Athena gazed upon the tree in satisfaction but did not utter a word.

4

Poseidon looked at the tree, then he looked at the saltwater   5
spring. He roared with laughter, which traveled out to sea. Finally
there was silence. Athena spoke: "This small tree is yet mighty. Oil
from its fruit will be one of the favorite offerings of the gods, and
rich men will bedeck themselves with it for the feast. Women will
use it to light the lamps and do the cooking. This oil will be prized
among all the lands, so the city will grow wealthy and renowned as
its merchants trade the world over. This is my gift."

Cecrops had little trouble making up his mind. He chose Athena   6
as the winner and named the city after her: Athens. And so it came
to be that Athena's gift provided prosperity to her city, which has
been honored for its beauty and wisdom ever since.

Source: Courtesy of Joanna Davis-Swing.

ISAAC NEWTON AND THE DAY HE DISCOVERED THE RAINBOW

by Kathleen Krull

On that particular day in the early 1660s, he was not yet Isaac Newton the greatest scientist ever. He was merely an unpopular, solitary, brilliant college student.

1

That day Newton spent a rare few hours outside, at the annual market near his college. He bought a toy—a prism, a piece of glass cut according to precise angles. Though he had next to no money, the prism was so cool that he promptly bought another.

2

Shortly afterward, the plague hit England hard, and the only way to avoid catching it was to avoid other people—not a problem for a guy like Newton. In 1666, at age 24, he was forced to leave college and retreat to his remote childhood home, Woolsthorpe Manor, with his prisms and other science toys.

3

While other students might have goofed off, Newton sat still . . . and thought. Which of the many puzzles in nature could he solve while he was waiting out the plague?

4

All was quiet except for the moaning of sheep. He lived in a time and place of no distractions—no Facebook, TV, cell phone, video games, newspapers, malls.

5

The sparkling prisms caught his eye. What if he could understand the nature of color—something more accurate than what he was being taught in college?

6

Ever since the ancient Greek Aristotle said so, scholars assumed that white light was one simple thing, uniform, solid. Color, therefore, was the product of white light mixed with black. Even those in Newton's day, like Robert Hooke, continued to insist that color was a mixture of light and darkness. Hooke had invented his own personal color scale, ranging from bright red, which he claimed was pure white light mixed with the tiniest amount of darkness, to soft blue and then black, which was darkness completely blocking out the light.

7

104

Newton didn't see how Aristotle or Hooke could be right. 8
After all, a white page with black writing did not appear in color
when viewed from a distance and the black and white blended. It
appeared as gray. So he set out to prove the experts wrong—one of
his very favorite activities.

The prism was the perfect tool for his experiment. Others, like 9
Hooke, were using prisms too, admiring the colors they projected
when sunlight fell on them. They believed that the prism itself was
somehow coloring the light. In their experiments they had placed a
screen close to one side of the prism and seen the spot of light come
out the other side as a mixture of color.

Newton suspected that more accurate results could be had 10
by moving the prism farther away. In his lonely study upstairs, he
positioned the prism at the far wall so that it was 22 feet from the
window. He let a skinny beam of sunlight pass through the prism.
He observed that the beam spread out into colored bands of light,
which he called a spectrum. The white light had split into different
colors. How?

Newton kept thinking. His theory was that each color was a wave 11
of light and that each wave had the ability to be refracted, or bent,
by something. A refracting substance, such
as a prism, could bend each wavelength
of light by a different angle or amount.
The shorter wavelengths—those toward
the violet end of the spectrum—were
being bent the most. The longer
wavelengths—those toward the red end
of the spectrum—were being bent the
least. Therefore, all the colors already
existed in white light, and the prism was
simply fanning them out according to their
ability to be bent. Color was a matter of
wavelengths radiating in a range visible to
the human eye.

Newton Not Always Right

You know how everyone always tells you *not* to stare directly at the sun? Young Newton hadn't heard this important advice when he did his earliest experiments with color. He wanted to know if colors would look different when he stared at the sun. So he stared, and sure enough, the colors did change. But then specks began flickering before his eyes, and he was haunted for days. After one of these bone-headed experiments, it took two weeks before he got his normal vision back. Why he didn't go blind has always baffled people.

Trying unnecessarily to correspond to the seven notes of the musical scale (a wrong turn on his part), Newton used the seven color names red, orange, yellow, green, blue, indigo, and violet for the segments of the spectrum.   12

But the important thing he discovered was that the white light contained all the other colors. This was huge.   13

He was forgetting to eat, forgetting to sleep. So far, so good.   14

Now, to prove that the prism was not coloring the light, Newton did an "Experimentum Crucis." No, this wasn't a spell stolen from Harry Potter, but what scientists call a crucial experiment.   15

Ever Since Newton

Though Newton laid the basics, scientists continue to debate color theory, often aided by artists. About 150 years after Newton, scientists began proposing a theory that three types of color receptors exist in the retina of the eye. In the 1960s, scientists proved the existence of these receptor cells, calling them cones. The three cones were sensitive to the red, blue, and green hues of the spectrum, and those hues can be blended endlessly. Today it is believed that the eye can perceive over 2.8 million different hues—more colors than even Newton could imagine.

Newton placed a screen in between the window and his prism, and he cut a slit in it. He allowed only the pure green light to pass through the slit.   16

Then he grabbed his second prism and placed it in the green light. If the prism was coloring the light, the green would come out a different color.   17

But the green light remained green. The prism had no effect.   18

Newton rarely smiled, but he might have then. There was no one he could brag to yet—his rundown farmhouse was about a mile from the nearest road. But he had just established that colors were governed by scientific principles, and he suspected the rest of the natural world was, too. Oh, and he had become the first person to really understand the rainbow.   19

It was time to go think some more under his apple tree. . . .   20

Source: Courtesy of Kathleen Krull.

MAKING SCIENTISTS INTO CLIMBERS

(Excerpt From *Secrets of the Sky Caves: Danger and Discovery on Nepal's Mustang Cliffs*)

by Sandra Athans

Editor's Note: *This piece is an excerpt from* Secrets of the Sky Caves *by Sandra Athans. The book describes a series of expeditions to the sky caves of the Mustang Cliffs, located in a remote part of the Asian nation of Nepal. The caves, built near the tops of steep cliffs, contain manuscripts and bones of the cliff dwellers, including a 2,000-year-old skull. Peter Athans and a group of scientists, scholars, and mountain climbers explored these caves from 2007 to 2013. Peter's sister, Sandra Athans, wrote about these expeditions.*

On the expeditions were Peter Athans, the leader; his wife Liesl and their two children; Mark Aldenderfer, an archaeologist; Charles Ramble, a scholar of Tibetan history; Jeff Watt, an expert on Himalayan art and history; and Kris Ericksen, a climber and photographer. This excerpt chronicles the group's dangerous climb to the sky caves and their discovery of the Bon manuscript written by scribes. The manuscript contained prayers, religious lessons, and an illustration of the founder of the Bon faith.

Scaling the unstable cliffs in Mustang is risky, even for world-class mountain climbers. For Charles Ramble and the other scholars, the risks were even greater. They are not trained mountain climbers.

It was important for the scientists to study the artifacts and caves on-site. Context, or the environment in which materials are found, can provide important clues about a discovery. For instance, Aldenderfer needed to examine the high cave cities up close. Ramble had to see the Tibetan papers as they lay in the cave. That way, they could note details that might be overlooked if they left it to the mountain climbers to collect and photograph materials for them. "History is very important," said Ramble. "You can't make up the past. You have to look very carefully at what the evidence is. The general lesson is, don't take anything at face value and don't accept anything without evidence."

To make the climbing easier for the scientist, the team selected its routes carefully. It tried to avoid areas that demanded advanced climbing skills. "We tried to access the caves by the safest route possible," said Kris Ericksen.   3

The climbing was especially hard for Ramble because he had a fear of heights. But he said, "When you want knowledge so badly, you can't let things get in the way. My fear of heights was not going to prevent me from accessing that cave."   4

To help Ramble overcome his fear, the climbers coached him as he climbed. Athans guided and encouraged him with instructions such as, "Face into the rock. Place your left foot first and then place your right hand on the yellow rock by your thigh. That's it, Charles."   5

Library in the Sky

Ramble made a successful climb. Once he was inside the cave, he took a deep breath. An instant later, he was again breathless. Several feet from the cave opening, a thick carpet of thousands of written pages lay before him. Some of the text had been created with woodblock printing. Other writing had been penned by hand. Some pages featured tiny paintings. The pages glistened in the natural light coming from the cave opening.   6

The papers were in shambles. They were covered with bird droppings and had been battered by harsh weather. Some of the paintings had been cut from their pages—stolen by looters some time before.   7

The team collected and lowered the papers in a climber's haul bag to the lamas at the base of the cliff. The explorers sent down thirty loads—eight thousand pages in all. Once he was safely down the cliff face, Ramble and the other team members set up a field lab in a tent at the base of the cliff. There, they photographed and scanned the entire collection of papers. The job took hours.   8

Ramble knows how to read ancient Tibetan. He saw that the papers in the cave were mostly from a single ancient manuscript. It contained information on the Bon faith. The lamas also knew ancient Tibetan. They helped Ramble translate the text into English.   9

To learn more about the manuscript, Ramble and the others searched for the last page. They hoped it contained information called a colophon. The colophons of ancient manuscripts often list the name of the person who owned the document, the name of the scribe—the person who did the writing and printing—and the date the document was created. 10

Scouring the thousands of pages for the colophon was a lot like searching for a needle in a haystack. But to everyone's amazement, the team members found it. The colophon revealed the name of the scribe who had written out the Bon text. It also named the nobleman who had hired him to write it. But it did not provide a date for the manuscript. 11

In addition to the manuscript, the team found other written materials in the cave. Members found a book of proverbs, or wise sayings, and a manual for solving legal disputes. With the help of the lamas, Ramble translated these documents too. 12

Editor's Note: Many expeditions to the Mustang Cliffs followed the one described in this excerpt. The human remains discovered in the caves have been stored in Mustang. A site that contains a cave mural has protective enclosures to keep the drawings safe. Charles Ramble continues to translate the Bon manuscripts, now stored in a Buddhist monastery in the village of Lo Monthang. Ramble works with scholars from Nepal and other parts of the world to translate the manuscript that interests students of religion. The scientific studies of the artifacts found in the caves are ongoing and will take many years to complete.

Available for download at **http://resources.corwin.com/readtalkwrite**

Reprinted from *Read, Talk, Write: 35 Lessons That Teach Students to Analyze Fiction and Nonfiction* by Laura Robb. Thousand Oaks, CA: Corwin, www.corwin.com. Reproduction authorized only for the local school site or nonprofit organization that has purchased this book.

NEW HORIZONS IN SPACE

by Seymour Simon

Many science fiction stories that I read when I was younger told of going to the moon, exploring Mars, and discovering thousands of planets circling distant stars in the Milky Way galaxy. These stories have become real, science fact not science fiction. Now, a new frontier in space is opening—mining for minerals on asteroids. This may soon become the latest science fiction to become true science nonfiction—and it may provide resources that we Earth people desperately need.

1

Mining for minerals in space is the process of finding and collecting minerals and other raw materials from asteroids, planetary moons, and other space objects near Earth. Working in space is very expensive and much of the equipment still has to be developed and designed, so it's not likely that this will happen right away. However, in November 2015, the United States Congress passed and the president approved a bill making mining legal in space. There are private companies working on this already.

2

But mineral reserves on Earth are limited and people are consuming them faster and faster. Based on known reserves and how fast we are using them in modern industry and food production, scientists estimate that many essential minerals could be exhausted on Earth in 50–60 years. These include important metals such as gold and silver (rare and expensive), platinum and palladium (precious metals used in electronics), tungsten, iron, nickel, copper, and aluminum (used to make cars and planes and many other things).

3

What Can We Do When We Run Out of These Crucial Substances?

Space mining is one possible solution to the problem. Some of these important minerals may be mined on asteroids and sent back to Earth for use in manufacturing and food production. The

4

minerals can also be used on the same asteroid where they are found to build solar-powered stations and satellites. Water from the ice on some of the asteroids can be processed into hydrogen and oxygen for rocket fuel and for humans to breathe.

Earth and the many thousands of asteroids circling the sun in our solar system were all created from the same basic elements when the solar system was formed. This means that asteroids have many of the same materials that are present in Earth's crust. Most of the asteroids orbit around the sun in a region between Mars and Jupiter called the Asteroid Belt. Other bunches of asteroids, such as the Trojans and the Greeks, are found in groups near the orbit of Jupiter, the giant planet of our solar system. Near-Earth asteroids and some comets travel into the inner solar system and pass close to or cross over the orbit of Earth.

5

How Would We Get There?
And How Would We Get Back?

Much of the rocket fuel needed to launch a spaceship is used just in takeoff from Earth. Fortunately, all of the asteroids have a much lower gravity than Earth and even the moon. So landing a spaceship on a low-gravity, near-Earth asteroid uses much less fuel than landing on the moon and is much easier than landing on Mars. This means that nearby asteroids are likely places for early mining trials.

6

There are three main types of asteroids.

7

- C-type asteroids have a lot of water (in the form of ice) as well as carbon and other minerals for fertilizers that can be used to grow food in space colonies for astronaut miners.

- S-type asteroids have little water but contain many valuable minerals. Scientists have estimated that even a small S-type asteroid, only 10 meters (about 11 yards) across, contains over a million pounds of different metals and over a hundred pounds of rare metals such as gold and platinum.

- M-type asteroids are rare but contain 10 times more metal than S-types.

In recent years, 12 asteroids out of 9,000 searched by a group of space scientists were identified as prospective sites that could be mined with present-day rocket and mining technology. Though rich with valuable resources, they are quite small, ranging in size from 2 to 20 meters (6.5 to 65.5 feet) in diameter. These asteroids could be propelled by rockets into a near-Earth orbit and then mined for essential elements.

8

Several companies are involved in space mining and asteroid research locating. One group, the B612 Foundation, is dedicated to protecting Earth from asteroid strikes. It conducts research to help detect asteroids that might strike Earth one day and to find the means to change their paths to avoid such collusions. Data gathered by this group could also be used to identify possible asteroids that could be used for collecting mineral resources.

9

Other private companies are making plans on how best to find and extract minerals from asteroids. In recent years NASA has mentioned that it is interested in studying whether it is possible to launch humans to land on asteroids. New spaceships would have to be developed that are different than the ones currently used to operate in Earth orbit or in the gravities of the moon and Mars.

10

One way or another, space mining might lower the cost and change the way we explore space. The abundance of water on some of the asteroids could be used to produce fuel to further explore more asteroids and return their mineral resources to help the people of Earth. The exciting science fiction magazines I read many years ago may become a gateway to new realities of science fact.

11

Source: Courtesy of Seymour Simon.

SNOW DAY

by Priscilla Cummings

"Blood!" Digger called out. "Brady! J.T.! Come quick!" 1

My friend and I looked at each other. Our mouths dropped and we 2
took off through the snow-covered field. It wasn't easy running in our
boots. We must've looked like two turkey buzzards the way we lifted our
feet up and down out of the snow and flapped our arms to get some
momentum going.

Just under a foot of powdery white flakes had fallen overnight, but it 3
was enough to cancel school. A snow day! We three called each other as
soon as we were up. We had to wait for J.T. to get some chores done on the
chicken farm where he lives. But then my mom made blueberry pancakes
so that gave me time to eat. I even got to thinking that Digger would like
some of those pancakes, too. Over at his house, the kids all just got up and
ate whatever was there. One time it was Goldfish crackers! Almost never
pancakes or eggs, so I knew he'd love an invite—and he did.

"Stop right there," my mom ordered, holding our empty plates as we 4
opened the door to go. "Digger, where are your gloves?"

He lifted his shoulders and let them drop. "I don't know," he said. 5

I hadn't noticed he wasn't wearing gloves. But half the time we 6
were outside in winter, Digger didn't have a hat or gloves on. He never
complained, though. I've always thought that Digger was pretty tough. We
were only in sixth grade and already he talked about how he was going to
be a Marine someday.

"Here," my mom said. She set down the plates and fetched a pair of 7
leather gloves I'd just gotten for Christmas. I hoped Digger didn't lose
them.

"Brady," Mom said when we were halfway out the door. "I know 8
this is a snow day and you boys want to have some fun. But it's also
your opportunity to get that science report done, so save part of your
afternoon, okay?"

I nodded, but no way was I going to write about dolphins on a snow 9
day!

Finally, we were out of there, closing the door quickly because my   *10*
yellow lab, Tilly, wanted to come, too, and this was one time when
we had to leave her home.

"Come on!" I shouted to Digger, not wanting to suffer Tilly's   *11*
whining.

We plunged into the snow and raced each other over across   *12*
our yard, onto the street, and finally up the long, curvy driveway,
already plowed, to Digger's grandfather's farm. It was maybe our
favorite place on the face of this earth. In warm weather, we made
tree forts in the woods, rode the hay bailer, slept in the barn with
bats, and sucked on raw, sour rhubarb from the garden. Winters,
with a fresh snow, we liked to go tracking, guessing which animals
had come through, trying to figure out where they came from and
where they went. If you wanted to track animals you had to do it
first thing while the tracks were fresh, and before the sun started
melting everything.

Right off, behind the barn, I saw what looked like fox paw   *13*
prints, evenly spaced because of the way the animal trotted. I'd
been seeing a fox lately, a big, bushy-tailed red one, and I was
eager to know where it slept overnight. J.T. wanted to find the fox,
too, so we started following its tracks. Digger picked up on two
deer and went in the other direction until we heard him holler,
"Blood!"

When we met up we saw right off the bright red splotches on   *14*
white snow.

"Think it got shot?" I asked.   *15*

"Better not have!" Digger exclaimed. "This land's posted. No one's   *16*
supposed to hunt here, not ever!"

Even though Digger's grandfather didn't have milking cows on   *17*
the farm anymore, he still had a few heifers. No way were hunters
allowed on his property.

"Still, it doesn't stop some people," I told him.   *18*

J.T. snorted, agreeing with me.   *19*

"If it did get shot, maybe we can find it and help," Digger said,   *20*
surprising me a little because I didn't normally think of him as soft
on animals.

So we set off following the blood trail. Weird, but a feeling of dread, a kind of queasiness in the pit of my stomach, came over me. I've often wondered since then: Can a person sense something bad is about to happen? *21*

The deer tracks took us all the way across the pasture and down a hill to the cow pond. It's a pretty big pond and what happened is that the wind blew some of the snow off the pond before it piled up, so there were patches of bare ice. Where there was snow, however, we saw an interesting crisscross of tracks. Maybe a lot of animals had already come seeking a drink. *22*

"Look!" I exclaimed to J.T. "The fox tracks again!" I followed them, walking fast and sliding some on the bare ice while J.T. and Digger pursued that wounded deer. *23*

Suddenly, about halfway across the pond, I heard a heavy *crack*! It was so loud it echoed in the hollow. *24*

I stopped immediately. I knew it was the ice. But there wasn't time to change course. The next crack tore through the frozen water like a giant zipper, the ice giving way beneath my feet. I sunk in fast and was sucked up to my armpits in cold, icy water. *25*

"Guys! Help!" I shouted. It was all I could get out before I was gasping and struggling just to keep my head above that frigid water. My boots, my lined jeans, my parka, they all weighed a ton. I slapped at the water and chunks of ice with my heavy, mittened hands but already I felt my limbs going numb. *26*

Seemed like a long time, but I know now it was mere seconds before my friends rushed toward me. *27*

"We're here!" Digger shouted. *28*

"Hold on!" J.T. called out. *29*

But the ice opened up in front of them and they had to backtrack fast. *30*

Digger circled swiftly around the growing hole in the ice. "Brady, can you get over to the edge here?" *31*

I tried to look at him. "I can't . . ." I mumbled because an amazing sleepiness was setting in and I could barely speak. *32*

"I'll get a branch!" J.T. shouted to Digger. *33*

"No time!" Digger yelled back to him. "Come here and grab my   *34*
feet!"

I didn't get what they were doing then. I was already fading out, I   *35*
think.

In one swift movement, Digger dove over the ice and stretched   *36*
out his bare hands toward me. J.T. kneeled behind, holding his feet.

"Grab ahold!" Digger yelled at me.   *37*

Weakly, I flailed in the water. The cold was paralyzing my arms and   *38*
hands.

"Do it *now*!" Digger hollered at the top of his lungs.   *39*

I hated it when he yelled at me. I forced my arms and hands with   *40*
everything I had and felt Digger's hands grab my own.

Next thing I knew he was hauling me out of that icy pond. Digger   *41*
peeled off my soaking wet parka while J.T. pushed my arms into his
dry one.

My feet felt like a ton of cold, wet cement had been plastered to   *42*
them, but those two guys walked me across the pond, halfway lifting
me, up the hill, across the field, and all the way back to Digger's
grandfather's house.

It was kind of a blur after that. Digger's grampa drew a warm bath   *43*
and I was stripped down and put in the water while phone calls were
made. Next thing I knew my mom and dad were there wrapping
me in towels and warm blankets and then dry clothes. It was later,
sitting in Digger's grandfather's living room, all of us sipping on hot
chocolate, shaking our heads and being thankful—even laughing
some—that I noticed the chip in Digger's front tooth.

An hour later, J.T. and I went home with Digger. We wanted to   *44*
see him get praised for being the hero, I guess. But that's not what
happened. At Digger's house, his truck driver dad was still asleep and
Digger's brother and sister had just spilled grape juice on the kitchen
table, which had Digger's mom peeved.

I knew Digger wasn't going to make a big deal out of what he'd   *45*
done, so in a loud voice I told his mom right there, "You won't
believe this, but Digger just saved my life! Pulled me out of the
frozen cow pond!"

"It was amazing!" J.T. chimed in.   46

But maybe we didn't look like we just escaped death. Not with   47
our clean, dry clothes and all.

Digger's mom paused in her cleanup task and looked up.   48
"That so?"

"Absolutely!" I assured her.   49

J.T. nodded like his head was going to fall off.   50

The corners of her mouth lifted, but she didn't have time to say   51
anything more because just then, Digger's dad came into the kitchen
rubbing his eyes and asked what all the commotion was about,
didn't we know he needed his sleep?

"Digger just saved my life!" I repeated.   52

"Yeah?" Digger's father squinted and scratched his bald head.   53

"Yeah. It was pretty incredible," Digger admitted. He smiled big,   54
the way he deserved to smile.

And just like that the expression on Digger's dad's face changed.   55
"What the heck?" he demanded. He walked over to Digger and
roughly lifted his son's chin. "You chip your front tooth?"

Digger felt it with his index finger. "Must have," he said, although   56
I'm pretty sure he already knew. "Huh. I guess 'cause I threw myself
on the ice."

"You knucklehead!" His father held his hands up like what was he   57
going to do with Digger and went to pour himself a cup of coffee.
"I ain't payin' to have that fixed. You do something stupid like that,
you pay for it."

The three of us stood there, silent—and stunned.   58

His dad took a sip of coffee and threw us a look.   59

"What?"   60

But no one spoke. The air seemed to have gone out of the room.   61

"Go on," his father said with a scowl. "You boys beat it! Digger, go   62
to your room."

J.T. and I got out of there fast. We knew better than to stick   63
around when Digger's dad got going. J.T. went on home and so did I.

I told my parents what happened and then went into the living   64
room, where I picked up the remote and sprawled on the couch.
My dad had an errand to run and my mom went back to cooking a

special meal for me, including my all-time favorite dessert, which is apple pie.

After a while, I turned off the TV because I couldn't get into it. 65
Instead, I went to my room to work on that dolphin report. I was looking through my notes, some I took from Wikipedia, when I reread how dolphins establish such strong social bonds that they will stay with other injured or ill dolphins, even helping them to breathe by bringing them to the surface if needed.

At first, it made me daydream about the wounded deer we'd been 66
following. Like what happened to it? And was another deer helping it? Then I got to thinking about Digger and I couldn't get it out of my head. I knew I had to do something.

Both Mom and Dad thought my idea was a good one. As soon 67
as that apple pie was done, we put it in a box, got in the car, and drove over to Digger's house.

Digger's mom let us in and there was Digger's dad, sitting in his big 68
chair watching a wrestling show on TV.

"We brought Digger a pie," I told them. 69

Digger's little sister and brother, LeeAnn and Hank, ran up to peer 70
in the box.

Hank's eyes grew large. 71

"It says his name!" LeeAnn exclaimed. "In frosting!" 72

I smiled because she didn't know how to read yet. "No," I told her 73
gently. "It says 'hero.' Your big brother saved my life today. I want to thank him."

"I'll go get him!" LeeAnn offered. And no one stopped her as she 74
rushed off to fetch Digger.

That's when my dad said to Mr. Griswald, "Look, we'd like to pay 75
to have that front tooth fixed."

Mr. Griswald finally got up out of his chair and Mrs. Griswald 76
turned off the TV.

"Y'all don't need to do that," he mumbled. 77

"Really, we'd like to," my mom said. "It's the least we can do." 78

"It's my fault Digger chipped his tooth," I added. 79

"Yeah, well, we'll see," said Digger's dad. He scratched his bald 80
head again and looked over at the pie.

Mom handed the box to Mrs. Griswald and I was giving her a carton of vanilla ice cream in a plastic bag when Digger came in, leaning back but pulled with both hands by LeeAnn and Hank.   *81*

I smiled at him. "How you doin'?"   *82*

"Okay," he said with a slight shrug, uncertain what was happening.   *83*

"They brung you a pie!" LeeAnn said excitedly. "Can we eat it now?"   *84*

We didn't stay long. I knew Mr. Griswald was eager to get a fork in that pie. I could only hope we'd made things a little bit better—if only for a while.   *85*

"Don't slip on the ice," Mom said as we left.   *86*

I glanced at her because it seemed like a funny thing to say to me after what had happened *and* because just then I was thinking about a pod of dolphins jumping through tropical water.   *87*

"Brady!" Digger called as we picked our way down the front steps.   *88*

When I turned he was handing me my gloves. "I forgot to give them back."   *89*

I waved him off.   *90*

"Keep 'em," I said. "Hey—and thanks again for saving my life."   *91*

Digger dropped his hand and squeezed the gloves. He took in and let out a deep breath. A few seconds passed.   *92*

"See you tomorrow," I said.   *93*

Source: Courtesy of Priscilla Cummings.

WHO CLIMBS EVEREST?

(Excerpt From *Tales From the Top of the World: Climbing Mount Everest With Pete Athans*)

by Sandra Athans

Everest is not a mountain for beginners. Mountaineers who attempt Everest have usually scaled other peaks in the Himalayas and other high mountain chains. 1

Most climbers make the journey as part of an organized group. Companies sometimes sponsor, or pay for, Everest expeditions. For instance, The North Face, a company that makes outdoor equipment, has sponsored Everest expeditions to test its climbing gear. The National Geographic Society, an educational organization, has sent climbers and camera crews up Everest to make documentary films. Sometimes climbers help scientists conduct experiments on the mountain. 2

Some people pay money to have experienced guides lead them up Everest. But that doesn't mean just anyone can sign up and pay to go to the top. Guide organizations insist that their clients have previous mountain climbing experience. Clients must also be in top physical shape. 3

Most expeditions on Everest include Sherpas. The Sherpas are an ethnic group that originated in Tibet and then moved to Nepal. They practice Buddhism, a common Asian religion. Climber Tenzing Norgay was a Sherpa. Many modern Sherpas are expert mountaineers who work for mountain climbing expeditions. Sherpa staff members set up climbing ropes, carry gear to high camps, assist with medical needs and rescues, cook meals, and more. 4

Adjusting to Thin Air

Scientists measure the altitude, or height, of landforms by their distance above the sea (sea level). At sea level, it is easy to breathe because the air is rich in oxygen. The higher you go above sea level, the less oxygen the air holds. We say the air at high altitudes is "thin" because it has less oxygen. 5

At about 5,000 feet (1,524 m) above sea level, our bodies begin   6
to sense a change in oxygen levels. People must breathe more
deeply and quickly to get the oxygen they need. Above 8,000 feet
(2,438 m), people can begin to suffer from high-altitude ailments.
These include headaches and coughs.

To keep from getting sick on Everest, climbers must acclimatize,   7
or adjust, to the low oxygen levels. Climbers make forays, or short
climbs up and down sections of the mountain, instead of trying to
climb to the top all at once. Forays help climbers acclimatize to the
high altitude.

Climbers Be Wary

Hold on to your balaclava! Wind gusts on Everest can exceed 250   8
miles (400 km) per hour. The winds come from the jet stream. This
strong current of air sometimes roars across the top of the mountain.
To avoid the worst of the jet stream, climbers usually tackle Everest
in early May or September. At those times, the jet stream blows
north of the Everest region.

On Everest, deadly snowstorms can kick up quickly, without   9
warning. One of the worst storms ever recorded occurred in 1996.
The storm engulfed the upper part of the mountain in snow. It killed
eight climbers. Journalist and mountaineer Jon Krakauer described
this "murderous storm" in his best-selling book *Into Thin Air*.

Altogether, bad weather has led to more than twenty deaths   10
on Everest. Even though climbers know the dangers they might
encounter, they believe the rewards of climbing Everest outweigh
the risks.

Aim 2

Teach Students to Read, Talk, and Write About Fiction

CHAPTER 4

Taking the Plunge

How to Talk and Write About Fiction

Stories are like oxygen; we need them to survive. Katherine Paterson (2010) explains it this way: "To understand and have compassion for others, we must begin by knowing ourselves, and that is the first gift of a great novel. . . . If we know ourselves and can love and respect ourselves, there is hope that we can reach out from ourselves and respect others." Stories not only enrich our lives but also build bridges of understanding.

Because we are the sum of our personal stories, stories help readers define the essence of who they are and hold the potential of connecting and bonding them to narratives. Readers see themselves in stories written by others, and it's these connections that enable them to learn more about themselves and characters from the past, present, and future. Therefore, weaving units of fiction into curriculum not only enables students to better understand other cultures but also helps raise their awareness of the personal stories that have shaped their own lives.

To deepen students' understanding of fiction and foster meaningful discussions, it's important to teach them about literary elements, literary devices, and genre, so they have a framework for thinking about fiction and the language to describe what they notice. As students participate in literary conversations about fiction, their knowledge of these concepts helps them dig deeper into texts, exploring layers of meaning. This kind of talk boosts their comprehension and also lays the groundwork for further exploration of ideas through writing. In this chapter, you'll find lessons and prompts that build students' comprehension through talk and informal writing about literary elements, literary devices, and genre.

Use your read-aloud materials to introduce students to literary elements and literary techniques.

Exploring and Analyzing Fiction With Literary Elements

Think aloud and show students how you go beyond merely stating the definitions of literary elements that appear in the list that follows by explaining how these elements function in a text. When students can connect literary elements to the texts they are reading, listening to, and viewing, they move beyond memorizing the definition of an element to showcasing their understanding. This type of thinking opens the door to analyzing fiction and making connections between and among literary elements in a narrative (see lessons on literary elements in Chapter 5).

Give students the handout Using Literary Elements (pages 125–126, and http://resources.corwin.com/readtalkwrite) so they can use it as a resource that clarifies terms. Have students tape the handout in their smart notebooks so it is easy for them to access when needed. You will find questions that scaffold students' analysis of literary elements in the lessons presented in Chapter 5.

Building Knowledge of Key Literary Techniques

Students should be aware of the literary techniques that follow, as each one can deepen their understanding of literary elements and heighten their enjoyment of the story. To foster literary conversations about these techniques, try these suggestions.

▶ **Think aloud** using a read-aloud text, showing how you use a specific literary technique to deepen your understanding.

▶ **Organize guided practice** by having students partner talk and/or participate in small-group discussions using a short text and then share what they've learned with the entire class.

▶ **Have a whole-class discussion** using a short text or a recently completed read-aloud text.

▶ **Encourage in-the-head conversations** about a literary technique while students read their self-selected books.

Some Key Literary Devices

Use the questions in italics under each technique to spark meaningful talk.

Flashback: An interruption of the sequence of events to present information about something that happened before the story began.

    Prompts: *Why did the author include this? Does the information create a better understanding of the protagonist? The antagonists? A problem? A conflict?*

Figurative Language: Language that takes readers beyond the literal meaning of words; also called figures of speech. Here are three common figures of speech.

Simile: A comparison of two dissimilar things that have one thing in common using *like* or *as*.

    Example: *Her eyes were cold, like steel.*

    Prompts: *How did the simile help you better understand the personality traits of a character? What did the simile explain about the theme? A conflict? How did the simile help you understand a character's decision or motivation?*

Metaphor: A comparison of two dissimilar things with one thing in common. A metaphor equates both items by using *is, was, are,* or *were*.

    Example: *The moon is a beacon for ships.*

    Prompts: *What did the metaphor show you about a character's actions? Words? How did the metaphor help you identify a main idea? A theme? Why did the metaphor provide insight into a character's decisions, motivation, or personality?*

Personification: Gives human feelings and abilities to an animal, object, or idea.

> **Example:** *The waterfall wept for the warrior's loss.*

> **Prompts:** *How does the figure of speech help you better understand a theme? What do you learn about a character from this figure of speech? How does the figure of speech provide insights into the antagonists? The settings? A conflict?*

Foreshadowing: Hints that the author drops to prepare the reader for an event that is to come. Foreshadowing can help the reader anticipate or predict the outcome.

> **Example:** *Lois Lowry foreshadows Jonas leaving the Community in* The Giver.

> **Prompts:** *Why do you think the author foreshadowed this event? How does being able to predict an outcome enable you to cope with a difficult event? How does foreshadowing raise your awareness of a conflict? Setting? Antagonist? Theme?*

Imagery: Strong verbs, specific nouns, and phrases that appeal to the senses and enable readers to visualize an event, a character, conflict, or setting.

> **Example:** *Priscilla Cummings uses a simile, strong verbs, and specific nouns to create imagery in the first three paragraphs of "Snow Day."*

> **Prompts:** *What did the imagery help you visualize? How did your visualization deepen your understanding of the protagonist? A different character? An antagonist? A conflict?*

Irony of Situation: An event occurs in a story that is the opposite of what the reader expects.

> **Example:** *In* The Giver, *when Jonas watches the video feed of release, he doesn't expect to see his father killing the newchild.*

> **Prompts:** *How did the irony make you feel? Explain why. Did the ironic event change your thinking about the protagonist? Antagonists? Conflicts? Settings? Did it help you better understand a main idea or theme? Explain.*

Verbal Irony: Words in a story are used to suggest the opposite of what they usually mean.

> **Example:** *In* Riding Freedom *(Muñoz Ryan, 1998), Ebeneezer shouts, "It ain't a pony ride out there in California," when Charlotte says she is leaving and moving to California. Ebeneezer uses verbal irony because a pony ride is easy, but riding and living in California will be tough.*

> **Prompts:** *Explain why the verbal irony was effective. What did the verbal irony cause you to think about? Did the verbal irony change your thinking about a literary element? Explain.*

Encouraging Students to Discuss Literary Elements and Techniques

Literary elements and techniques can be turned into prompts that foster talk about fictional texts. You'll find prompts in the lessons in Chapter 5. In addition, use or adapt

Using Literary Elements

Antagonists

Forces that work against the protagonist and create tension in a literary text. There are two kinds of antagonists:

External: nature, other characters, decisions, actions, and interactions

Internal: thoughts within the character's mind and emotions

Understanding how the protagonist copes with antagonists can offer insight into his or her personality, conflicts faced, and themes.

Climax

The moment or point of greatest intensity in the plot. Short stories usually have one climax, but novels can have small climaxes as the plot unfolds. The major climax is near the end. The climax, the highest point of the action, can deepen comprehension of plot details and also offer insights into themes.

Conflicts

Struggles or differences between opposing forces such as protagonist and nature, two characters, protagonist and a specific event or situation, or an internal conflict within a character. Some conflicts become problems. For example, the inner conflict of deciding whether to drive in a snowstorm leads to a problem when the person's car becomes stuck in a snowdrift on a desolate road. Observing how characters deal with inner conflicts and conflicts with other characters and/or a setting can reveal much about their personalities and the themes of the story.

Crisis

This is related to the climax—it's the moment when the protagonist must finally make some essential decision about who she is or what to do.

Denouement

Events that resolve the climax in a novel, short story, or drama; often referred to as the outcome. Understanding the outcomes of a narrative can lead to figuring out themes and central themes and deepen readers' understanding of how the plot brought them to back to a feeling of normalcy.

Diction

Whether you consider this a literary element or literary technique, diction is an underappreciated aspect of literature. How characters speak—the words they choose, their cadences, the degree to which they speak—all offer important clues to what they want and need, and who they are.

Other Characters

Observing how other characters relate to, dialogue with, and interact with the protagonist can deepen our knowledge of all their personalities as well the themes in a story.

Plot

Events that occur in a text and enable readers to observe characters in diverse situations. Plot supports an understanding of theme, conflicts, setting, and characters' personalities. Often referred to as rising action, the plot in a text builds from the opening of the story to a high point of interest, called the climax.

(Continued)

Point of View

This refers to who is narrating the story.

- A first person narrator is often the protagonist, and the author uses first person pronouns: I, me, mine, we, us, our, ours.

- An objective narrator acts like an observer who sees and records information and events from a neutral perspective and uses third person pronouns: he, she, it, they, them, their, theirs.

- An omniscient narrator knows everything about the characters, their conflicts and problems, decisions and motivation, thoughts and feelings. Told from the third person point of view, it uses these pronouns: he, she, it, they, them, their, theirs.

Protagonist

The main character in a text who has problems to solve. Observing how the protagonist interacts with others, makes decisions, and tries to solve problems offers insight into this character's personality and motivations.

Problem

Something that gets in the way of a character's desire or goal and requires an action or decision to overcome, such as whether to risk diving from the high board as required by the PE teacher when you're a weak swimmer or lying to your parents about where you've been to avoid punishment and then coping with the guilt. Problems require characters to figure out solutions such as having no money for food, or coping after a twister or fire destroyed their home. How characters tackle problems and deal with their inability to resolve some can provide readers with deep insights into personality and decision-making processes.

Setting

The time and place in which a story takes place. A short text can focus on one setting while longer texts have multiple settings. How characters function in and react to a setting can deepen readers' understanding of characters' motivation and personality traits.

Symbolism

Short story writers and novelists sometimes select physical objects to signify the emotions and abstract ideas they are trying to communicate. Symbols often recur and don't always appear in the exact same way. Authors might use an object (a lighthouse, a locket) the weather in general or particular aspects of nature (sunlight; fog; darkness).

Theme

This is a statement about people and life that the author makes with the narrative. In folk and fairy tales, theme is frequently stated as a moral or lesson at the end of the story.

the prompts that follow to stimulate partner talk, small-group and whole-class discussions, and in-the head-conversations.

Ten Open-Ended Prompts

- Evaluate how a character responds to a specific situation. Describe the situation and the character's reaction; then assess what happened.
- Predict what you think will happen next and give evidence from the book that supports your prediction.
- Explain how foreshadowing or flashback deepened your understanding of a character or conflict.
- Identify a problem and explain how the character solved it.
- Identify a decision the character made and evaluate whether it was a good or poor decision. Use text evidence to support your thinking.
- Choose two antagonistic forces and show how they worked against the protagonist.
- Choose a character, list two to three personality traits, and cite evidence from the book that helped you identify the traits.
- Show how another character or an event changed the main character and explain the change you observed.
- Identify two characters who like each other or don't get along. Use text evidence to explain their relationship.
- List four to five significant events from a book in sequence and explain why each one was significant. To explain significance, you can link the event to a theme, a setting, a character's decision, or a solution to a problem or conflict.

Characteristics of Fictional Genres

Introduce students to the fictional genre or genres that they are studying. Understanding the characteristics of these genres can improve students' reading comprehension because while reading, they can draw on the schema they've developed of what to expect from a particular genre, such as historical fiction, folk tale, and fantasy (Anderson, Pichert, & Shirey, 1983). By knowing that each genre has its own features, purposes, and conventions, then combining this knowledge with the common thread of literary elements that runs through all fiction, students become more secure navigating the text (Duke & Purcell-Gates, 2003).

The following chart details the characteristics of genres most commonly taught in middle and high school. All genres lend themselves to a discussion of literary elements as discussed earlier in the chapter. Here I have provided specific prompts for each genre that guide students to explore the characteristics particular to that genre.

To introduce a genre that students are unfamiliar with or to review a genre they've studied before, use the chart as a guide for teaching a genre's characteristics. In addition, you can select discussion prompts for partner talk, small-group discussions, and whole-class discussions whether students read the same material or different texts within a genre. The prompts for discussion work well with a read-aloud as you invite students to turn-and-talk. Students can also use their independent reading to occasionally respond to one or two prompts related to the genre of their book in their notebooks.

Some reproducibles that go with the lessons in Chapter 2 ask students to discuss the genre of their book because understanding genre is one key part of comprehension.

	CHARACTERISTICS	PROMPTS FOR DISCUSSION
...on	• Includes all literary elements. • Setting, plot, characters, and problems all could happen today because they are real and relevant to students' lives. **Example:** *Esperanza Rising* by Pam Muñoz Ryan	• Show how the protagonist's problems are realistic and similar to those you or your friends might have. • Identify a problem and a conflict and show how each one is realistic. • In real life, an event or person can change the course of another's life. How did an important event and/or a character change the protagonist? • What are two themes in the book? How do they relate to issues students today face, such as growing up, peer pressure, friendship, or family relationships? Use evidence from the book to support each theme statement.
Historical fiction	• Includes all literary elements. • Plot events take place in settings that are in the past. • Plot and problems link to the social, economic, or religious issues of the time. • Characters can be historical figures placed in imaginary situations or fictional characters living through researched events. **Example:** *Lyddie* by Katherine Paterson	• Identify the historical period and discuss three unique aspects of it. • What do you learn about family life and relationships during this historical period? • How are the protagonist's problems different from yours? Choose one problem that is different and link it to the historical period the book is set in. • How do people cope with economic problems such as scarcity of food, money, or jobs?
Science fiction	• Includes all literary elements. • Takes place in the future and predicts what society will be like at that time. • Setting can be Earth, space, or a different planet or universe. • Warns readers about an abuse of important issues in their society. • Uses technology and science familiar in today's world and projects what it will be like in the future world. **Example:** *The Giver* by Lois Lowry	• What scientific advances do you see in the society? How do these advances affect the characters' actions and decisions? • Are problems the characters face similar to or different from problems you face? Explain and give examples. • What present-day issues and problems does the author deal with? Compare the author's view to your own. • What warnings does the author give? Is there hope for humanity? Explain. • How do people fit into this society? Are they subordinate to machines? Is there a class system? Has democracy vanished? Identify changes and provide reasons for each one. • Does the book offer hope? Explain.
Mystery	• Includes all literary elements. • Centers on solving a crime or strange occurrence. • Investigating the crime or situation is the protagonist, who is like a detective. • Includes red herrings—plot events that confuse the reader and deter her or him from figuring out the crime. **Example:** *Peeled* by Joan Bauer	• How does the author build suspense and excitement? Give two to three examples from the book. • What is the mystery that must be solved? What clues helped you solve it? • Why did the protagonist become involved with the mystery? • How does danger affect the decisions and actions of the protagonist/detective? • What were one or two red herrings?
Fantasy	• Includes all literary elements. • Includes supernatural elements such as talking animals and objects or fantastic creatures.	• Explain two supernatural elements in the story by showing how each one affected plot, conflict, or the protagonist.

GENRE	CHARACTERISTICS	PROMPTS FOR DISCU...
Fantasy (cont.)	• Has a hero or heroine who takes a journey to learn about self and/or help others. • Set in a world that isn't real but is believable to readers. • Explores and calls attention to issues in our society that need to be reflected upon. **Example:** The Harry Potter Series by J. K. Rowling	• What special powers ... possess? How does ... in the story? • What does the protagonist/hero learn a... himself or herself? About life? • Describe the world or worlds the protagonist lives in and moves through. What problems do you see in these worlds? Give two examples. • Is there a struggle between light and dark or good and evil? Explain the struggle and how it affects the protagonist. • How do the journey and tasks of the protagonist/hero change him or her? • What themes does the story deal with?
Folktale	• Includes all literary elements. • Can explain how something came to be, such as the creation of the world. • Reflects the customs and beliefs of a group of people. • Has people and animals as characters. • Has a hero or heroine who must solve a difficult task. • Includes a struggle between good and evil. • Often has events happen in threes, using the magic number three. • Provides a moral or lesson for readers. **Example:** "Jack and the Beanstalk"	• Would you rate the protagonist heroic? Explain why. • What are the forces of good? The forces of evil? Are they antagonists? Explain why. • Can you find examples of the magic number three? How do these deepen your understanding of plot? Conflict? • What are the tasks the hero or heroine must complete? How do these tasks change him or her? • What is the moral or theme of the folktale? • What do you learn about the culture the folktale represents? What's valued? • What does the folktale explain?
Myth	• Includes all literary elements. • Reflects a specific culture. • Told as if it is fact. • Has gods and goddesses with supernatural powers and human characteristics. • Explains creations and events in nature. • Provides lessons or morals about people, nature, war, courage, and so on. • Can be a symbolic interpretation of the world. **Example:** "Phaethon, Son of Apollo"	• Discuss the human and supernatural characteristics of the gods and goddesses. • Compare and contrast two different gods or heroes. • What lessons does the myth teach? • What force of nature does the myth explain? How is this done? • What symbols does the myth contain? Explain two to three and show how each one links to the theme.
Short story	• Includes all literary elements. • Has fewer characters than a novel. • Focuses on one incident. • Covers a short period of time. • Moves the plot quickly to a climax. • Can be realistic, historical, science fiction, fantasy, or mystery. **Example:** "The Lottery" by Shirley Jackson	• What is the story's point of view? How does point of view affect the plot? Your understanding of characters? • What is the one incident the story focuses on? How does the incident relate to the protagonist and theme? • What background information do you learn about the protagonist and his or her problem?
Narrative poetry	• Includes all literary elements. • Can be a traditional ballad that is usually sung but also written; unknown author. **Example:** "Lord Randall" • Can be a literary ballad that tells a story; the author is known. **Example:** "God's Judgment on a Wicked Bishop" by Robert Southey • Can be an epic poem that tells a long story. **Example:** The Iliad and The Odyssey by Homer	• Is the poem a traditional ballad or literary ballad? Explain. • Who is the protagonist and what is the problem? • Identify two key antagonists and explain the role each plays. • What are the climax and return to normalcy? • Discuss figurative language and how it deepens an understanding of theme, conflict, or setting.

From Talk to Writing

In addition to the rich and varied discussions about reading you integrate in daily lessons, it's important to have students do some writing about their talk. The process of writing about their literary conversations helps them better remember the ideas they discussed, serves as an informal assessment for you, and provides a wealth of ideas for them to explore in longer pieces of writing. The research on writing to improve comprehension is clear; see the box on page 131. Having students write about their literary conversations has the added benefit of being a sort of scaffold to students writing in response to reading independently. The talk provides a way of rehearsing ideas; students can then draw on these experiences as they think through a text independently in writing.

Brief Writing Tasks to Follow Talk

Here are the types of writing you can ask students to do in their reading notebook after they talk.

- ▶ Quick, short responses after a turn-and-talk
- ▶ Lists of the key points of partner-talk, small-group discussions, and whole-group discussions
- ▶ Notes that document in-the-head conversations, either in the reader's notebook or on a bookmark (see page 56)
- ▶ Responses to guiding questions and open-ended prompts and questions that were explored during a literary conversation
- ▶ Summaries of the discussion
- ▶ Reproducibles that prompt students to reflect on their discussion, such as those found on pages 41–44

These short pieces of writing can help you evaluate students' level of understanding of a literary element, technique, or genre and their ability to infer to explore layers of meaning in a text. For example, consider this summary paragraph written by fourth grader Ebony after her group discussed the section where Shiloh fights with a German shepherd. The question the group wrote for their discussion is *How does Marty feel about this crisis?*

> *One crisis is when Shiloh and the German Shepard get in a fight. Marty ran straghit for Shiloh's pen and his dad closely followed. Marty could have left the dog to die. I think that Marty made the right choice to do what he did—take the dog to Doc Murphy with his dad. Otherwise Shiloh would have died and Marty really cares for Shiloh and wants to save him. Marty also feels guilt 'cause he left Shiloh in a pen on the mountain to hide the dog. Marty didn't think about dangers for Shiloh. All he could think was he wanted to keep Shiloh and he had to hide him.*

Have students write about their reading in their smart notebooks (see pages 18–19) and on the reproducibles that are part of the lessons in Chapter 5.

Note the inferences Ebony makes as a result of the group's discussion. She understands the guilt Marty feels and also sees that Marty didn't think of the consequences of hiding Shiloh.

Teaching Tip: Get Students' Notebook Ready

Have three to four students quickly pass out smart notebooks. Then ask students to head a page so that their notebook is ready to receive writing after talking.

The Research on Writing to Improve Reading Comprehension

In 2010, the Carnegie Corporation published *Writing to Read: Evidence for How Writing Can Improve Reading* (Graham & Hebert, 2010), a landmark study with a meta-analysis that showed students improve their comprehension when they write about their reading. Based on the data, Steve Graham and Michael Hebert developed recommendations for the kinds of writing that boosts reading comprehension:

> You can download a free copy of this report by going to www.carnegie.org.

- Reading responses that express personal reactions and analyze and interpret the text
- Summaries
- Notes about a text
- Answers to questions about a text
- Asking questions about a text and then answering them

As you can see, these types of writing mirror the kinds of talking students do during literary conversations. When we ask students to write about their conversations, we are scaffolding their ability to write about reading independently.

Writing About Reading

According to Graham and Hebert (2010), writing can enhance reading in three ways:

▶ Improves the comprehension of texts

▶ Strengthens students' reading skill

▶ Boosts students' analytical thinking

What follows is a summary of Graham and Hebert's recommendations for using writing to improve reading. In the report, the authors discuss each recommendation and the data behind it.

1. Have students write about texts they read in science, social studies, and language arts.

2. Teach students process writing and the skills they need to create a text.

3. Increase the amount of time that students write at school. When students produce their own texts, reading comprehension improves.

Unfortunately, the actual writing that goes on in middle and high school classes today still focuses on fill in the blanks, worksheets, copying teachers' notes, and formulaic essay structures (Applebee & Langer, 2011; Gillespie & Graham, 2011; Graham & Hebert, 2010). The research on the importance of writing and its correlation to reading comprehension suggests that the request for more writing time at school is a clarion call. However, the kinds and amounts of authentic writing about reading that students do at school needs to be reevaluated and revised.

For writing to improve students' understanding of texts, four qualities or components need to be in place (Applebee & Langer, 2011a, 2011b). These qualities hold true for short and informal writing about reading and for more structured types of writing such as analytical and explanatory essays.

1. **Ownership:** Students choose what they will write about.

2. **Teacher support:** Students understand what the writing looks like because the teacher has modeled the process.

3. **Collaboration:** Teachers help students and peers help one another move from talking about reading to writing about reading. This includes scaffolding the writing and pairing up students so they can support one another.

4. **Internalization:** Through observations and listening and guided practice, students can complete different writing tasks on their own as well as transfer them to different situations.

Students can experience success with writing about reading if they *talk, and then write*, as the lessons in this book advocate. William Zinsser (1993) said this about the relationship between writing and learning: "Writing is a form of thinking, whatever the subject" (p. vii). Writing about reading is like talking on paper. Writing can shape oral texts into ideas that raise students' awareness of what they comprehend as well as communicate their thinking to others.

The final section of this chapter contains a lesson that uses talk and writing to deepen students' understanding of how making inferences while reading can enrich their understanding and interpretation of texts they read and view.

Data on Writing to Improve Reading

"For instance, when elementary grade students are directed to write about material they are reading (versus students who mainly read and reread or study this material), their comprehension of the text jumps 24 percentile points, whereas writing about content material presented in class results in a 9 percentile-point jump on measures of learning (Graham, Harris, & Santangelo, 2015)" (Graham & Harris, 2016).

The Importance of Inferring

"Snow Day" by Priscilla Cummings

"Snow Day" by Priscilla Cummings features the three characters—Digger, J.T., and Brady—from her outstanding novel *Red Kayak* (2006). The snow day puts the three in a situation where instant choices must be made. The boys' experience and the way Brady's and Digger's families deal with it invite readers to infer in order to deepen their interpretation of the story and the relationship between Digger and Brady.

Making inferences while reading is one of the most important reading strategies because when writers show with details instead of telling, they expect readers to infer. Instead of writing, "Digger is courageous," a sentence that tells readers what to think, Cummings shows readers by providing details about how Digger saves Brady's life.

The first important concept about making inferences that readers need to understand is that an inference is unstated or implied—it's not explicitly written in the text. To infer, readers use narrative elements such as dialogue to make inferences. In the lesson that follows, students make inferences using dialogue, actions that characters take, and interactions between characters. The student handout Prompts for Inferring (page 137) discusses additional ways readers infer with fiction. Students can refer to the handout when asked to infer using guided and independent reading texts. It's also a great refresher course for students to review before making inferring the focus of in-the-head conversations. You can use "Hoops Tryouts" (page 93) and/or "Coming Clean" (page 86) to provide students with continued practice with inferring.

This lesson includes turn-and-talk for quick exchanges and partner talk for literary conversations about inferring using the three narrative elements. Partners remain the same throughout the lesson.

Planning the Lesson

To plan this lesson, I followed the process described earlier in this chapter. In addition to building prior knowledge and presenting an interactive read-aloud, I divided the reading and thinking about the story into two parts. I wanted students to focus on the accident and then the aftermath and how it affects both families.

Included are text-specific prompts to help students zoom in on parts of the story they can use to infer. Since the goal is for students to infer independently, use these prompts only if students appear to struggle. In addition, accept all inferences that students offer as long as they can support each one with text evidence.

I'm always prepared for a lesson to derail, especially if it's the start of the year and I don't know my students' reading ability that well. No problem. If students struggle working through a section on their own, simply return to the interactive read-aloud format and continue to model inferring until students show you they are proficient and can infer on their own; see the Pause and Reflect box on the next page for details.

Materials

"Snow Day" by Priscilla Cummings; smart notebooks; Prompts for Inferring

(Continued)

(Continued)

Lesson Guidelines

Day 1

Prepare Students to Read; Assess Knowledge of Inferring *(15–25 minutes)*

▸ Ask students to turn-and-talk about what they do when they have an unexpected day off from school.

▸ Have students write about their conversation in their smart notebooks.

▸ Invite a few students to share what they wrote.

▸ Give students a piece of paper, have them put their name at the top, and ask them to explain what an inference is and give an example of what they do to make an inference about a character.

▸ Collect the papers and end the lesson.

Pause and Reflect on Students' Knowledge of Making Inferences

Before continuing with Day 2 of the lesson, review students' papers and separate them into two groups: those who understand inferences and those who show confusion or misunderstandings about inferences. You know students understand inferring if they write that an inference is implied or not stated in the text and that they can study a character's dialogue, inner thoughts, decisions, motivation, actions, or relationships with other characters to infer. If you have any students who do not know what an inference is, take a day to do a small-group interactive read-aloud with them while the rest of the class is reading independently. This intervention will build their inferring stamina. Remember that some students will need more than one lesson on making inferences before they can work with a partner or small group. While the rest of the class reads or writes independently, continue to support these students until they have enough understanding to complete the lesson on inferring.

After two to three interventions using "Snow Day," include all students in the lesson that starts on Day 2. Even if some students still feel tentative with making inferences, practicing with a partner and participating in a small-group discussion about a familiar text can enable them to better understand this strategy.

Interactive Read-Aloud to Build Inferring Skills *(15 minutes)*

• Read the first three paragraphs aloud; then pause to think aloud to model how you make an inference: Here's what I say:

> *The word "blood" combined with the phrase "our mouths dropped" helps me predict that this day will have suspense, mystery, and excitement. A prediction is a type of inference that uses text details to infer what might happen next.*

• Read aloud paragraphs 4 to 7; then pause to model inferring again, saying something like:

> *The exchange between the mom and Digger helps me make inferences about both. Mom is a woman in charge—the word "ordered" helps me make that inference. She also cares because she doesn't want Digger to be in the snow and cold without gloves, so she gives him a pair. I can also infer that Digger's family is short of money and that's why he doesn't have a hat or gloves. Or it could be that Digger wants to show how macho he is. As I read on, I'll be able to figure this out.*

- Point out that the inferences you made in each part you read aloud were unstated—not in the text. Also point out that you used words, actions, and interactions to infer.
- Read aloud paragraphs 8 to 11. Ask students to turn-and-talk and make one inference and offer text support. Here's what fifth graders inferred:

Mom is practical—she wants Brady to use the time to finish his science report.

Brady is polite but does what he wants. He nods and agrees about the report, but thinks he won't do it.

As soon as you can, bring all students together for the following lesson on inferring, using "Snow Day." If you find that some students still need scaffolding to infer, then continue to help them until you can gradually turn the inferring process over to them.

Students Infer Using Partner Talk *(25–35 minutes)*

Day 2

▶ Distribute copies of "Snow Day."

▶ Read aloud or have students read silently to the first stop.

▶ Invite students to partner talk (4 minutes):

Discuss the gist of the story with your partner.

▶ Read aloud or have students read the text a second time, prompting students to think carefully this time about characters' words, actions, and interactions, since they will be using these elements to make inferences.

▶ Ask students to partner talk (5 minutes):

Talk with your partner and make one inference based on words spoken, actions, or interactions between characters. Be sure to offer text support.

▶ Circulate among pairs and provide support when needed with prompts such as:

What do you learn about grandfather's land? How do the boys react to Brady falling into icy water? What can you say about the boys' reactions to Brady falling into a hole in the ice?

▶ Make a T-chart and project it onto a whiteboard or use chart paper. Have students share their inferences and text support. Here are two inferences that fifth graders offered.

INFERENCE	TEXT SUPPORT
Digger follows the law.	Says his grandfather's land is posted—no hunting, and see blood near fox tracks.
Digger and J.T. know about hypothermia.	Both take Brady's wet clothes off; J.T. gives Brady his dry parka and doesn't think about himself getting cold.

Continue Partner Talk for Making Inferences *(20 minutes)*

Day 3

▶ Have students retrieve their copies of "Snow Day" and continue using partner talk to infer (10 minutes).

(Continued)

(Continued)

▶ Invite students to share inferences they made up to the first stop, ensuring they can support them with text evidence (5 minutes).

▶ Debrief by asking students to turn-and-talk and discuss one way inferring connected them to this part of "Snow Day," and have students share.

Day 4

Students Infer Using Part 2 of the Text *(25–30 minutes)*

▶ Have students retrieve their copies of "Snow Day." Read aloud or have students read silently from the first stop to the end to get the gist. Ask them to turn-and-talk to discuss the gist (5 minutes).

▶ Read aloud or have students read the text a second time, prompting students to think carefully this time about characters' words, actions, and interactions, since they will be using these elements to make inferences. Ask students to partner talk (10 minutes):

> *Talk with your partner and make two inferences based on words spoken, actions, or interactions between characters. Be sure to offer text support.*

▶ Circulate among pairs and provide support when needed with prompts such as:

> *What do you learn about Digger's parents from their reactions? What do Brady's words tell you about his feelings toward Digger? Why do Brady and his parents return to Digger's home? How do you know the reactions of Digger's parents bother Brady? What do you learn about the Griswald family?*

▶ Invite students to make a T-chart in their smart notebooks and record their two inferences, then share different ones with the class (10–15 minutes). Here are a couple of the inferences fifth graders made.

INFERENCE	TEXT SUPPORT
Brady and J.T. feel proud of Digger for saving his life and want Digger's parents to feel the same way.	The boys brag about Digger, call him a hero and amazing, but the parents only see the chip on Digger's front tooth.
Brady cares about Digger having to pay for fixing his tooth and knows that the Griswalds are too poor to fix the tooth.	Brady makes a plan, tells his mom and dad, and they offer to pay for fixing the tooth.

Since making inferences is a natural part of reading fiction, it's important to repeat lessons like this during the school year. Middle grade and middle school students will need to revisit this strategy many times before they absorb and internalize it to the point they can infer while reading independently.

Have students use the Prompts for Inferring handout (page 137) as a resource. When your lesson focuses on inferring with specific narrative elements, such as dialogue and actions, point students to the prompts on their handout. Before asking students to complete guided practice on inferring, review all or a specific section of the handout after you've modeled that type of inferring with a read-aloud text. Remind students to review their handout before having in-the-head conversations about inferring, using instructional level or independent reading materials. The goal is for students to become familiar with the prompts, internalize them, and use them automatically while reading.

Prompts for Inferring

You can infer using a character's dialogue and inner thoughts:

- What do the character's inner thoughts reveal about his or her feelings and/or personality?
- What does dialogue tell you about each character's feelings? About the personality traits of each?

You can infer using characters' actions and interactions:

- Cite an action a character takes and infer the personality trait and/or motivation that it reveals.
- Study two characters' interactions and explain what these reveal about each one.
- What do you learn about a character from the actions he or she has taken?

You can infer using a character's decisions and motivation:

- Why did a character make a key decision?
- Show how an important decision shaped or changed the character's personality.
- What does a character's motivation reveal about his or her personality?

You can infer using settings:

- What information do you learn about a character because of setting?
- How does a specific setting affect a key decision?
- How does setting contribute to a change in a character?

You can infer using conflicts:

- Explain how and why a conflict changes a character's personality.
- What do you learn from the choices a character makes during a conflict?

You can infer using key plot events:

- Choose a key plot event and discuss how it affected a character.
- Consider how one plot event led to several other events.

Available for download at http://resources.corwin.com/readtalkwrite

Reflect on Your Teaching

Use the following question/prompts for in-the-head conversations with yourself or discussions with colleagues.

▶ What kinds of informal writing about reading do you include in lessons? What do you learn about students' reading comprehension from their writing?

▶ How much do your students know about the characteristics of fictional genres? Discuss ways you enlarge students' knowledge of genre characteristics and why this supports reading comprehension.

▶ How does the research about writing about reading affect helping students move from talk to writing?

Don't Miss Reading and Learning From: *Mini-Lessons for Literature Circles* by Harvey Daniels and Nancy Steineke, Heinemann, 2004.

CHAPTER **5**

Going Deeper
How to Analyze Literary Elements

The lessons in this chapter start with the teacher modeling how to think about and apply literary elements to a text. It's crucial for students to hear and observe what the teacher, who has reading expertise, does while reading. Watching and listening build students' mental model of what reading fiction is like. Armed with that mental model, students can practice talking and writing about literary elements because they have begun to internalize the process.

Kinds of Talk to Use in the Lessons

The nature of the task and the time you have determine the type of talk that students use. Turn-and-talk is short and ideal when you read aloud. Partner talk works well for guided practice and when pairs read different texts. Most of the time you'll use a brief turn-and-talk in conjunction with other types of literary conversations.

Offer Students Guided Practice

Once you've modeled a lesson on literary elements, it's time for students to have literary conversations during guided practice so you can determine whether all students understand the lesson or if there are some who need extra help. While students practice, circulate and pause to help those who need a 2- to 3-minute conversation. You can support students who require more time by scheduling a 5-minute conference when the rest of the class works independently on reading and writing.

Moving From Talking to Writing

You don't have to ask students to write each time they turn-and-talk or engage in another type of talk. However, the research of Graham, Harris, and Santangelo (2015) points to a large increase in comprehension when students write about texts they read. Therefore, after longer conversations, I suggest that you invite students to list the key points of the discussion, write a short summary paragraph about it, or offer their opinion about literary elements or techniques.

Review the material about guided practice on page 8. For each lesson the teacher reads the text out loud or students read the story twice: once for the gist and a second time to better recall details.

Literary Elements and Five Kinds of Conflict

Conflicts supply stories with energy and tension and affect other literary elements. Use a read-aloud text to model each type of conflict and familiarize students with them. As you teach protagonist and antagonist, setting, plot, climax, and other literary elements, help students understand how conflict affects each one.

Bundling Literary Elements

Literary conversations bring deep analytical thinking to lessons on literary elements. To help students experience the interplay among literary elements, the lessons in this chapter combine them and invite students to analyze protagonist and antagonist together as well as connect conflict, setting, and plot to illustrate how these elements work in concert to deepen comprehension. By bundling literary elements, the lessons mirror the way readers naturally link elements while reading fiction.

Selections Used in Literary Elements Lessons

If not all of your students can read the selections in this chapter, then read them out loud so everyone can participate. However, if you select a piece for a lesson you've created, make sure all students can read it, or find an alternate selection for them that deals with the same ideas.

- "Snow Day" by Priscilla Cummings
- "How Athens Got Its Name" Retelling by Joanna Davis-Swing
- "Hoops Tryouts" by Anina Robb
- "Coming Clean" by Anina Robb

Teaching Tips for Literature-Based Lessons

As you prepare to teach the following lessons, make class sets of texts and handouts for each lesson. Students should always have the handout for guiding discussions available: Guidelines for Discussion and Prompts That Keep a Discussion Moving Forward. Remind students to consult the guidelines if they notice a discussion faltering. If the text that goes with a lesson works for all students in your class, then students can read it independently. If not, you can read the text aloud.

Most of the lessons use two types of talk. I often start with turn-and-talk to warm up students' thinking and then move to another kind of talk. Remember that it's not always necessary to share after a turn-and-talk when you hear and observe that all students "get it." As students discuss, accept any response as long as students paraphrase the text to support their position with specific details or with inferences that use details. Use the same partners throughout a lesson, and make sure every student has a copy of the materials for the lesson.

Circulate and listen carefully as students talk; share suggested time limits in each lesson. However, know that your students might need more or less time, so adjust accordingly.

Understanding the Five Types of Conflict

1. Person vs. Person: The protagonist experiences conflicts with another character.

   Example: In *The Giver*, Jonas develops a conflict between himself and his father after he watches the video feed showing his father "release," or kill, the smaller newborn twin.

2. Person vs. Society: Conflicts arise from institutions like school, home, or the law.

   Example: In *Bud, Not Buddy*, Bud Caldwell has been an orphan since he was 6. But he runs away from a foster home after being abused by the family.

3. Person vs. Nature: A natural disaster such as a twister or a blizzard causes conflicts.

   Example: In *Drowned City* by Don Brown, Hurricane Katrina is a natural disaster that affects all the people in New Orleans.

4. Person vs. Fate: An event beyond the protagonist's control causes conflicts: the character's family situation, the death of one or both parents, being homeless, and so on.

   Example: In *Terrible Typhoid Mary*, by Susan C. Bartoletti, the fact that Mary is a carrier of typhoid fever is something she did not purposefully do, nor can she change or control it.

5. Person vs. Himself/Herself: Internal conflicts arise from emotions, difficulty making a decision, or acting to resolve a conflict.

   Example: Charlotte in *Riding Freedom* doesn't want to behave like a proper girl; she wants to do what boys can do, like drive a stagecoach and vote. Charlotte turns this gender conflict into a plan that lets her lead life, in the 1800s, on her terms.

Protagonist and Antagonists

What It Is

The protagonist is the main character who has one or more problems to solve. Antagonists work against the protagonist; create tension, conflicts, and problems; and can be characters in a story, emotions like fear, or natural forces like earthquakes.

How It Helps

Analyzing these literary elements helps students

- See that the protagonist and antagonists drive the plot.
- Understand the concept of both internal and external antagonists.
- Infer the protagonist's personality traits and the story's themes.

Introducing the Concept of Protagonist and Antagonists

▶ Think aloud with a read-aloud text to identify the protagonist, problems he or she faced, and how they are solved.

▶ Use a read-aloud that has external and internal antagonists on another day to develop the concepts further. Invite students to turn-and-talk and identify characters who are antagonists, as this is concrete and easier (3–4 minutes).

▶ Continue modeling with short read-alouds until students are proficient at identifying a variety of antagonists and protagonists. Have students practice choosing antagonists from

  ○ **External forces:** characters, the weather, nature, setting, an event

  ○ **Internal feelings:** fear, jealousy, insecurity, etc.

▶ Give students Prompts That Support Understanding Protagonists and Antagonists (pages 152–153) for help identifying external and internal antagonists.

Prompts

▶ Identify the protagonist and his or her problems; identify how they are solved.

▶ Use the protagonist's dialogue and interactions to infer his or her personality traits.

▶ Show how antagonists change the protagonist.

▶ Identify one conflict and show how the protagonist deals with it.

▶ Compare and contrast the protagonist to a character who is an antagonist.

Reflect and Intervene

▶ Have students use Prompts That Support Understanding Protagonists and Antagonists as you help them and when they work with a partner or alone.

▶ Make sure students understand the protagonist and antagonists.

▶ Review the directions if students don't understand them.

STUDENT BEHAVIORS	POSSIBLE SCAFFOLDS
Has difficulty identifying the protagonist	• Think aloud and show how you identify the protagonist using a read-aloud text. Explain that the name of the protagonist is repeated throughout a chapter. Show how you identify the protagonist's problems. • Use a short text the student can read; have the student identify the protagonist. • Use a short text. State the problem and have the student find the protagonist. Reverse the strategy, name the protagonist, and have the student state the problem.
Is unable to pinpoint internal antagonists	• Ensure that the student understands *internal* and that it applies to a character. • Think aloud and show how you identify a character's feelings based on what he or she does and says. Invite the student to do this with a different text. • Choose a passage; have the student reread it and figure out the protagonist's emotions and/or inner thoughts.
Needs help with showing how antagonists work against the protagonist	• Think aloud with a recently completed read-aloud text and explain how antagonists work against the protagonist. • Use a short text and ask the student to identify the antagonists and, one by one, show how each works against the protagonist.

Assessing Students' Understanding of Identifying the Protagonist and Antagonists

1. Use the two reproducibles: The Protagonist and External Antagonists (page 146) and The Protagonist and Internal Antagonists (page 147).

2. Use the reproducible for English language learner (ELL) and special education students: Examples of Protagonists and Antagonists (page 148).

3. Use the Teacher's Checklist for Literary Elements (pages 149–151).

Supporting English Language Learners

▶ Help students understand the concept of protagonist and antagonists; start with real-life situations like moving, forgetting homework, or disagreeing with friends; move to texts when students understand.

▶ Think aloud using picture books or short texts. Show how you analyze protagonist and antagonists, then invite students into the discussion.

▶ Pair up ELL students for extra practice.

Reproducibles

The Protagonist and External Antagonists (page 146)

The Protagonist and Internal Antagonists (page 147)

Examples of Protagonists and Antagonists (page 148)

Teacher's Checklist for Literary Elements (pages 149–151)

Teaching Protagonist and Antagonists

"Hoops Tryouts" by Anina Robb

Organize students into groups of 4 to 6 so they can engage in turn-and-talk and small-group discussions. If you feel students have little to no knowledge of the topic of the story, then have them turn-and-talk to activate prior knowledge before you read aloud. When a story is short, you might want to complete the read-aloud during one class, as this lesson does. If it's longer, you can divide the story into two parts and complete it over consecutive days.

This story appeals to this age group because they are into sports, have self-esteem problems just as Brian does, and like Brian will work diligently to overcome internal and external antagonists to meet a seemingly impossible dream.

Materials

"Hoops Tryouts" by Anina Robb; smart notebooks; Prompts That Support Understanding Protagonists and Antagonists

Understanding Protagonist and Antagonists *(40–45 minutes)*

▶ Organize students in groups of 4 to 6.

▶ Ask students to turn-and-talk to the person on their right to activate prior knowledge for the story by asking (2–3 minutes):

  What is the meaning of "hoops"? What do you know about basketball?

▶ Read aloud or have students read silently to the first stop.

▶ Ask students to turn-and-talk for 3 minutes. Say something like*:*

  Who is the protagonist? What problem does he or she face? Why is this a problem?

▶ Ask for a pair to share what they discussed. Then say something like:

  Is there anything another pair wants to add?

▶ Read aloud to the second stop.

▶ Organize students in small groups of 4 to 6 and tell students to use the Prompts That Support Understanding Protagonists and Antagonists (pages 152–153).

▶ Ask half of the small groups to take about 7–8 minutes to explore the problems in the story. Say something like this:

  What additional problems is Brian facing? How does he deal with these problems?

▶ Have the rest of the small groups explore antagonists in the story. Say something like this (7–8 minutes):

  Identify two external and two internal antagonists and explain how each works against Brian.

◗ Invite students from the groups that discussed Brian's problems to share. Call for students to add any ideas (2–3 minutes).

◗ Ask students from groups that discussed antagonists to share, and invite students to add ideas (7–8 minutes).

◗ Connect the discussions by asking groups to discuss (10 minutes):

How does each external and internal antagonist affect Brian's problems and decisions?

◗ Have students share key points of their small-group discussions.

◗ Read to the end of "Hoops Tryouts."

◗ Ask students to turn-and-talk and comment on this quote (2 minutes): "Brian decided the thing to do was make himself look good—to take all the work that he had put in the last few weeks and show it off—not for Matt or his brother or his mom but for himself."

◗ Close the lesson by asking students to volunteer and share their feelings about and reactions to the story's ending and then write their reactions in their smart notebooks.

Notes to Yourself About Teaching the Lesson

_____

_____

_____

_____

_____

_____

_____

_____

_____

_____

_____

The Protagonist and External Antagonists

Name _____ Date _____

Title _____ Author _____

Video or Film Clip _____

Directions: Choose and answer four of the following prompts/questions in your notebook or on separate paper. You can use a print or eBook or a video or film clip.

1. Identify the genre of your book and offer evidence that supports your choice. How did understanding the genre assist your comprehension of the text?

2. Name the protagonist and one key problem he or she faces as well as two additional problems. If the problems are connected, explain how and why.

3. Are the protagonist's problems similar to your problems? To the problems of a main character in a different book you've read? Explain your answer with text evidence.

4. Name two external antagonists and show how each one creates tension and works against the protagonist.

5. Compare and contrast the protagonist with another character in the text, a character who is an antagonist.

6. Show how an external antagonist is a cause, and then list the effects that result.

The Protagonist and Internal Antagonists

Name _____ Date _____

Title _____ Author _____

Video or Film Clip _____

Directions: Choose and answer four of the following prompts/questions in your notebook or on separate paper. You can use a print or eBook or a video or film clip.

1. Identify the genre of your book and offer evidence that supports your choice. How did understanding the genre's characteristics sharpen your comprehension of the problems the protagonist faces?

2. Name the protagonist and one key problem he or she faces as well as two additional problems. If the problems are connected, explain how and why.

3. Name the internal antagonists that the protagonist wrestles with as he or she tries to solve problems and cope with conflicts. Then, choose one problem and one conflict, and explain how the internal conflicts help or thwart the protagonist's efforts.

4. Compare and contrast the protagonist's internal antagonists with the way he or she interacts with and talks to other characters.

5. Does the protagonist overcome any of his or her internal antagonists? Choose one or two and explain how.

Examples of Protagonists and Antagonists

Name _____ Date _____

Title _____ Author _____

Video or Film Clip _____

Directions: Using a short text you've recently completed or a section of your instructional reading book, answer these questions in the space provided below:

1. Define *protagonist* and give an example of the protagonist from your text. Explain how you know this person is the protagonist.

_____

_____

_____

_____

_____

_____

_____

_____

_____

2. Explain the role of an antagonist. Choose a character in your text who is an antagonist, and show how that character works against the protagonist.

_____

_____

_____

_____

_____

_____

_____

_____

_____

_____

Teacher's Checklist for Literary Elements

Name _____ Date _____

Directions: Check those items you're monitoring by observations or by reading smart notebook entries. Complete the checklist three times during the year to monitor progress.

Key: R = Rarely; S = Some of the Time; U = Usually; N/O = Not Observed

DATE			SKILL	NOTES
			Defines protagonist.	
			Gives an example of the protagonist to a literary text.	
			Defines external antagonists.	
			Defines internal antagonists.	
			Shows how external antagonists work against the protagonist.	
			Shows how internal antagonists work against a conflict, setting, and plot events.	
			Defines setting.	

(Continued)

(Continued)

DATE			SKILL	NOTES
			Shows how setting affects characters' actions and words.	
			Defines five kinds of conflict.	
			Explains different kinds of conflicts.	
			Shows how a conflict affects the protagonist.	
			Identifies settings.	
			Shows how setting affects conflicts and characters.	
			Defines climax and denouement or return to normalcy.	
			Explains climax in a short story.	

(Continued)

(Continued)

DATE			SKILL	NOTES
			Identifies small climaxes and the final climax in a novel or long text.	
			Identifies a return to normalcy.	
			Shows the protagonist's personality traits.	
			Shows how and why the protagonist changes.	
			Defines theme.	
			Identifies themes and supporting details.	

Additional Comments

_____

_____

_____

_____

_____

Prompts That Support Understanding Protagonists and Antagonists

You can analyze the protagonist and problems faced:

- What do you learn about the protagonist's family? Friends? Self-image?

- What is the main problem the protagonist wrestles with? Does he or she resolve this problem? How?

- What motivates the protagonist to deal with his or her problems?

- What character traits does the protagonist have that enable him or her to cope with problems?

- How do external antagonists change the protagonist from the beginning to the end? Show what the protagonist's personality and feelings are like at the beginning and then at the end.

- What does the protagonist learn about himself or herself by solving problems and confronting the antagonist?

You can analyze the antagonist's character if it's a person:

- What do you know about the antagonist's history? What key experiences helped shape his or her personality?

- What motivates the antagonist? What goal or desire is he or she trying to achieve?

- How would you describe the antagonist? Use details and dialogue from the text to support your description.

- What does the antagonist value? How does this affect his or her decisions?

- What internal feelings does the antagonist have? Why do you think he or she has these feelings? How do they affect the antagonist's actions?

- How does the antagonist affect the protagonist?

You can analyze how the antagonist affects the plot:

- What is the main conflict in the plot? How is the antagonist involved?

- What are the key events in the plot? How is the antagonist involved?

- How is the conflict resolved? What is the antagonist's role in the resolution?

- What actions or reactions of the antagonist affect the events of the story?

You can analyze how the antagonist interacts with the protagonist and other characters:

- What is the relationship between the antagonist and the protagonist? How does this relationship affect the plot?

- How do the antagonist and the protagonist interact with each other? What do the interactions reveal about the character and motivations of each?

- Does the antagonist have friends or allies? What are these relationships like? How do they help you better understand the antagonist?

(Continued)

- Does the antagonist interact with other characters? What do these interactions reveal about the character of the antagonist?

- What is the source of the conflict between the protagonist and the antagonist? Compare and contrast how the antagonist and the protagonist view the conflict.

You can analyze how the antagonist affects the setting:

- Identify the key settings in the story. Which settings does the antagonist shape? Why do you think those particular settings are used?

- How does a particular setting influence the protagonist? Is there a setting where he or she feels more powerful and in control? Where he or she feels vulnerable? Explain why and how this power and control affect other story elements.

- How do the settings relate to the antagonist and the mood or tone of the story?

You can analyze how internal and external forces serve as antagonists:

- What internal conflicts get in the way of the protagonist achieving his or her goals? Does an intense fear or other feeling hamper the protagonist? Show how this internal conflict affects the protagonist's decisions, motivation, and ability to act.

- Does the protagonist have an illness or physical challenge to manage? How does it affect his or her plans and goals?

- What role do natural forces, such as a geographic feature, the weather, or a natural disaster, play in the plot? How do they affect the protagonist?

- What external events, such as war, holidays, or even a school assembly or competition, play a role in the plot? How do they affect the protagonist?

You can analyze how antagonists deepen your understanding:

- How do antagonists help you understand the plot?

- Show how understanding the antagonists enables you to determine and support themes.

- What do you notice about the antagonists?

- How do antagonists enable you to understand the personality of the protagonist? Provide evidence.

- How are antagonists connected to settings in the story? What do these connections help you understand about theme, plot, conflicts, and the protagonist?

Conflict, Plot, and Setting

What It Is

Conflict is the interaction between the protagonist and antagonists; there are five kinds of conflict (see page 141). Conflict develops the plot, a series of connected events that have a beginning, middle, and end. It also affects the setting.

How It Helps

Analyzing these literary elements helps students

- Understand that plot, setting, and conflict cause a story's rising action.
- Recognize that the plot can contain more than one type of conflict.
- See that conflicts can change the direction of the plot.

Introducing Conflict, Plot, and Setting

▶ Make sure that students understand the term *conflict* as the tension caused by the relationship between the protagonist and antagonists.

▶ Give students a copy of Applying Five Types of Conflict to Texts (page 159) to use as you introduce each type using a read-aloud text.

▶ Think aloud how each type of conflict drives the plot in read-alouds.

▶ Discuss setting and the place and time of a story, and connect to the plot and a conflict.

Prompts

Identify three types of conflicts in the text and give an example of each one.

▶ What is the source of the conflict the protagonist experiences? How is it resolved?

▶ Identify an internal conflict the protagonist faces and show how it affects his or her actions.

▶ Choose two external conflicts from a completed text; explain how each conflict moves the plot forward and provides insights into the protagonist.

▶ Choose an internal conflict the protagonist overcomes, describe it, and explain how the protagonist overcomes it.

▶ Choose two settings and explain the insights they provide about a conflict, the protagonist, or two antagonists.

Reflect and Intervene

Use scaffolds to deepen students' knowledge of the five types of conflict, plot, and setting and the interconnectedness of these literary elements.

STUDENT BEHAVIORS	POSSIBLE SCAFFOLDS
Has difficulty identifying a specific type of conflict	• Review the basic kinds of conflicts. • Engage the student in a discussion of each type, and have the student offer examples. • Pinpoint one or more of the five types of conflict the student can't identify, and discuss how to identify the conflict in a text. • Have the student read a short text and think aloud to show how he or she identifies the specific conflict. • Have the student practice with an instructional-level text.
Is unable to link conflict to plot	• Model how you link conflict to plot using a read-aloud text or a short video. • Find a plot event in the student's instructional reading text, and have the student identify the conflict that is part of the event. • Point the student to a specific plot event in a short text he or she has read, and ask the student to identify the conflict.
Finds identifying internal conflicts difficult	• Start by discussing emotions such as fear and jealousy and how these can create conflicts. • Use the student's instructional reading text and have him or her identify feelings the protagonist experiences; link the feelings to inner conflicts.
Finds identifying changes in setting a challenge	• Use texts to ensure the student understands that setting can be hinted at or specific. • Use a read-aloud text to show changes in setting. • Have the student use a short text and point out different settings.

Assessing Students' Understanding of Setting and Conflict

1. Have students list the highlights of a partner or small-group discussion in their notebooks.

2. Use the reproducibles Conflict, Plot, and Setting (page 158) and Applying Five Types of Conflict to Texts (page 159).

Supporting English Language Learners

▶ Show the types of conflict in daily life—without using names. Use school situations: breaking a rule, criticizing clothing or hair style, deciding how to treat a new student, and so on.

▶ Think aloud to show the types of conflicts students find difficult; use a read-aloud text.

▶ Show students a short video; ask them to identify conflicts.

Reproducibles

Conflict, Plot, and Setting (page 158)

Applying Five Types of Conflict to Texts (page 159)

Prompts for Setting, Plot, and Conflict (page 160)

Teaching Conflict, Plot, and Setting

"Coming Clean" by Anina Robb

This is an excellent story to teach students about conflict because it contains four types.

Person vs. Himself/Herself: Jasper vs. himself

Person vs. Person: Jasper vs. Savion

Person vs. Society: Jasper vs. the boys who are the skate park regulars

Person vs. Fate: Jasper vs. his home situation that creates a need to help Papi

These conflicts shape the outcome of the story and Jasper's decision to "come clean" and tell his papi the truth.

The lesson includes turn-and-talk, partner talk, and a whole-class discussion. I chose whole-class discussion because it affords students an opportunity to hear how their peers identify different conflicts, each conflict's relationship to a setting, and how the conflicts affect the protagonist.

Materials

"Coming Clean" by Anina Robb; smart notebooks; Applying Five Types of Conflict to Texts

Lesson Guidelines

Day 1

Prepare Students to Read *(15 minutes)*

▶ Write the four kinds of conflicts that are in this story on the blackboard or post them on a whiteboard; review each one. Give an example of each from a read-aloud text (see examples at the beginning of this lesson).

Day 2

Preteach Vocabulary; Read for the Gist;
Explore Conflicts on Resource *(30–35 minutes)*

▶ Introduce the term *bodega* and explain that it is a small, neighborhood grocery store in an urban area.

▶ Have students read the story, or read it aloud if it is beyond your students' instructional reading levels.

▶ Invite students to turn-and talk and discuss the gist, share key points, and write three to four points in their smart notebooks (10 minutes).

▶ Have students partner talk (10 minutes):

  1. Discuss the first three types of conflict listed in the handout, Applying Five Types of Conflict to Texts, determining if they apply to "Coming Clean."

  2. Be sure to identify the protagonist and the conflict.

▶ Ask students to use their resource and turn-and-talk to identify the conflict that's fated—that's beyond Jasper's control (3–5 minutes).

▶ Hold a brief whole-class discussion about the conflict that Jasper can't control.

Whole-Class Discussion *(20–25 minutes)*

Day 3

▶ Ask students to retrieve "Coming Clean" and reread it, or you read it aloud again.

▶ Start the discussion with a guiding question, such as:

How does the setting influence the conflicts?

▶ Summarize students' ideas halfway through and at the end of the whole-class discussion.

▶ Here are some ideas eighth-grade students discussed:

The bodega is a setting that causes the conflict between Jasper, Savion, and the other guys because the store had candy that they wanted to steal with Jasper's blessing.

The skate park causes a conflict in Jasper. He wants to be part of the group that goes there. He's desperate to belong and decides to let Savion and the others steal from his dad's store.

Jasper wakes up when he sees his dad mopping floors and he's letting his friends steal candy. Jasper has big guilt. He decides to tell his dad.

▶ Debrief by asking students to partner talk to identify two things that worked during the whole-class discussion and one area they could improve (5 minutes).

Notes to Yourself About Teaching the Lesson

_____

_____

_____

_____

_____

_____

_____

_____

Conflict, Plot, and Setting

Name _____ Date _____

Title _____ Author _____

Directions: Answer the prompts below using "Coming Clean" by Anina Robb. Use the back of the paper if you need more room.

1. Identify a key conflict in the story and explain the specific nature of the conflict.

_____

_____

_____

_____

_____

2. Describe the plot event the conflict develops; include the setting of the event.

_____

_____

_____

_____

_____

3. Show how the protagonist resolves the conflict. If the conflict isn't resolved, explain why.

_____

_____

_____

_____

_____

Applying Five Types of Conflict to Texts

Name _____ Date _____

Title _____ Author _____

1. List and explain the five types of conflict.

_____

_____

_____

_____

_____

_____

_____

_____

_____

_____

_____

_____

2. Identify two to three types of conflicts in your book and clearly show why each one fits in a specific category.

_____

_____

_____

_____

_____

_____

_____

_____

_____

_____

_____

_____

_____

Available for download at **http://resources.corwin.com/readtalkwrite**

Prompts for Setting, Plot, and Conflict

You can analyze Person vs. Person conflict and its connection to settings and plot events.

- Who is the antagonist creating the conflict for the protagonist? What does the character do and/or say that develops conflict?

- Does the conflict result in a change of setting?

- How does the protagonist react to the conflict?

- Does the conflict change the plot? Explain why or why not.

- How does the protagonist resolve the conflict?

- Does the conflict change the protagonist's relationship with the character? Explain.

- What images does the author use to describe an important setting? How do these images relate to the conflict that takes place in the setting?

You can analyze Person vs. Society conflict and its connection to settings and plot events.

- Identify the historical period that's the backdrop of your book. Did school, laws, epidemics, customs, traditions, or money issues create conflicts? Choose a conflict that relates to society during the period your book takes place in and describe the conflict, explain why it arose, and explain how it connects to the plot and setting.

- In science fiction authors often warn readers about technology and beliefs in today's world by projecting them far into the future. Explain a warning the author gives and show how it becomes a conflict in the story.

You can analyze Person vs. Nature conflict and its connection to settings and plot events.

- How does nature create conflicts that lead to problems for the protagonist? Choose one conflict and a problem that grows out of the conflict, and explain how the protagonist deals with them.

- Show how a natural disaster affects the lives of the protagonist and other characters.

You can analyze Person vs. Fate conflict and its connection to settings and plot events.

- Are there conflicts beyond the protagonist's control, such as his or her birth family, a physical condition he or she was born with or developed due to a random event, such as an accident? Why does this element create conflict for the protagonist?

- Choose a conflict that is beyond the protagonist's control and explain how the conflict connects to the plot and settings.

- Fated conflicts can affect the protagonist's personality and outlook on life. Choose one such conflict and explain how it affects the personality of the protagonist and two choices he or she makes that enable him or her to cope with the fated problem.

You can analyze Person vs. Himself/Herself conflict and its connection to settings and plot.

- What are significant emotions the protagonist wrestles with as the story unfolds? Why and how do these emotions become antagonists, causing conflict and problems?

- Does an incident or event replay in the protagonist's mind to cause problems for him or her to solve?

- Is making a decision a challenge for the protagonist? When does this challenge arise? How does it cause conflict? Explain a conflict it causes and how the protagonist deals with it.

....

Identifying Themes

What It Is

A theme is a lesson about life, people, the environment, and so on that can be inferred from the plot, characters, conflicts, and antagonists; it threads through an entire story. A theme is not unique to a specific text; it doesn't name characters or places, and it can apply to other texts.

How It Helps

Analyzing these literary elements helps students

- Reflect on the author's purpose.
- Infer themes they can connect to their own lives.
- Understand the purpose and context of key details in the text.

Introducing the Concept of Theme

Introduce finding themes using the three steps below. Have students copy the steps in their notebooks as a resource.

1. Identify the topic using one word or a short phrase. A short phrase for "Coming Clean" could be *a struggle between right and wrong*.

2. Determine what the story teaches about the topic by asking a question: *What does "Coming Clean" teach about right and wrong?*

3. Write a theme that expresses the message of the piece without naming characters or other text-specific details. Here's a possible theme: *Guilt over cheating and lying to a person you love can make you do the right thing and tell the truth.*

Prompts

- How does an external or internal conflict reveal a theme?

- Reflect on what the protagonist says and does to compose a theme statement.

- Show how the author uses symbols or figurative language to lead you to an important theme.

- Explain how the protagonist deals with a conflict, and develop a theme.

- Consider the lessons about life the story teaches, and develop a theme from these lessons.

Reflect and Intervene

- Make sure the students understand theme.

- Use a read-aloud text and the three steps above to think aloud and show students how you develop a theme statement.

- Ask students to follow the three steps for finding theme, listed above, using a short text; offer support as needed.

- Continue having students practice finding themes until they "get it."

(Continued)

(Continued)

Assessing Students' Understanding of Identifying Themes

1. Have students complete the reproducible Composing Theme Statements (page 165).

2. Invite students to have an in-the-head conversation using a bookmark (see pages 53–55) so you can evaluate what they do and don't understand about theme.

Supporting English Language Learners

▶ Make sure students understand the concept of theme.

▶ Use a read-aloud text to review themes.

▶ Give students a short text to read. Think aloud and show pairs or a small group how you figure out the theme, then ask them to try with a different section of text.

▶ Organize students into pairs; have them use a short text to find a theme.

Reproducible

Composing Theme Statements (page 165)

Notes to Yourself About Teaching the Lesson

_____

_____

_____

_____

_____

_____

_____

_____

_____

_____

Teaching Theme
"Snow Day" by Priscilla Cummings

"Snow Day" is a short story with many themes about friendship, families, and nature. Students can consider what characters say and do, their decisions, and motivation to figure out important themes.

Students use turn-and-talk, partner talk, and small-group discussions to identify themes and develop theme statements. Organize students in groups of 4 to 6 so they have a partner for turn-and-talk and partner talk.

Small-group discussions are ideal for digging into a story to identify themes because students have the opportunity to collaborate, risk sharing ideas, and observe the thinking of peers.

Materials

"Snow Day" by Priscilla Cummings; smart notebooks

Lesson Guidelines

Preparing Students to Read *(30–40 minutes)*   Day 1

▶ Have students turn-and-talk about this question (3–4 minutes):

What kind of an event could cause you to put your life in danger?

▶ Invite students to share their ideas.

▶ Have students read "Snow Day," or you read it aloud, for the gist.

▶ Ask students to partner talk, discuss the gist, and share their ideas (8–10 minutes).

▶ Ask partners to share the key points of the story with the whole class.

Using Small-Group Discussions to Find Themes *(30–40 minutes)*   Day 2

▶ Have students retrieve their copies of "Snow Day" and their smart notebooks.

▶ Review the three steps for finding themes (page 161). Give an example of the process using a read-aloud text you have recently completed (5–8 minutes).

▶ Reread "Snow Day" to improve students' recall of details.

▶ Ask students to choose a group facilitator for small-group discussions who will use the prompts on Prompts for Moving a Discussion Forward.

▶ Invite groups to use the three steps to find two themes and text support for each one using "Snow Day" (10 minutes).

▶ Ask students to use a T-chart to write a theme statement and text support in their smart notebooks. Following are two themes eighth graders shared.

THEME STATEMENT	TEXT SUPPORT
An accident can turn joy into horror.	Brady falls into icy water and is in danger of freezing.
Friends help each other in times of danger.	Digger immediately helps Brady out of the icy water without thinking of the danger to himself.

(Continued)

(Continued)

| **Day 3** | **Finding More Themes With Small-Group Discussions** *(20 minutes)* |

▶ Have students retrieve their copies of "Snow Day" and their smart notebooks.

▶ Ask students to use the same group facilitator as on Day 2.

▶ Have groups use the three steps to find two additional themes and text support for each one (10–15 minutes).

▶ Ask students to set up a T-chart in their smart notebooks and write two themes and text support, and share with the entire class.

▶ Invite students to complete the checklist My Role in a Small-Group Discussion (page 49). You can complete a checklist for group members you observed: Teacher's Checklist for Assessing Small-Group Discussions (page 48).

▶ Here are additional themes eighth-grade students identified:

THEME STATEMENT	TEXT SUPPORT
Empathy for others can change lives.	Brady's empathy for Digger pushes Brady to enlist his parents' help by paying to fix Digger's chipped tooth.
Unexpected expenses can cause resentment between child and parents.	Mr. Griswald tells Digger he did a stupid thing by chipping his tooth to help Brady.
A father's unleashed anger toward a child can cause the child to feel anxious and worried.	Mr. Griswald sends Digger to his room and is very angry about his chipped tooth.

Notes to Yourself About Teaching the Lesson

_____

_____

_____

_____

_____

_____

_____

_____

Composing Theme Statements

Name _____ Date _____

Title _____ Author _____

Directions:

1. Use the steps in the box below to collect information from your book.

2. Discuss the information with your partner or group.

3. Jot notes under Steps 1 and 2.

4. Use your notes to develop two theme statements.

> **Step 1:** Identify the topic using one word or a short phrase.
>
> **Step 2:** Determine what the story teaches by asking a question that uses the word or short phrase from Step 1.
>
> **Step 3:** Write two themes that could apply to other texts, statements that capture the message or life lesson you inferred from events in the story related to the topic. Don't include names of characters or places in your text.

Use your notes to find two themes in your text and write the theme statements below.

1. _____

   _____

   _____

   _____

   _____

2. _____

   _____

   _____

   _____

   _____

Planning and Writing a Summary: Fiction

What It Is

Summarizing is a selective process that asks students to choose the key points in a text and organize them into a paragraph along with a title.

How It Helps

- Requires students to select key details and omit insignificant ones.
- Leads students to identify themes in a story.
- Encourages students to apply their knowledge of genre and literary elements.

Lesson Guidelines

Day 1

Model Planning a Summary *(15 minutes)*

▶ Use a read-aloud text to model how you use the summarizing form to generate ideas for a summary; think-aloud, offering details you'd include under each category: Somebody-Wanted-But-So.

▶ Demonstrate how to transform talk into notes for each category.

▶ Review the rubric, explaining that it provides your expectations.

Day 2

Model Writing a Summary *(20 minutes)*

▶ Model how you use your notes for Somebody to write one to two sentences that also contain the title and author of the piece. This becomes the opening of the summary.

▶ Continue using notes to compose sentences for each category.

▶ Create a title for your summary using a detail from your notes.

▶ Read your summary out loud, modeling how to revise for improved word choice, varied sentence openings, proper usage, and correct punctuation.

▶ Demonstrate how to check your summary against the rubric and revise as necessary.

Days 3 and 4

Students Plan and Write Summaries *(20–35 minutes)*

Some students can complete the process in one class, but others will need two classes. Invite students who finish early to read. Circulate and offer on-the-spot support.

▶ Organize students into partners.

▶ Give out the rubric for summarizing fiction and the reproducible Somebody-Wanted-But-So: Fiction.

▶ Discuss your expectations for partner talk—focus on important details.

▶ Ask partners to use the summary form and rubric to discuss each part of the summary.

▶ Have students jot notes on their form and raise their hands when they're ready for you to approve the plan. If a plan is complete, have the student start writing the summary on his or her own. Support students who need more details with specific feedback.

Reflect and Intervene

When students have difficulty planning and writing a summary for fiction, consider the following suggestions as you scaffold the process for them. The art of summarizing supports writing book reviews and presenting book talks.

- Talk with the student to ensure that he or she can recall details from the material.
- Ask the student to reread a short text or chapter if there's little recall of details. If limited recall persists, give the student an easier text.
- Help the student translate talk into jotting notes for each item by modeling how you do this with the first item. Then invite the student to write notes for the second item and so on.
- Model how you use the first item to compose one or two sentences that include the title and author.
- Have the student turn notes for the second item into one to two sentences.
- Continue supporting the student until he or she can complete the process independently.

Assessing Plans and Summaries

1. Use the rubric on page 173 to assess students' notes and their summary.
2. Use the reproducible Somebody-Wanted-But-So: Fiction that students have completed.
3. Use students' written summary.

Supporting English Language Learners

- Have students summarize a short chapter or short text, and make sure they can read it with ease.
- Help students at the planning stage by talking about each item on the form with them before they jot notes.
- Ask students to summarize longer chunks of texts once they show they can successfully summarize short texts.

Reproducibles

Somebody-Wanted-But-So Summary: Fiction (for grade-level and above students) (page 171)

Somebody-Wanted-But-So Summary: Fiction (for ELL and special education students) (page 172)

Rubric for a Somebody-Wanted- But-So Summary: Fiction (page 173)

Teaching Summary: Fiction

"Hoops Tryouts" by Anina Robb

By inviting students to collaborate in planning and writing a summary for a fictional text, you provide them with a mental model of the planning process and show them how the plan makes writing the summary easy.

Students use turn-and-talk and partner talk to discuss and understand the story, then use turn-and-talk to collect notes for the plan. Have students continue with turn-and-talk as they transform notes into sentences for the summary and create a title.

Materials

"Hoops Tryouts" by Anina Robb; Somebody-Wanted-But-So reproducible; notebook paper

Lesson Guidelines

Day 1

Reading "Hoops Tryouts" *(40 minutes)*

▶ Invite students to turn-and-talk and discuss this question:

> *How can trying out for a position on a basketball team be a challenging experience?*

▶ Have students share their ideas.

▶ Invite students to read "Hoops Tryouts" or read the story out loud to them for the gist.

▶ Ask students to partner talk and discuss the gist.

▶ Have students reread "Hoops Tryouts" or reread the story to them.

▶ Invite students to use partner talk to discuss the problems the protagonist faces.

Day 2

Collaborative Note Taking *(20 minutes)*

▶ Have students skim "Hoops Tryouts" to refresh their memory.

▶ Give students a copy of the Somebody-Wanted-But-So reproducible.

▶ Think aloud and write the notes you take for Somebody. Here's what I write:

> *Brian is the protagonist. He's short but wants to make the BB team.*

▶ Invite students to turn-and-talk; create and discuss notes for Wanted, But, and So; and share with the class. Explain that students should not give away the outcome. Here are agreed-upon suggestions from fifth graders:

> *Wanted: Brian wanted to grow taller; he wanted to make the basketball team; he practiced.*

> *But: The coach pairs Matt Lesh and Brian at the tryouts. Matt always picks on Brian for being short and thinks he's the best BB player 'cause he's tall.*

> *So: Brian uses his hard work and tries to outperform Matt at every tryout station.*

Collaborative Summary Writing *(40 minutes)*

▶ Model how you use your notes for Somebody to write a topic sentence that includes the title and author. Tell students that notes can be turned into one to three sentences. Here's what I write on chart paper:

In Anina Robb's "Hoops Tryouts," Brian, the protagonist, wants to make the seventh-grade basketball team and show that practice and preparation can overcome his short height.

▶ Ask students to partner talk and turn notes into sentences for each section. Record their notes on chart paper or project them onto a whiteboard.

▶ Have students reread and suggest a title for the summary. The title some of my students chose is "Does Practice Pay Off?"

▶ Here's the completed collaborative summary:

Does Practice Pay Off?

In Anina Robb's "Hoops Tryouts" Brian wants to make the seventh-grade basketball team and show that practice can overcome his short height. Brian wants to grow taller so he stretches his legs every day. He wants to make the basketball team. At the tryouts, the coach pairs Matt Lesh with Brian. This is a nightmare for Brian because Matt always picks on Brian for being short. Matt sees himself as the tallest and best basketball player in seventh grade. Brian puts his fear of Matt aside. He decides to use his hard work to be better than Matt at every tryout station.

▶ Have students turn-and-talk about how the notes helped them write the summary and share their ideas.

Notes to Yourself About Teaching the Lesson

_____

_____

_____

_____

_____

_____

_____

Somebody-Wanted-But-So Summary: Fiction

Name Lucien

Date February 2016

Title "How Athens Got Its Name"

Author Joanna Davis-Swing

	NOTES
SOMEBODY: Name the protagonist.	Creops-half man half snake-king of goat farmers and bee keepers in Greece
WANTED: State a conflict/problem or goal the protagonist faced.	To find a patron god or goddess for his city so Zeus set up a contest between Poseidon and Athena
BUT: Explain a conflict that worked against the protagonist.	Athena's gift of the olive tree won over Poseidon's gift of salt water seas.
SO: Show how the conflict was resolved without giving the ending away.	The olive tree made Athens a booming city. Olives gave people food, oil to offer gods and rub on men's skin, to light lamps and use to cook.

Summary

Contest Winner

The Greek myth, "How Athens Got Its Name" explains how the goddess Athena became the patron of Athens, the city named for her. Creops half man and half snake became King of a city of goat farmers and bee keepers. The gods had fights over who would be the patron of Creops city that was prophesed to be successful. Zeus hated the fighting so he said the contest was between Athena and Poseidon who had to present a special gift to the city. Athena's gift of the olive tree won over Poseidon's gift of salt water because olives give food to people, oil to offer the gods, and oil to light lamps and cook meals. The gift of the olive tree helped Athens become a booming city that people also honored for its beauty.

Robb's Comments: Notice that Lucien gave his summary a title that reflects its main point: the contest and its winner. The notes taken before writing the summary asked Lucien to select details and do his thinking before writing. You can see how the notes supported writing the summary and enabled him to focus on things like varying sentence openings and using strong verbs. I avoid focusing on spelling errors, but first celebrate what really worked. I do expect students to spell the Greek names correctly if they are in the myth. Lucien can reread his piece and correct the spelling of *prophesied*.

Somebody-Wanted-But-So Summary: Fiction

Completing Notes Independently

Name _____ Date _____

Title _____ Author _____

Video or Film Clip _____

Directions:

1. Use a short text, one to three chapters from a novel, or the entire book.

2. Talk about each element for summarizing by having an in-the-head conversation or a short conversation with a partner.

3. Jot notes on the form.

4. Use separate paper and turn your notes for each item into one to two sentences.

5. Create a title for your summary.

	NOTES
SOMEBODY: Name the protagonist.	
WANTED: State a conflict/problem or goal the protagonist faced.	
BUT: Explain a conflict that worked against the protagonist.	
SO: Show how the conflict was resolved without giving the ending away.	

Write your summary on a separate sheet of paper. Turn in your notes with your summary.

....

Somebody-Wanted-But-So Summary: Fiction

Completing Notes With a Partner

Name _____ Date _____

Title _____ Author _____

Video or Film Clip _____

Directions:

1. Work with a partner who has read the same material.

2. Use a short text, or one chapter from a novel.

3. Talk about each element for summarizing by having a short conversation.

4. Jot notes on the form.

5. Use separate paper and turn your notes into one to three sentences.

6. Create a title for your summary.

	NOTES
SOMEBODY: Name the protagonist.	
WANTED: State a conflict/problem or goal the protagonist faced.	
BUT: Explain a conflict that worked against the protagonist.	
SO: Show how the conflict was resolved without giving the ending away.	

Write your summary on a separate sheet of paper.

Rubric for a Somebody-Wanted-But-So Summary: Fiction

	4	3	2	1
Plans	Detailed notes support each category.	Detailed notes support three of the four categories.	Detailed notes support one to two categories.	Notes not detailed but general.
Title	Short; catches reader's attention; announces topic.	Announces topic.	Uses "Summary."	No title.
Opening	Includes title and author.	Leaves out title or author.	Leaves out title and author.	Leaves out title and author.
Summary Details	Includes key text details in sentences for each category; includes an inference from text details.	Includes key text details for three of the four categories.	Includes key details for two of the four categories.	Lacks key details in three or more categories.
Wrap-Up	"So" sentence ties summary together and doesn't reveal the ending.	"So" sentence is very general but ties summary together.	"So" sentence wraps up summary but gives away ending.	"So" sentence gives away ending and doesn't tie together the summary.
Writing Conventions	Uses complete sentences; varies sentence openings; uses strong verbs and specific nouns.	Indents paragraphs; varies sentence openings; needs to revise some verbs and nouns.	Contains two run-ons; sentence openings the same for several sentences; uses weak verbs and specific nouns.	Contains several run-ons; most sentences start same way; needs to work on verbs and nouns.

Compare and Contrast Notes

What It Is

When students compare and contrast, they reflect on how two characters, settings, conflicts, or other literary elements are alike and how they differ.

How It Helps

- Enables students to think about literary elements by making connections between two elements in the same text or in different texts.
- Helps students understand conflicts, characters' decisions, dialogue, and personality traits more deeply.

Lesson Guidelines

Day 1

Modeling How to Compare and Contrast *(15–20 minutes)*

- ◗ Review the meaning of *compare* and *contrast*. Explain how understanding the likenesses and differences of two characters or other literary elements can deepen readers' understanding of conflict, decisions, and characters' personality traits.
- ◗ Think aloud with a read-aloud text to show how you compare and contrast two different characters, settings, and so on.
- ◗ Model how you use what you've learned by comparing and contrasting to deepen your understanding of a conflict, decisions, and/or a character's personality traits.

Day 2

Guided Practice With Compare and Contrast: Character *(20–25 minutes)*

- ◗ Have students use a completed short text or a recently completed read-aloud and partner talk to compare and contrast two characters.
- ◗ Discuss your expectations for partner talk. Circulate and listen to students talk; provide on-the-spot support when needed.
- ◗ Ask partners to discuss what compare and contrast taught them about the characters, conflicts in the story, and decisions characters made.

Day 3

Guided Practice With Compare and Contrast: Setting *(20–25 minutes)*

- ◗ Review your expectations with students.
- ◗ Have students partner talk to compare and contrast two different settings.
- ◗ Ask partners to discuss what setting reveals about conflicts, characters' decisions, and personality traits.
- ◗ Have students complete one of the reproducibles for compare and contrast on pages 178 and 179.

Reflect and Intervene

Try the following scaffolding suggestions. Once students can compare and contrast, they can use this strategy to write paragraphs and essays and to give a speech that compares and contrasts specific literary elements.

- Make sure students understand what both terms mean.

- Use a think-aloud with one of your read-aloud texts or a short text students have read, and show how you use story details to explain how two characters are alike and different. Do the same for setting.

- Help students apply these terms to a short text that they can understand and read with ease, and have students practice until they can compare and contrast independently.

- Partner a student who requires extra support with a student who "gets it," and have them practice using a text both can learn from and read.

- Have students complete a reproducible with your support or the support of a peer.

Assessing Students' Venn Diagrams

1. Use the Teacher's Checklist for Compare and Contrast (page 180) for assessing students' thinking on their Venn diagrams.

2. Evaluate student work on Compare and Contrast in Two Parts (see page 179).

Supporting English Language Learners

- Make sure students understand the meaning of *compare* and *contrast*.

- Have students complete one of these concepts at a time using instructional reading materials.

- Pair up ELL students reading the same short text, and have them talk to compare and contrast two characters or settings and complete the reproducible Compare and Contrast in Two Parts.

Reproducibles

Compare and Contrast: Venn Diagram (page 178)

Compare and Contrast in Two Parts (page 179)

Teacher's Checklist for Compare and Contrast (page 180)

Notes to Yourself About Teaching the Lesson

_____

_____

_____

_____

_____

_____

Teaching Compare and Contrast Notes

"How Athens Got Its Name"
Retelling by Joanna Davis-Swing

The Greek myth "How Athens Got Its Name" is an excellent text for introducing and practicing compare and contrast because it's about Athena and Poseidon giving gifts to a city they both hope will be named after them. Students can compare and contrast the Greek god and goddess as well as the gifts they offer, and then determine why Athena won the contest.

Greek myths might be a new genre for these students, so make sure you take the time to build their background knowledge. Once students have completed the lesson, consider having them read other Greek myths as well as myths from different cultures. Ask your school librarian to help you find materials your students can read for instruction and independently.

Materials

"How Athens Got Its Name"; Compare and Contrast: Venn Diagram; Compare and Contrast in Two Parts; Teacher's Checklist for Compare and Contrast

Lesson Guidelines

Day 1

Build Students' Background Knowledge *(30–40 minutes)*

▶ Help students understand that the main characters of myths are gods and goddesses, heroes and heroines with great powers, and human beings. Often, the gods and goddess act like human beings, showing anger and jealousy toward one another. Think aloud and say something like:

The main characters of myths are gods and goddesses, heroes and heroines with great powers, and human beings. Myths tell a story. The story can explain something in nature like thunder and lightning, how human beings and animals were created, or how something in the environment such as rivers and mountains appeared.

▶ Read aloud a myth about Athena and one about Poseidon; discuss their history and role as an Olympian god and goddess, and the symbols they carry and/or wear. An excellent resource is *D'Aulaires' Book of Greek Myths* (D'Aulaire & D'Aulaire, 1992).

▶ Ask students to partner talk to discuss what they learned about Athena and Poseidon.

Day 2

**Read "How Athens Got Its Name"
Out Loud and Have Students Reread It** *(30 minutes)*

▶ Read aloud or have students read "How Athens Got Its Name."

▶ Have students partner talk and take turns retelling the story. Encourage them to skim parts of the myth that have information on each of the four prompts listed below in order to present detailed retellings. Ask partners to take turns retelling.

1. How did the idea of having a contest begin?

2. Describe what Poseidon looks like and the gift he offers.

3. Describe what Athena looks like and her gift.

4. Explain why you think the judges give Athena the prize.

▶ Have students turn-and-talk to discuss what this myth explains and to share their ideas with the group.

Compare and Contrast Athena and Poseidon and Their Gifts *(30 minutes)*

▶ Give these prompts to students to help them, and have them partner talk to discuss how Poseidon and Athena and their gifts are alike and different.

1. Show how Athena and Poseidon are alike.

2. Explain how Athena's and Poseidon's gifts differ. Explain who and what each gift helps.

▶ Circulate and listen to students, stopping to help partners.

▶ Ask pairs to share their discussions.

Have Students Complete Compare and Contrast: Venn Diagram or Compare and Contrast in Two Parts *(about 20 minutes)*

▶ Circulate and offer students suggestions and support.

▶ Have students read to their partner what they wrote to make sure it's complete.

▶ During a planning period, complete the Teacher's Checklist for Compare and Contrast based on students' written work on the reproducible.

Notes to Yourself About Teaching the Lesson

_____

_____

_____

_____

_____

_____

_____

Compare and Contrast: Venn Diagram

Name _____ Date _____

Title _____ Author _____

Directions:

1. Choose two characters or two settings from your book.

2. Write on the left and right side of the Venn the names of each character or setting.

3. Note on the left and right sides of the Venn elements that differ.

4. Write in the overlapping part of the Venn elements both have in common.

5. Reread the Venn and think about what you learned about a conflict, a character's decisions, and/or a character's personality traits.

Explain what you learned about a conflict, a character's decision, and/or a character's personality traits.

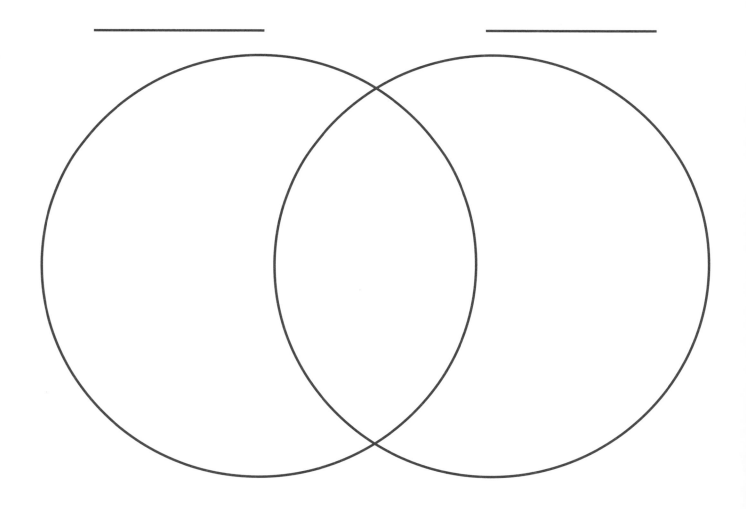

Compare and Contrast in Two Parts

Name _____ Date _____

Title _____ Author _____

Directions:

1. Choose two characters, two settings, two items, or two conflicts.

2. Show how they are alike and different using the headings on this form.

3. Explain what you learn from comparing and contrasting about a conflict, a character's decision, and/or a character's personality traits.

Name both characters or settings.
Jot, in a list, how they are alike.

Name one character or setting and show how it differs.	Name a second character or setting and show how it differs.

Explain what you learned about a conflict, a character's decision, and/or a character's personality traits.

Teacher's Checklist for Compare and Contrast

Name _____ Date _____

Title _____ Author _____

What students compared and contrasted: _____

Comparing

_____ Talks with a partner to discuss likenesses.

_____ Uses specific text details to show how two characters, settings, or other pairs of literary elements are alike.

_____ Makes inferences to show how two characters, settings, or other pairs of literary elements are alike.

_____ Uses comparing to deepen his or her understanding of a conflict, a character's decisions, and/or a character's personality traits.

Contrasting

_____ Talks to a partner to discuss differences.

_____ Uses specific text details to show how two characters, settings, or other pairs of literary elements differ.

_____ Makes inferences to show how two characters, settings, or other pairs of literary elements differ.

_____ Uses contrasting to deepen his or her understanding of a conflict, a character's decisions, and/or a character's personality traits.

Additional Observations and Comments

_____

_____

_____

_____

_____

_____

_____

_____

Schedule a 5-minute conference if necessary on _____

Aim 3

Teach Students to Read, Talk, and Write About Nonfiction

6

Taking the Plunge

How to Talk and Write About Nonfiction

If textbooks are the main or only informational texts that students read in Grades 4 and up, we are shortchanging them. Textbooks have facts, facts, and more facts, and often, as a fifth grader said, "leave out the story—all the great stuff." Yet it's the true stories and the narrative elements in informational books that bond and connect readers to them (Newkirk, 2014).

Skilled and award-winning nonfiction writers do extensive research to find mysteries, true accounts, snippets of diaries, and recorded conversations to weave into their writing. Nonfiction can be as creative as fiction and includes figurative language, dialogue, and the writer's strong voice—combined with true stories—elements that engage readers and motivate them to continue reading (Duke, Caughlan, Juzwik, & Martin, 2011; Fletcher, 2015; Newkirk, 2014).

To deepen students' understanding of nonfiction, it's helpful to teach them about text features such as diagrams, photographs, and captions because these features often clarify information in the text or add related and important information. In addition, to better navigate nonfiction texts, students need knowledge of text structures such as description (which helps students visualize to understand) and sequence (which can aid students' comprehension of the order of a series of events or a process such as cell division); see page 188 for more on text structure and comprehension. Inviting students to talk about nonfiction texts supports their recall of details, increases their understanding of text features and structures, develops their appreciation of narrative elements, and, most important, builds their knowledge.

Seven Tips for Inspiring Students to Have Literary Conversations About Nonfiction

These tips work best with partner talk. Students can work with a partner in their guiding reading or literature circle groups, or the teacher can select partners. Partners can be reading the same book or different books in the same genre, and books can be for instruction or for independent reading.

1. Ask Students to Complete a Preview Before Reading. To build prior knowledge, have students reflect on and discuss the cover illustration, the title of the book, and the table of contents. Then have them read the first chapter of a book or first page of a short text, including text features (see page 187 for a list of text features). To extend the preview, students can try to connect chapter titles to what they have learned from the preview.

2. Have Students Talk to Set Reading Purposes. Having a purpose for reading not only can make the reading engaging, but also helps students determine what's important. With nonfiction texts, a first purpose for reading can come from questions raised during the preview, or students can use the title of a chapter and read to discover why the author used that title. Help students understand that purposes can change while they continue reading. It's helpful to invite students to adjust their reading purpose before starting a new chapter or a chunk of text.

3. Invite Partners to Check Out and Discuss Chapter Titles. Since chapter titles usually point out a key theme and/or main ideas in the chapter, the title can help students identify theme and/or main ideas along with the details that support it.

4. Teach Students to Talk About the Context Clues for Tough Vocabulary. Nonfiction often contains words that are unfamiliar to students. There are six different types of context clues (see page 184). Students can avoid letting an unfamiliar word stump them by discussing it with a partner and using context clues to figure out meaning. To support their partner talk, give students the handout Six Kinds of Context Clues (page 184 and available for download at http://resources.corwin.com/readtalk-write). The more students meet a word while reading, the better they'll understand how it works in different situations or contexts.

5. Ask Students to Talk About Making Inferences. With informational texts students can infer using details and narrative elements the author includes. With biography, making inferences is often similar to fiction, and in addition to details, students can use dialogue, inner thoughts, problems, conflicts, and antagonists.

6. Have Students Discuss Interpretive, Text-Dependent Questions. Discussing interpretive, text-dependent questions can deepen students' recall of information, text features, and structures (see pages 12 and 74 for more guidelines).Teach students how to skim to locate details that answer questions by identifying key words in a question and skimming a text to find those words. In addition, students can use chapter titles to locate information that answers a question.

7. Solve Problems With Close Reading and Talking. A close read can help "unconfuse" confusing passages and enable students to understand figurative language and how it links to main ideas and/or themes, new information, and vocabulary. Close reading asks students to reread and analyze a passage phrase by phrase and sentence by sentence in order to link ideas and improve your comprehension. (See Close Reading Guidelines for Informational Text on page 185 and http://resources .corwin.com/readtalkwrite).

Teach Six Kinds of Context Clues

The vocabulary demands in nonfiction texts challenge readers, and many of the words, because they are topic specific, are new to students. Therefore, it's important to provide students with the tools for using context to unlock an unfamiliar word's meaning. Think aloud as you read aloud to show students how you use context clues to figure out tough words in nonfiction. Be explicit and state the kind of clue you're using.

Have students partner talk during guided practice as they use context clues to figure out the meanings of unfamiliar words.

s and Synonyms: The author gives a definition or uses a similar word immediately after or close ...liar word. A definition or synonym follows a comma, a dash, or words such as *or, is called, that is*, and *in other words*.

> **Example:** From *Terrible Typhoid Mary* by Susan C. Bartoletti: *In her wake are many cases of typhoid fever, she having unwittingly **disseminated**—or as we might say, **sprinkled**—germs in various households.*

2. Concrete Examples: The author offers an example that helps you figure out the word's meaning. Examples can be found in the sentence, in a new sentence or following these words or phrases: *for example, such as,* and *especially*.

> **Example:** From "Isaac Newton and the Day He Discovered the Rainbow" by Kathleen Krull: *A **refracting** substance, such as a prism, could bend each wavelength of light by a different angle or amount.*

3. Restated Meanings: Sometimes the author defines a difficult word by restating its meaning in simpler terms. Often commas set off the word from the meaning. You'll also find the meaning of a word stated after words and phrases such as *or, that is,* and *in other words*.

> **Example:** From *Tales From the Top of the World* by Sandra Athans: *To keep from getting sick on Everest, climbers must **acclimatize**, or adjust, to the low oxygen levels.*

4. Comparison: The author uses a comparison to help you understand a tough word.

> **Example:** From *Drowned City* by Don Brown: *The police were as **stranded** as the people who need their help* (p. 34).

5. Words or Phrases That Modify: Modifiers such as adjectives, adverbs, or relative clauses can have clues to a word's meaning. A relative clause begins with *who, which, that, whose,* or *whom* and often explains or extends an idea or word in the main part of the sentence.

> **Example:** From "Isaac Newton and the Day He Discovered the Rainbow" by Kathleen Krull: *He [Newton] observed that the beam spread out into colored bands of light, which he called a **spectrum**.*

6. Conjunctions That Show Relationships and Link Ideas: Coordinating and subordinating conjunctions show relationships and help you link unknown words and ideas to known words and ideas. *And, but, or, not, for*, and *yet* are coordinating conjunctions. Common subordinating conjunctions are *when, if, since, whenever*, and *because*.

> **Example:** From "New Horizons in Space" by Seymour Simon: *Planet earth **and** the many thousands of asteroids circling the sun in our solar system were all created from the same basic material **when** the solar system was formed.*

In addition to the vocabulary demands of nonfiction, students will find that knowledge and understanding of text features and text structures can also support recall, comprehension, and analytical thinking.

....

Close Reading Guidelines for Informational Text

When you're reading a text, assume that every word and phrase carries meaning. If you're unsure of what something means, do a close reading.

If it's a difficult word . . .

- Look carefully at the word. Are there any prefixes, suffixes, or roots you recognize? Think of their meaning.
- Reread the sentences before and after the one containing the difficult word. Do they contain any clues to what the word means? If not, back up and read the entire paragraph; continue and read the paragraph that comes after the tough word.
- Is there a glossary you can consult? Are there any text features, such as charts or photographs and captions, that provide clues to the word?
- Have you seen or heard the word or phrase? In what situation? Can you recall what the word or phrase meant in the specific situation?

Dig Deeper

- Can you connect the word or phrase to information that came before it? To what you know and have learned from the preview, from other books, or in another class?
- Why do you think the writer uses this particular word or phrase?
- How does this word or phrase relate to the tone, main idea, or theme of the text?
- What is the significance of this word or phrase in relation to other ideas in the sentence or paragraph?

If it's a difficult sentence, paragraph, or section . . .

- Read each sentence word by word, chunking phrases and making sure you know what each one means. If a particular word gives you trouble, use the strategies above to figure it out.
- Paraphrase each sentence by saying it in your own words.
- Continue rereading and paraphrasing each sentence. When you get to the end of a paragraph, retell it for yourself. If you can't retell several details, then reread the paragraph and try retelling it again.
- Continue rereading and retelling paragraphs. When you get to the end of a section, retell it for yourself. Try to think of the main idea of the section.

Dig Deeper

- Consider the themes of the text. How does the sentence, paragraph, or section relate to them?
- Why do you think the writer includes this sentence, paragraph, or section in the text?
- How does this sentence, paragraph, or section connect to the title?
- How does this sentence, paragraph, or section connect to other parts of the text?
- What inferences can you make from this sentence, paragraph, or section?

Recap What You Understand

- Try restating some main ideas and a theme. If you can do this and recall details, then you've attained your close reading goal.

Mining Text Features for Information

An engaging way to teach students about nonfiction text structures is asking them to explore features in books that you have checked out from your school's library. Ask the school librarian to provide enough nonfiction books, including picture books, so that each pair has a text.

Lesson Guidelines

Day 1

Partner Talk to Explore Text Features *(30–40 minutes)*

▶ Organize students into partners.

▶ Invite partners to select one book from those displayed.

▶ Give pairs 10–15 minutes to browse through the book and identify text features.

▶ Have pairs talk about each feature they find, using these questions:

What do you learn from the feature?

How does the feature help you better understand the topic?

▶ Ask pairs to choose two features they'd like to share. Selecting two means that if someone has already shared a feature, they have a second one to use.

▶ Make a list of features on your computer and post the list onto a whiteboard.

▶ Call for questions from students about specific features.

Day 2

Analyze Text Features to Build Comprehension *(30 minutes)*

▶ Use the same partnerships that you organized on the first day. Partners use the same book they used on Day 1.

▶ Give each pair one text feature.

▶ Ask students to partner talk to explain the feature and discuss how it can improve recall and understanding and help readers in general.

▶ Type students' responses into your computer and project them on the whiteboard.

▶ Invite all students to read the explanations and offer additional ideas.

Day 3

Build Knowledge of Text Features *(15–20 minutes)*

▶ Give each student a copy of Nonfiction Text Features (page 187 and available for download at http://resources.corwin.com/readtalkwrite).

▶ Have students use partner talk to compare the resource with what they collaboratively wrote for each feature, and display these on a whiteboard.

▶ Invite students to use their handout to add and/or adjust ideas on the text that's projected onto the whiteboard.

Asking students to create their own list of text features and explain how each one supports readers shows that you respect students' expertise and collaborative thinking. It also gives students ownership of the process and deepens their understanding of features because they explored them and then explained each one.

Nonfiction Text Features

Each feature includes an explanation of how it can help recall, understanding information, locating details, and/or connecting ideas.

- **Afterword:** This contains information about a person or event that occurs after the end of the book. Knowing what happened satisfies your curiosity, brings closure to a series of events, and lets you see the results of decisions, conflicts, the impact of nature, and so on.

- **Bibliography:** This list at the end of the book cites the books and magazines the author used to write the book. A list of sources lets you know how much research the author completed as well as the accuracy of the information.

- **Boldface Type:** This is the darker type used for titles and headings. Key vocabulary can also be in boldface type. This feature calls your attention to words or phrases and indicates they are important. Boldface titles and headings enable readers to quickly locate specific information to prove a point, answer questions, or study for a test or quiz.

- **Glossary:** This alphabetic list of important terms explains tough or unusual words found in the text. It usually comes near the end of the book. Sometimes a glossary entry also includes guidelines for pronouncing the word, offering quick help when you can't figure out a word's meaning using context.

- **Index:** This alphabetic list of key words, topics, and names of people and places in the text comes at the end of the book. Next to each item is a page number or several page numbers, referring you to the places in the book where the idea or person is mentioned. The more page numbers an index entry has, the more details you can find about that topic. Scanning the index for a specific topic can let you know how much information you'll find in a book because the index is more detailed than the table of contents.

- **Maps:** These help you visualize the location of a place the author discusses. They also allow you to follow the path of an explorer, pilot, or rescue effort and can enable you to better understand how distances and geography can create hardships, challenges, and dangers.

- **Introduction:** This part of a text can explain how the author conceived of the idea as well as recognize others who helped the author gather information. Here, you learn about the extent of the research and interviewing the author did, and this can help you evaluate the accuracy of the information in the book.

- **Photographs and Captions:** These supply an image of an object or person and can give extra information about the topic. Captions are one or two sentences that explain the photograph. Having a visual can help you understand a difficult concept and deepen their understanding of new information.

- **Quotes and Interviews:** These features can be in sidebars or on a section of the page separate from the story. Quotes and interviews give the exact words of a person. These can provide anecdotes and stories about a person or topic that can help you remember details and connect ideas.

- **Sidebars:** These are boxes containing information on a page of a book or magazine article that didn't quite fit into the text but that the author wanted to include. Sidebars can contain a list of fascinating facts, quotes, a part of an interview, a newspaper clipping, or a letter. The additional information in a sidebar can help you better understand the topic and identify a main idea or theme.

- **Table of Contents:** This provides chapter titles and page numbers. It's also an overview of what you will find in the text.

- **Time Line:** This feature provides visual images and the sequence of a person's life, key historical events, or events that led to an invention or medical breakthrough. This feature can include key dates in a person's life. It can also cover the dates of key events in a historical period such as the Middle Ages or the Renaissance or a major war such as World War II. Time lines can have photographs, illustrations, and short write-ups under each date.

Available for download at **http://resources.corwin.com/readtalkwrite**

Identifying Text Structures to Build Understanding

It's the content that authors are trying to communicate that determines the text structure they use. Most often, a paragraph or section of text contains more than one text structure. For example, a descriptive paragraph might also include sequence and/or cause/effect. In fact, description is usually a part of each text structure. Text structure can help students comprehend a text as well as skim and locate information. Review these structures and the meanings each can develop by using the lessons in this chapter.

▶ **Description:** Helps students visualize or picture what a place, an event, a historical period, an invention, a setting, or a person looks like. When students can visualize something from their reading, it shows that they understand it and can recall the information.

▶ **Sequence:** When the author writes about something in the order it happened, it helps students see and understand connections among events. Not only does sequence supply the chronological order that something occurs in, but it also enables readers to visualize and understand complex ideas such as mitosis, developing photographs, and so on.

▶ **Compare/Contrast:** This text structure shows students how two items are alike and how they differ. These can be people or characters, settings, problems, information, and events. Compare/contrast can deepen students' understanding of ideas in a text and a person's personality traits, and it can help them find main ideas and themes.

▶ **Cause/Effect:** The cause comes before the effect or effects and shows how words, nature, decisions, problems, actions, and events can cause other things to happen. By understanding the relationship between a cause and the resulting effect(s), readers deepen their knowledge of events, settings, the decisions a person makes, as well as the obstacles he or she faces.

▶ **Problem/Solution:** The author presents a problem and then helps readers understand one or more solutions. This structure helps students search for an answer after the author states the problem and helps them gather the main points of a passage.

▶ **Question/Answer:** Sometimes a paragraph opens with a question, or there's a question within the paragraph, and the author offers answers. This structure provides students with an inquiry model of reading informational texts: Raise a question and read on to explore the answer.

▶ **Main Idea/Details:** A paragraph can open or end with the main idea, the most important idea in a paragraph or section of text. However, there are times when you will have to use details in one or more paragraphs to infer the main idea. Understanding main ideas can help students figure out themes as well as connections among main ideas.

Teaching Text Structures

What follows is a generic lesson that works for teaching the text structures one at a time so students gain a deep understanding of each one.

Materials

You can use excerpts from *Tales From the Top of the World* by Sandra Athans that includes these structures: description, cause/effect, compare/contrast. Or use "New Horizons in Space" by Seymour Simon, which includes these structures: problem-solution, cause/effect, description. The selections are on pages 119 and 109, respectively, and are available for download at http://resources.corwin.com/readtalkwrite. Or you can choose passages from your read-aloud texts or texts students are reading for instruction.

Lesson Guidelines

Introduce Text Structure With a Read-Aloud *(15–20 minutes)*

Day 1

▶ Read aloud a short text that features a clear example of the text structure you want to introduce.

▶ Think aloud about the text structure, noting how you determine what it is and how it helps you better understand the text. Here's what I say for the section "Adjusting to Thin Air" from *Tales From the Top of the World*:

> *The cause is climbing to 5,000 feet above sea level; the effects are people have to take deep breaths to get enough oxygen.*

▶ Organize students into partners for guided practice.

▶ Give each pair a short text they can learn from and understand that features the target text feature.

▶ Invite students to read the text, then use partner talk to identify the specific text structure and discuss how it helped them understand the information.

▶ Share words that signal the structure if the author uses them (see the chart on page 190 and the handout on Text Structures and Signal Words on page 191). Ask students to find signal words in the text if the author has used them. For example, Seymour Simon uses signal words for problem-solution in paragraph five in the first sentence: *Space mining is one possible **solution** to the **problem**.*

Continue Guided Practice *(10–15 minutes)*

Day 2

▶ Continue guided practice using different texts until students are secure with a structure.

Text Structures and Signal Words

Quite often, authors write without using signal words. This means that students have to use meaning to determine structure.

> **Example of Cause/Effect Using a Signal Word:** From "Defying Gravity: Mae Jemison" by Anina Robb: *Because of her love of dance and a salute to creativity, Mae took a poster of the Alvin Ailey American Dance Theater with her along on her historic space flight.*

(Continued)

(Continued)

Robb's Comments: The signal word *because* introduces the cause: Mae Jemison wanted to honor dance and creativity on her space flight. The effect was that she took a poster of the Alvin Ailey American Dance Theater with her on the historic space flight.

> **Example of Cause/Effect Without Signal Words:** "How Ada Lovelace Leaped Into History" by Kathleen Krull: *Annabella kept an iron grip on her daughter's days, from the moment Ada awoke at 6 a.m. until bedtime. She hired an army of top-notch scholars to educate Ada at home on every subject—except poetry. The emphasis was on facts, logic, and all branches of math, as well as languages and other subjects useful to know.*

Robb's Comments: The cause is that Ada's mother, Annabella, kept a tight grip on her daughter's day. The effects are that she hired scholars to teach Ada all subjects except poetry, and the emphasis of Ada's learning was logic, facts, and math. Notice that Kathleen Krull does not use any of the cause/effect signal words, but readers can still spot the cause/effect relationship.

DESCRIPTION	SEQUENCE	COMPARE/CONTRAST
for example, like, as, such as, some characteristics are	until, now, before, first, last, after, then, next, on, finally, at	however, but, instead of, on the other hand, similar to, different from, compared to, same as, as opposed to
CAUSE/EFFECT	**PROBLEM/SOLUTION**	**QUESTION/ANSWER**
because, since, therefore, so then, as a result, not only, but, for this reason, due to	one reason is, a solution, a problem, as a result, outcome is, issues are, solved by, therefore	how, why, when, what, where, who, how many, it's possible, it could be that

Notes to Yourself About Teaching the Lesson

_____

_____

_____

_____

_____

_____

_____

Text Structures and Signal Words

Description: Helps you visualize or picture what a place, an event, a historical period, an invention, a setting, or a person looks like. When you can visualize something you read, it shows that you understand it and can recall the information.

Sequence: When the author writes about something in the order it happened. Sequence helps you see and understand connections among events. Not only does sequence supply the chronological order that something occurs in, but it also enables you to visualize and understand complex ideas such as mitosis, developing photographs, and so on.

Compare/Contrast: Shows readers how two things are alike and how they differ. This can be people or characters, settings, problems, information, and events. Compare/contrast can deepen your understanding of specific elements in a text.

Cause/Effect: The cause comes before the effect or effects and shows how words, nature, decisions, problems, actions, and events can cause other things to happen. By understanding the relationship between a cause and the resulting effects, you deepen your knowledge of events, settings, the decisions a person makes, and the obstacles he or she faces.

Problem/Solution: Shows you a problem and then helps you understand one or more solutions. This structure helps you search for an answer after the author states the problem and therefore gather the main points of a passage.

Question/Answer: Sometimes a paragraph opens with a question or there's a question within the paragraph, and the author offers answers. This format also provides you with a model of how to read informational texts: Raise a question and read on to explore the answer.

Main Idea/Details: A paragraph can open or end with the main idea. However, there are times when you will have to use details in one or more paragraphs to determine the main idea. Understanding main ideas can help you figure out themes as well as identify main ideas and discover connections among them.

From Talk to Writing

Talk can assist students as they unpack meaning from informational texts and other nonfiction genres. Use partner talk and/or small-group discussions when students are reading the same text or different texts on the same topic or about the same person. Comparing different texts on the same topic or about the same person provides opportunities to talk about why events were omitted.

Ten Open-Ended Prompts for Talking and Writing About Nonfiction

- What new information did you learn about a topic?
- Identify and explain the author's point of view, especially when reading different texts on the same topic or about the same person.
- Explain how three text features helped you better understand the topic.
- What are two main ideas? Were they stated in the first or last sentence? Did you infer to find main ideas?
- How does the book's title connect to the themes of the book?
- What text structures contributed to your understanding? Explain how.
- Why was a biography written about this person?
- What obstacles did the person face? Choose two, and explain the obstacle and how the person overcame it.
- What event and/or person affected decisions the person made?
- How did this person change from the beginning to the end of the book?

Understanding the Structure of Nonfiction Genres

Some reproducibles that go with the lessons in Chapters 6 and 7 ask students to discuss the genre of their book or reading materials because understanding genre is one key part of comprehension.

Since text structure plays an important role in comprehending material, introduce students to the genre structure of each type of nonfiction text they will read in order to build and enlarge their schema (Anderson, Pichert, & Shirey, 1983). Knowing the difference between a newspaper and a magazine article or a memoir and a biography enables them to use structure to predict, to raise questions, and to improve comprehension (Duke et al., 2011).

GENRE	CHARACTERISTICS	PROMPTS FOR DISCUSSION
Informational text	• Presents information about a topic • Includes narrative elements such as anecdotes, dialogue, snippets of journal entries, archaeological or space mysteries, etc. • Argues for a position • Includes text features and structures • Uses extensive research to present information • Has a bibliography of sources	• Why were you drawn to this topic? • What new information did you learn? • Does the text have a bibliography? What conclusions could you draw from it? • What is the author's purpose? Give two examples to support your position. • If the purpose is to persuade you, what ideas does the author use that do this? • How do text features improve your understanding? Select three and explain what you learned from each one and how each one supported your understanding. • What questions does this book raise but not answer? Give one example. • Did your book change your thinking on the topic? Explain. • Does the author weave opinions into facts? Give a few examples.
Biography	• Contains these literary elements: main person who is the protagonist, antagonists, plot, conflicts, problems, themes • Written about a famous or infamous person by a different person • Can be from birth to death or focus on one part of the person's life • Based on extensive research of that person • Has a bibliography of sources	• Why is this person famous or infamous? • Discuss three to four personality traits that enabled this person to reach his or her goal. • What are two to three problems the person had to overcome? Explain how he or she dealt with each problem. • Were there people and events that helped this person realize his or her dream? Choose one person and one event, and explain how each impacted the person. • What do you admire or dislike about this person? Explain. • How did this person affect the lives of others during his or her times? • Does this person have an effect on our times? Explain. • How extensive was the author's research? Explain how you know this. • What people or events were antagonists to the person? Choose one person and one event, and show how each was an antagonist. • What are two to three themes your book presented?

(Continued)

(Continued)

GENRE	CHARACTERISTICS	PROMPTS FOR DISCUSSION
Memoir	• Contains these literary elements: main person, antagonists, plot, conflicts, problems, themes • Includes part of a person's life • Written by the person • Helps readers see events through that person's eyes • Written in first person • Leaves out information • Using memory, the writer recounts events • Includes recalled conversations	• Why do you think the author shared his or her life story? • What does the author want you to think about him or her? Explain. • Were there any times that you felt the author was stretching the truth? Discuss one or two. • Discuss two problems the author faced and how he or she dealt with each one. • What did you learn about the author as a person? Give three examples. • What are some themes the author presented? • How do other people in the memoir view the author? • What were two key antagonists in the author's life? Describe each one and explain how it worked against the author.
Magazine article	• Can include narrative elements • Focused on one aspect of a topic; can have one of these purposes: inform, explain, analyze, persuade, advise • Has a headline or title and headings that divide the article into sections of text • Can contain some text features such as photographs, map, or diagram • Text can be written in column format • Has a bibliography of sources	• What drew you to the topic of this article? • What is the purpose? Give examples that illustrate the purpose. • What new information did you learn? • Did you disagree with any information? If you did, discuss two points. • Does the article contain text features? What did you learn from these? • Choose two text features and explain how each one helped you understand the point and purpose of the article. • What are three main ideas the article presented?
Essay	• Can argue, explain, persuade, express an opinion, describe something, compare and contrast, analyze • Includes narrative elements • Length is short: about 3 to 20 pages • Addresses a topic or answers a question • Can be personal or autobiographical • Can be a photographic essay • Has a title, introduction, body, and conclusion • May include a bibliography of sources	• What is the purpose of the essay? To argue, compare/contrast, analyze, express an opinion, persuade, etc.? • Does the essay have more than one purpose? Identify each one and give an example. • How does the author organize the information? How is the order important to the point being made? • What are two to three main ideas? • What is a key theme? Give evidence to support the theme. • What does the conclusion keep you thinking about? • If it is a photographic essay, what do you learn from the photos? How do they make you feel? Explain.

GENRE	CHARACTERISTICS	PROMPTS FOR DISCUSSION
Journalism	• Includes narrative elements • Provides information on current events • Can have a local focus • Contains advertising • Written by reporters who investigate topics • Includes features other than news: photographs, comics, advertisements, editorials, letters to the editor, op-ed pieces, etc.	• What is the headline for the article? What is the focus of the article: local, national, or international news? • What information did you learn from the article? • What are two main ideas this article presents? • Did the article change your thinking? Explain how. • What questions does the article raise but not answer? Use the Internet to find answers to one or two questions.
Speech	• Can educate, inform, entertain, argue for a point of view, be a call to action • Can combine some or all of the above categories • Includes narrative elements • Should be short and easy to listen to and understand • Needs to engage the audience	• What is the purpose of the speech? To educate, inform, explain, entertain, argue for, present a call to action? Does it achieve its purpose? Explain. • How does the speech catch and hold your attention? • Do you agree or disagree with the content of the speech? Explain why. • Why do you think the author felt compelled to give the speech? • Are there points that you feel need clarification? Choose two and explain why.

Reflect on Your Teaching

Use the following question/prompts for in-the-head conversations with yourself or discussions with colleagues.

◗ How do text features support comprehension of nonfiction?

◗ Why is it important to teach students about text structures?

◗ Why should you expose students to several nonfiction genres?

Don't Miss Reading and Learning From: *Reading and Writing Genre With Purpose in K–8 Classrooms* by Nell Duke, Samantha Caughlan, Mary Juzwik, and Nicole Martin (2011).

CHAPTER 7

Going Deeper

How to Analyze Nonfiction

Literary conversations using informational texts and biography can lead students to explore meanings that bring depth and excitement to studying nonfiction. In Chapter 3 (pages 62–66) I discuss mining texts for teaching topics and provide templates you can use as you plan. We all have a bank of teaching topics that our schools and districts require, so as I read texts to use for instruction, I'm always considering the type of lesson that would work best with each one. Of course, other lessons can be taught with a text, but there are times when the main focus is apparent. Take Seymour Simon's "New Horizons for Space"—the entire article builds on the problem-solution text structure, though it could also be used to teach explicit main ideas, taking notes, or the theme of change. As you read short and long texts you plan to use for instruction, try to identify the concept that jumps out at you—that's most likely the one to use.

Teaching Tip: Finding Short Texts for Students to Discuss

Put a magazine title into a search engine and learn more about the contents and how to order copies.

Cobblestone Magazine: history articles, Grades 4–8

Dig Into History Magazine, Grades 4–8

Scholastic News: current events, Grades 5 and 6

Junior Scholastic: social studies/current events, Grades 6–8

Scholastic Scope: nonfiction, fiction, plays, Grades 6–8

Science World: nonfiction articles, Grades 6–10

Scholastic Action: materials for below-grade-level readers, nonfiction, Grades 6–12

Smithsonian TweenTribune: science, technology, national and world news, Grades 5–6 and 7–8

Time Edge: digital resource that ties history and science to current events, Grades 5–8

The lessons in this chapter show you how to teach students to take notes as well as how to use text structure to boost comprehension. You'll also explore a lesson on finding explicitly stated and inferred main ideas. In addition, I provide two lessons that help students analyze the personalities, decisions, and achievements of people they read about in biographies and other nonfiction texts. One lesson examines obstacles a person faces, and one identifies the personality traits a person cultivates in order to reach a goal. This type of teaching moves students beyond recalling facts to using the facts to critically think about and interpret informational texts and biographies.

Teaching Tips for Text-Based Lessons

As you prepare to teach the following lessons, make class sets of texts and handouts for each lesson. Students should always have available the Guidelines for Discussion (page 17) and Prompts That Keep a Discussion Moving Forward (page 25). Remind students to consult these resources if you notice a discussion faltering. If the text that goes with a lesson works for all students in your class, then students can read it independently. If not, you can read the text aloud.

Most of the lessons use two types of talk. I often start with turn-and-talk to warm up students' thinking and then move to another kind of talk. Remember that it's not always necessary to share after a turn-and-talk when you hear and observe that all students "get it." As students discuss, accept any response as long as students paraphrase the text to support their position with specific details or with inferences that use details. Use the same partners throughout a lesson and make sure every student has a copy of the materials for the lesson.

Circulate and listen carefully as students talk; share suggested time limits in each lesson. However, know that your students might need more or less time, so adjust accordingly.

Nonfiction Selections Used With Lessons

"Who Climbs Everest?" (Excerpt From *Tales From the Top of the World: Climbing Mount Everest With Pete Athans*) by Sandra Athans, fifth-grade reading level

Excerpt From *Secrets of the Sky Caves: Danger and Discovery on Nepal's Mustang Cliffs* by Sandra Athans, fifth-grade reading level

"How Ada Lovelace Leaped Into History" by Kathleen Krull, seventh-grade reading level

"Isaac Newton and the Day He Discovered the Rainbow" by Kathleen Krull, seventh-grade reading level

"Defying Gravity: Mae Jemison" by Anina Robb, seventh-grade reading level

"New Horizons in Space" by Seymour Simon, ninth/tenth-grade reading level

Taking Heading Notes and Finding a Main Idea

> **What It Is**
>
> This lesson asks students to jot down important ideas about a text in their own words.
>
> **How It Helps**
>
> Taking notes helps students
>
> - Set a purpose for reading.
> - Select essential details from a text.
> - Identify a main idea in a paragraph or section (see more about main idea on pages 203–204 and 224–225).
> - Recall details and information in preparation for assessments.

Introducing Note Taking for Informational Texts

While there are many ways of taking notes, I prefer to use *heading notes*, a simple and straightforward format. Students can use headings in texts to organize their notes in two ways:

1. Write headings in smart notebooks and jot notes under each one.

2. Create a T-chart with about three inches on the left side for headings, leaving more room on the right side for notes.

To teach students how to take heading notes, follow this procedure:

▶ Explain that having a purpose for reading helps readers determine important ideas.

▶ Show students how to preview a nonfiction text using the title and headings to set a reading purpose. Here's what I say for *Tales From the Top of the World: Climbing Mount Everest With Pete Athans:*

> *The book's title tells me it's about Everest. The heading "Who Climbs Everest? Adjusting to Thin Air, Climbers Be Wary" helps me set my reading purpose: to find out about who can make this climb and why climbers should be cautious.*

▶ Have students read the entire selection and use a brief partner talk to discuss the reading purpose. It's important to understand content prior to taking heading notes.

▶ Model how you take heading notes by writing the heading of the first section at the top of the page.

▶ Reread the section of text, keeping in mind your purpose. Then skim the text to find notes to record under the heading. Here's a sample of what I jot:

> *beginners can't climb Everest; most climbers part of a group; companies sponsor climbs to make documentary movies; people hire and pay guides to make the climb; guides insist people have climbing experience*

▶ Reread notes to find the main idea. For the "Who Climbs Everest?" section of text, I write:

When I reread these notes, I see that Everest is a tough climb; people need experience on other mountains. Here's the main idea: To climb Everest, people must have previous experiences with mountain climbing.

▶ Have students practice until they can take heading notes independently.

Reflect and Intervene

If you notice that some students aren't taking notes or seem unsure about what to write, try some of the following scaffolds.

IF STUDENTS HAVE TROUBLE . . .	POSSIBLE SCAFFOLDS
Previewing and setting purposes	• Ask students to tell you how the preview and setting purposes for reading help recall and note taking. • Think aloud with the students' text; show how you preview and use preview information to set a purpose. • Invite pairs to preview and set purposes; listen to them and offer suggestions. • Have students practice until they can preview and set purposes independently.
Reading and discussing	• Discuss why it's important to read the entire selection before taking notes. • Have students read silently and discuss. • Change the text if students can't recall details.
Determining key details	• Think aloud and show how you use your reading purpose to determine one key detail. • Invite students to find the additional key details. • Return to modeling if students have difficulty. • Continue practicing until students identify key details independently.
Paraphrasing the author's words	• Explain that paraphrasing, using their own words, illustrates understanding. • Model paraphrasing a short passage. • Have students practice paraphrasing. If they continue to struggle with this, try an easier text.

Assessing Taking Notes for Informational Texts

1. Use one or both reproducibles: T-Chart Notes (page 201) and Discover the Main Idea (page 202).

2. Use students' completed notes in their smart notebooks.

Supporting English Language Learners

▶ Give students a short passage so note taking doesn't overwhelm them.

▶ Work with groups of 4; support them as they preview, set purposes, and read.

▶ Have students discuss the text and practice paraphrasing passages you select.

▶ Guide and support students as they jot notes.

▶ Have students work with ELL partners and move them to independence.

Reproducibles

T-Chart Notes (page 201)

Discover the Main Idea (page 202)

Notes to Yourself About Teaching the Lesson

_____

_____

_____

_____

_____

_____

_____

_____

_____

_____

_____

_____

_____

_____

T-Chart Notes

Name _____ Date _____

Title _____ Author _____

Directions:

1. Work with a partner.

2. Talk to your partner to preview a short text you are both reading and to set purposes.

3. Read the text using your preview and purposes to discuss important details.

4. Take notes on your own using the T-chart format.

HEADING	NOTES

Discover the Main Idea

Name_____ Date_____

Title_____ Author_____

Directions:

1. Read the text using your preview and reading purpose to pinpoint key details.

2. Write each heading, reread the section, and take notes under it using the T-chart format.

3. Reread the notes under each heading to figure out the main idea and write it in the spaces provided below.

HEADING	NOTES

Main Idea

_____

_____

_____

_____

Taking Heading Notes and Finding a Main Idea

"Who Climbs Everest?" (Excerpt From *Tales From the Top of the World*) by Sandra Athans

Organize students into partners; use partner talk for heading notes. Partner talk helps students set purposes for reading. After reading with a purpose in mind, students can partner talk to clarify the text's meaning and identify important ideas related to their reading purpose. Students take notes independently, but you can have them share and discuss their notes to find the main idea until they can do this independently. Have students practice talking about their reading with a partner until you feel they can move to having in-the-head conversations about previewing to set reading purposes, reading the text and thinking about information relating to their purpose, and jotting notes. Students develop the responsibility for the entire note-taking process at different times. Have students use partner talk until they can work independently.

Materials

Copy of the excerpt from *Tales From the Top of the World*; smart notebooks

Lesson Guidelines

Set a Purpose for Reading; Read and Discuss the Text *(20–30 minutes)*	**Day 1**

▶ Give students a copy of the excerpt from *Tales From the Top of the World*.

▶ Show students how you preview to set a reading purpose for each section using headings. Jot each purpose on the board. Here's what sixth graders suggested:

Purpose 1: Who can climb Everest?

Purpose 2: Is adjusting to thin air important?

Purpose 3: Why are climbers cautious?

▶ Remind students to think of the purpose of each section of the text as they listen to or read it; read aloud or have students read the text.

▶ Invite students to partner talk to discuss the gist of each section.

▶ Show students how you choose and paraphrase important details and jot notes for the first section: "Who Climbs Everest?" (see page 204 for examples).

▶ Field student's questions and close the lesson.

Take Heading Notes; Find Main Idea *(25–35 minutes)*	**Day 2**

▶ Have students retrieve their copies of the excerpt from *Tale From the Top of the World* and their smart notebooks.

▶ Remind students of their purpose for reading the second section: Is adjusting to thin air important?

(Continued)

(Continued)

▶ Have students reread the text and partner talk to discuss the reading purpose.

▶ Ask students to write notes under the text's section heading in their smart notebooks. Here is the heading as well as some notes from sixth graders:

Heading: Who Climbs Everest?

Notes: high altitudes have thin air—air with less oxygen; around 5,000 ft. above sea level people find breathing tough; at 8,000 ft. they get headaches and coughs; people climb and stop to adjust to altitude changes.

▶ Show how you reread notes to find a main idea. Ask:

What is the author saying about these details?

▶ Say something like:

One main idea is to warn climbers about altitude sickness.

▶ Have partners use the general topic and their notes to find a main idea. Here's what sixth graders said:

Climbers won't get sick if they stop and rest and get their bodies adjusted to higher and higher altitudes.

Day 3

Model Taking Heading Notes With a T-Chart Using "Climbers Be Wary" *(25 minutes)*

▶ Remind students of their purpose for reading the third section: Why should climbers be cautious?

▶ Have students read and discuss this section.

▶ Provide students with a model of taking heading notes using a T-chart.

T-Chart Notes

HEADING	NOTES
Adjusting to Thin Air	high altitudes have thin air—air with less oxygen
	around 5,000 ft. above sea level people find breathing tough

▶ Have students choose a format and continue to take notes with other texts.

Thinking About Issues: Obstacles

What It Is

Obstacles can be conflicts, settings, or internal and/or external antagonists—anyone or anything that blocks what the person wants to achieve.

How It Helps

- Helps students understand that overcoming obstacles can make a person strong, change his or her life, or impel him or her to achieve something.
- Illustrates that everyone copes with obstacles.

Introducing the Concept of Obstacles

- ▶ Ask students to turn-and-talk about obstacles and share with the class.
- ▶ Use students' ideas to show that obstacles are part of everyone's life and that studying obstacles people faced and how they overcame them to reach a goal can provide students with a model to emulate.
- ▶ Explain that internal and external antagonists, conflicts, and settings can become obstacles.
- ▶ Help students see that people don't overcome every obstacle; it's the trying that builds strength.

Prompts

- ▶ Identify an obstacle; classify it as internal or external.
- ▶ Show how the obstacle blocks the person's goal.
- ▶ What personality traits enabled the person to overcome an obstacle?
- ▶ How did coping with an obstacle change a person?
- ▶ Identify a conflict and explain how it was an obstacle.
- ▶ Show how a setting became an obstacle.
- ▶ Choose two obstacles; show how each changed the person.

Reflect and Intervene

Try the following scaffolds if students have difficulty finding and analyzing obstacles.

(Continued)

(Continued)

IF STUDENTS HAVE TROUBLE . . .	POSSIBLE SCAFFOLDS
Identifying internal obstacles	• Make sure students understand that internal obstacles are in their mind and emotions. • Give students examples of emotions (fear, jealousy) and internal obstacles (no self-confidence, how siblings treat you). • Model identifying internal obstacles using your read-aloud. • Have students practice using an instructional-level text.
Identifying external obstacles	• Make sure students understand external obstacles are outside of the person: a storm, a car wreck, failing a subject. • Model identifying external conflicts using your read-aloud. • Invite students to practice identifying external obstacles using instructional texts.
Identifying conflicts that are obstacles	• Review the five kinds of conflicts. • Model conflicts that students have difficulty with using a read-aloud; explain why the conflict is an obstacle. • Use a different read-aloud; ask students to identify conflicts and show how each one is an obstacle. • Ask students to practice identifying conflicts in their instructional texts and show how each one is an obstacle.
Identifying settings that are obstacles	• Use a read-aloud to think aloud and explain how a setting becomes an obstacle. • Have students practice pinpointing a setting, explaining how it is also an obstacle using their instructional reading text.
Showing how dealing with or overcoming obstacles can change a person's life	• Think aloud with a read-aloud text and model how dealing with overcoming obstacles changed a person's life. • Ask students to identify an obstacle a person dealt with using their instructional reading text and show how the obstacle changed the person's life. • Have students continue practicing using instructional reading texts until they can work independently.

Assessing Students' Understanding of Obstacles

1. Use one or both of the reproducibles: Overcoming Obstacles (page 208) Conflicts as Obstacles (page 209).

2. Assess what students write about a prompt in their smart notebooks.

Supporting English Language Learners

- Make sure students understand what an obstacle is. Discuss with examples of life experiences such as moving to a new country, leaving friends, and learning a new language.

- Review internal obstacles such as fear and jealousy and external obstacles such as an illness, a physical challenge, or loss.

- Complete an interactive read-aloud; show how you identify obstacles (see pages 210–211). Invite students to participate after you've modeled.

- Organize ELL students into partners, and give them a text they can read with ease. Have pairs identify two obstacles and show how each worked against a person.

- Continue asking partners to practice, and gradually move students to independence.

Reproducibles

Overcoming Obstacles (page 208)

Conflicts as Obstacles (page 209)

Notes to Yourself About Teaching the Lesson

ercoming Obstacles

Name _____ Date _____

Title _____ Author _____

Directions: Identify two obstacles the person overcame; explain what he or she did to overcome the obstacle and how this changed the person. Do this by completing the three columns below.

NAME OF PERSON	OBSTACLES	HOW OVERCOMING CHANGED THE PERSON

Conflicts as Obstacles

Name_____ Date_____

Title _____ Author _____

Directions:

1. Choose one of the conflicts listed in the box below.

   Five Kinds of Conflicts

   Person vs. Himself/Herself

   Person vs. Person

   Person vs. Society

   Person vs. Nature

   Person vs. Fate

2. Name and describe the conflict, and show how it affected the person's goals or ability to cope with life.

_____

_____

_____

_____

_____

_____

_____

_____

_____

_____

_____

_____

MODEL LESSON 7.2

Teaching About Obstacles

"How Ada Lovelace Leaped Into History" by Kathleen Krull

Studying the obstacles a person deals with works well with biographies as students read about real people who faced obstacles that shaped and changed their lives. Students can use turn-and-talk and partner talk to raise their awareness of the obstacles a person faced, which obstacles a person overcame, and whether coping with obstacles changed the trajectory of a person's life, setting him or her on a path to fame. Closing a lesson with a whole-class discussion can show students their classmates' thinking as well as invite them to use what they learned about obstacles to discuss how each one shaped and/or changed the person's life.

Materials

"How Ada Lovelace Leaped Into History"; smart notebooks

Lesson Guidelines

Day 1

Prepare to Read "How Ada Lovelace Leaped Into History" ***(10–15 minutes)***

- Teach students about the romantic poet Lord Byron, the father Ada Lovelace never knew. Use a search engine to find information about Byron that you can share with students.
- Ask students to partner talk to discuss how computers have changed our lives and to share their ideas (5 minutes).

Day 2

Read for the Gist ***(25 minutes)***

- Give students a copy of "How Ada Lovelace Leaped Into History."
- Read out loud to paragraph 17 or have students read it silently.
- Have students partner talk to discuss the gist of the first part (5–6 minutes).
- Ask students to share what they learned from this first reading with the whole class.

Day 3

Reread to Identify Obstacles ***(30–40 minutes)***

- Organize students into partners.
- Reread out loud "How Ada Lovelace Leaped Into History" or have students reread to the first stop, and ask students to focus on pinpointing obstacles.
- Have students partner talk to identify obstacles in this part of the text and how each obstacle affected Ada, her mother, or Babbage (10–15 minutes).
- After students hear ideas with the entire class, ask them to set up a T-chart in their notebooks and write the person's name and the obstacle faced on the left and its effects on the right. Here's one that seventh graders shared.

PERSON'S NAME AND OBSTACLE	HOW OBSTACLE AFFECTED PERSON AND OTHERS
Ada's mom was a control freak	Ada had no choices growing up. No friends or brothers or sisters. She was lonely and alone. Her mother chose all of her studies—making Ada do math, science, and logic helped her work on "Thinking machines."

▸ Hold a whole-class discussion using a guiding question: *How did obstacles shape Ada's life?* (8 minutes)

▸ Summarize the discussion halfway through and at the end.

Guided Practice on Identifying Obstacles *(35–40 minutes)*

▸ Read out loud or have students read from the first stop to the end of the biography.

▸ Invite students to turn-and-talk to discuss the gist (4 minutes).

▸ Reread the section of text.

▸ Have students partner talk to identify obstacles in this part of the biography and discuss how each one affected Ada or Babbage (10–15 minutes).

▸ Ask students to set up a T-chart in their smart notebooks and identify two obstacles and how each affected the person.

▸ Invite students to share obstacles they identified. Here's one that seventh graders offered:

PERSON'S NAME AND OBSTACLE	HOW OBSTACLE AFFECTED PERSON AND OTHERS
Ada didn't know algebra	Made her frustrated. Had to get Babbage's help. She felt "dismay" and "botheration" but kept trying until she understood Babbage's machine.

▸ Hold a whole-class discussion using this guiding question (10 minutes):

Which obstacles changed the course of Ada's life? Explain why.

▸ Summarize the discussion halfway through and at the end.

▸ Have students jot the key ideas of the discussion in their smart notebooks.

Teaching the Problem-Solution Text Structure

What It Is

Problem-solution is a text structure that authors of biography and informational texts use.

How It Helps

Understanding this text structure helps students

- Know to search for solutions when a problem is presented.
- Comprehend the information better because they are familiar with the text structure.
- Understand that problem-solution can also be read as cause-effect and that this doesn't affect meaning; it's a shift in terminology.

Introducing the Problem-Solution Text Structure

▶ Think aloud to show problem-solution in a text and explain that it helps comprehension because knowing there's a problem causes readers to search for the solution.

▶ Explain that authors can use these signal words to point to problems and solutions: *one reason is, a solution, a problem, as a result, outcome is, issues are, solved by, therefore.*

▶ Show students that problem-solution can be part of an entire text, as in Seymour Simon's "New Horizons in Space," or used in one or more sections of a text.

▶ Think aloud and show that other text structures—description, compare and contrast, sequence—often accompany problem-solution.

▶ Help students understand that sometimes problem-solution can also be viewed as cause-effect, but that this doesn't affect meaning. For example, in "New Horizons in Space," the problem—mineral reserves on earth are limited and being used up rapidly—can be viewed as a cause whose effect (or solution) would be space mining, but the resulting information is the same.

Prompts

▶ What solutions does the author present? Evaluate them.

▶ Why does the author use other text structures such as description, sequence, or compare and contrast along with problem-solution?

▶ Describe a problem in the text that can't be resolved presently, and explain why.

▶ What new information did you learn from the text?

▶ Explain why you agree or disagree with the author's points.

▶ Share one to two parts of the text that could be read as cause-effect or problem-solution.

▶ Identify a problem that is unresolved and explain why.

▶ What does the problem-solution structure help you understand about the author's purpose for writing the text?

Reflect and Intervene

If students have difficulty using a text structure to navigate a text, try these scaffolds:

▶ Make sure that students understand problem-solution by thinking aloud using a read-aloud text.

▶ Ask students to read a section of a text that uses problem-solution signal words. Have them find the words and use them to pinpoint the problem and solution(s).

▶ Give students a short text to read and have them identify two to three problems and solutions. If a problem is unresolved, have the students explain why.

▶ Think aloud to show students that problem-solution can also be viewed as cause-effect.

▶ Have students practice using problem-solution to understand key details and the author's purpose until they can work independently.

Assessing Students' Understanding of Problem-Solution

1. Assess the writing about problem-solution that students completed in their smart notebooks.

2. Use the reproducibles Reflecting on Problem-Solution (page 214) and Problem-Solution and Cause-Effect (page 215).

Supporting English Language Learners

▶ Think aloud and share some real-life problems and solutions to help students better understand this structure. You can use having the flu, breaking a leg, being low on gas, or preparing for tryouts for a team.

▶ Think aloud and show students how you figure out a problem in a text and the solution.

▶ Organize ELL students into pairs. Give them a short text that's accessible; have them read and discuss it and pinpoint at least two problems and the solution for each. Have partners practice until they reach independence.

Reproducibles

Reflecting on Problem-Solution (page 214)

Problem-Solution and Cause-Effect (page 215)

Reflecting on Problem-Solution

Name _____ Date _____

Title _____ Author _____

Directions: Choose one of the following prompts/questions and give examples from your text to support your response. Write your answers below.

1. Describe a problem in your text that was unresolved. Explain why the problem did not have a solution. Provide a solution and explain why it could work.

2. What new information did the problems raised in the text teach you? How do these problems and their solutions affect people today?

_____

_____

_____

_____

_____

_____

_____

_____

_____

_____

_____

_____

_____

_____

_____

_____

_____

Problem-Solution and Cause-Effect

Name _____ Date _____

Title _____ Author _____

Directions: Describe two problems and their solutions from the text, and show how each one can also be read as cause-effect.

_____

_____

_____

_____

_____

_____

_____

_____

_____

_____

_____

_____

_____

_____

_____

_____

_____

_____

_____

_____

Teaching Problem-Solution

"New Horizons in Space"
by Seymour Simon

For students to read deeply and analytically about the problem-solution text structure, have them reflect on solutions presented and evaluate them. Doing this transforms a lesson from identification to analytical thinking. This lesson invites students to use turn-and-talk and partner talk and closes with a whole-class discussion that asks students to evaluate the different solutions in Seymour Simon's article "New Horizons in Space." Whole-class discussion is ideal for this phase of thinking because it offers students multiple opportunities to hear their peers' ideas and analyses, raise questions, clarify their own thinking, and evaluate solutions.

Materials

"New Horizons in Space" smart notebooks

Lesson Guidelines

Day 1

Build Prior Knowledge and First Reading *(20–25 minutes)*

▶ Organize students into pairs.

▶ Preteach *horizons* and *asteroids*.

▶ Read aloud or have students read the section that discusses the three main types of asteroids, paragraph 6.

▶ Have students use partner talk to understand each type of asteroid; ask them to discuss why asteroids might be valuable to humankind.

▶ Invite students to share their thoughts on asteroids with the whole class (4–5 minutes).

▶ Read aloud the entire piece or have students read it to get the gist.

▶ Have students partner talk to discuss the gist (4 minutes).

▶ Ask students to share their thoughts on the gist (4–5 minutes).

Day 2

Reread and Analyze Text Structure *(25–35 minutes)*

▶ Reread out loud or have students reread the entire text.

▶ Have students partner talk to identify two problems and evaluate any solutions in this section. Here's what seventh graders said:

A problem is that Congress and the president passed a bill saying we could mine in space, but we don't know how to do that yet. People are working to find one. No one knows how long this will take so maybe there needs to be other solutions.

▶ Read aloud to the second stop or have students read.

▶ Invite students to partner talk to find problems, solutions, and evaluate the solutions. Seventh graders shared this:

The problem is that on earth we are running out of gold and silver and lots of other metals. The solution is to start mining space. This seems way in the future and if we run out soon, this solution won't help.

◗ Have students turn-and-talk to identify a problem-solution structure that can be identified as cause-effect. Here's what eighth graders suggested:

Problem or Cause: Minerals on our planet are limited.

Solution or Effect: Mine important minerals on asteroids and ship them to earth.

◗ Ask students to write in their smart notebooks two problems and possible solutions they saw from the beginning of the text to the end of the second stop, evaluate one solution, and share with the class.

Guided Practice and Whole-Class Discussion *(25–35 minutes)*

◗ Reread out loud or have students reread "New Horizons in Space" from the second stop to the end.

◗ Have students partner talk to identify two possible solutions to running out of precious and rare substances (10 minutes).

◗ Engage students in a whole-class discussion.

◗ Start the whole-class discussion using this guiding question (10–15 minutes):

What happens if we run out of precious and rare metals and substances? Evaluate one solution.

◗ Summarize points halfway through and at the end of the discussion.

◗ Ask students to list a solution they think can work in their notebooks and explain why. Then have them share these (5–7 minutes).

Notes to Yourself About Teaching the Lesson

_____

_____

_____

_____

_____

_____

_____

_____

_____

Personality Traits and a Person's Achievements: Biography

What It Is

Personality traits are a set of characteristics that help define a person and enable the person to reach his or her goals. Readers infer personality traits from a person's talk, decisions, actions, and interactions with others. Doing this can show students the common traits of people who change their lives and the lives of others through their work and inventions.

How It Helps

Analyzing personality traits helps students

- Understand how personality affects decisions.
- Recognize that certain personality traits help people reach their dreams and goals.

Introducing the Concepts of Personality Traits and a Person's Achievements

- ❯ Make sure students understand the difference between personality traits and physical traits.
- ❯ Think aloud with a read-aloud text to show how you infer personality traits by studying a person's talk, decisions, actions, and interactions with others. Ask:

  What personality trait does this dialogue (or any other element) reveal?

- ❯ Think aloud using a read-aloud text to show students how personality traits connect to a person's goals, achievements, and conflicts. For example, in Kathleen Krull's "Isaac Newton and the Day He Discovered the Rainbow," persistence is one of Newton's personality traits, and it was persistence that enabled him to prove that colors exist in white light.
- ❯ Continue modeling how to infer personality traits and connect them to a person's achievements and goals with short biographies until students can infer personality traits.

Prompts

- ❯ What can you infer about personality by studying inner thoughts and dialogue?
- ❯ What actions does the person take that reveal personality traits?
- ❯ What do you learn about a person from his or her interactions with others?
- ❯ How does dealing with challenges affect personality?
- ❯ How does the person cope with conflicts? What does this show about his or her personality traits?
- ❯ Are there key decisions the person made that affected his or her personality? Explain.

Reflect and Intervene

If students have difficulty identifying personality traits, try these scaffolds:

▶ Think aloud with a read-aloud text and focus on the following elements one at a time. Each time you model an element, have students practice it with your read-aloud text or with a short, accessible text.

  o Internal talk and/or dialogue

  o Decisions

  o Actions taken

  o Interactions with others

  o Adversity

▶ Have students practice the element with your support using a short, accessible biography.

▶ Continue to think aloud and have students practice until they can infer personality traits with a specific element.

▶ Stay on the same element until students show you they can work independently.

▶ Pair up students for continued practice inferring personality traits with an element that requires more practice.

▶ Think aloud using a read-aloud text to show students how personality traits connect to a person's goals, achievements, and conflicts.

Assessing Students' Understanding of Analyzing Personality Traits and How They Shape Decisions

1. Use analysis of a person's personality traits in students' smart notebooks.

2. Use one or both of the reproducibles: Inferring Personality Traits (page 220) and Personality Traits and Achievements (page 221).

Supporting English Language Learners

▶ Helps students understand the difference between physical traits and personality traits by providing examples of each.

▶ Create a chart of personality traits with students' input based on short biographies you read aloud.

▶ Read aloud short texts that reflect the cultures of your students, and think aloud to show how you infer personality traits from talk, actions, decisions, interactions with others, etc.

▶ Pair up ELL students and have them use a short, accessible text. First, have them figure out personality traits from words. When students can do that, move to actions, then decisions, etc.

▶ Continue having students practice until they can infer personality traits independently.

Reproducibles

Inferring Personality Traits (page 220)

Personality Traits and Achievements (page 221)

Inferring Personality Traits

Name _____ Date _____

Biography Title _____ Author _____

Person's Name _____

Directions:

1. Choose three of the following elements and use each one to infer a personality trait for the person in the biography you read.

   Internal talk and/or dialogue

   Decisions

   Actions taken

   Interactions with others

   Adversity

2. Ask yourself: What personality trait does this element show?

3. Complete the T-chart below.

SUMMARIZE ELEMENT	PERSONALITY TRAIT IT REVEALS
1.	
2.	
3.	

Personality Traits and Achievements

Name _____ Date _____

Biography Title _____ Author _____

Person's Name _____

Directions: Choose two personality traits that the person in your biography had and explain how each trait helped him or her achieve a goal.

Personality Trait _____

Explain how the trait helped the person achieve a goal in the space below.

_____

_____

_____

_____

_____

_____

_____

Personality Trait _____

Explain how the trait helped the person achieve a goal in the space below.

_____

_____

_____

_____

_____

_____

_____

_____

Teaching Personality Traits

"Defying Gravity: Mae Jemison" by Anina Robb and "Isaac Newton and the Day He Discovered the Rainbow" by Kathleen Krull

Knowing the personality traits of a person enables students to determine how his or her traits support reaching goals. Inferring personality traits can be difficult at first, but with practice, students internalize the process and can apply it to independent reading.

Partner talk is ideal for this lesson because it's easier for students to risk sharing ideas with one person than with a group. The lesson has two parts: teaching the process and providing guided practice.

Materials

"Defying Gravity: Mae Jemison"; "Isaac Newton and the Day He Discovered the Rainbow"; smart notebooks

Lesson Guidelines

Day 1

Review Inferring to Identify Personality Traits; Read for the Gist *(20–25 minutes)*

▶ Organize students into pairs.

▶ Ask students to turn-and-talk about personality traits using these prompts:

What elements will you study? Use one element at a time to figure out personality traits for the protagonist of a biography.

▶ Here's what fourth graders said:

What a person is like—kind, mean, bossy

Study what someone says, does, and acts with others.

▶ Read aloud or have students read "Defying Gravity: Mae Jemison" for the gist.

▶ Have students partner talk to discuss the gist (7 minutes).

Day 2

Reread Biography and Identify Personality Traits *(20–25 minutes)*

▶ Reread the biography or have students reread it and think about Jemison's personality traits.

▶ Use partner talk to have students determine two to three personality traits for Jemison (10–15 minutes). Here are some traits fourth graders shared:

Fearless—'cause she talked back to her kindergarten teacher. She said "No, a scientist!"

Strong—didn't change her mind when her kindergarten teacher said that she meant a nurse.

Creative and *athletic*—she studied all kinds of dance.

Smart—she graduated high school at 16.

▸ Have students set up a T-chart in their smart notebooks. Write the personality trait on the left side and support from the biography on the right side.

▸ Ask students to select two personality traits that helped Jemison reach her goals, write these on the T-chart, and provide text support for each one.

Linking Personality Traits to Goals and Achievements *(20 minutes)*

▸ Think aloud to show students how you link one of Jemison's personality traits to a goal and/or achievement. Say something like:

> *Mae was strong in her beliefs and smart. She was a good listener and smart to consider her mother's advice. Strength, intelligence, and hard work helped her become a doctor.*

▸ Invite students to partner talk and determine the traits Jemison had for the NASA astronaut program. Ask students to share ideas (10–12 minutes).

▸ Ask students to partner talk and identify the traits that helped Jemison become the first African American female astronaut and write their analysis in their smart notebooks. Here's what a fourth grader wrote:

> *She used traits like hard working and studying a lot from dance and medical school to be an astronaut. Dance made her body strong, that helped her be an astronaut. She was fearless to her kindergarten teacher and that helped her get on the space shuttle.*

Guided Practice With "Isaac Newton and the Day He Discovered the Rainbow" *(35–45 minutes)*

▸ Organize students for partner talk.

▸ Read aloud or have students read the biography twice, once for the gist and a second time for Newton's personality traits.

▸ Invite students to partner talk to determine Newton's personality traits. Have them focus on inner thoughts, talk, actions taken, and adversity (10–15 minutes).

▸ Ask students to share what they learned about Newton's personality traits; post their ideas on a whiteboard using the T-chart format.

▸ Have students partner talk to discuss Newton's personality traits that enabled him to discover the spectrum (10 minutes).

▸ Invite students to share their ideas.

Identifying Main Ideas

What It Is

The main idea is the key point or the point the author wants you to remember most in a paragraph or section of text.

How It Helps

- Develops students' ability to synthesize key details.
- Improves comprehension and recall.
- Encourages close reading of text as students look for and synthesize details into a main idea.

Introducing the Concept of Main Ideas

▶ Explain that the main idea is the key point of a paragraph or section of text.

▶ Explain that in nonfiction each paragraph has a main idea supported by details and connected to the overall topic. Sometimes the main idea is stated in the first or topic sentence or the last sentence of a paragraph.

▶ Think aloud using a read-aloud text and the prompts that follow to show students how you find the explicitly stated or inferred main idea.

▶ On another day, tell students that sometimes readers have to infer the main idea in the paragraph or section of text.

Six Steps for Identifying Main Ideas

1. Read the paragraph.

2. List the details.

3. Use the details to figure out the general topic.

4. What is most important about the topic?

5. Is the main idea in the topic sentence? In the last sentence? If not, use details to infer the main idea.

6. Write the main idea.

Prompts

Here are four prompts that support inferring the main idea:

▶ What is the general topic of the paragraph or section?

▶ What does the section's heading say about the general topic?

▶ What key details relate to the general topic?

▶ Reread the information in Steps 1 to 3 and infer the main idea.

Reflect and Intervene

The lesson shows students how to determine explicitly stated and inferred main ideas, which in turn deepens their understanding of the text's content.

IF STUDENTS HAVE TROUBLE . . .	TRY THESE SCAFFOLDS
Finding explicitly stated main ideas	• Using a text students can read, show them how you use the prompts on page 224 to identify main ideas the author explicitly states. • Have students practice reading paragraphs from an accessible text and tell you what the writer is saying about the topic. Then ask them to find the stated main idea. • Pair up students and have them find explicitly stated main ideas using part of a text at their instructional reading level. Have students use the prompts on page 224 to guide their thinking.
Inferring the main idea	• Review that an inference is implied and not stated in a text. Use a read-aloud text to model this for students. • Give students the details of a paragraph from an accessible text and ask them to use these to infer the main idea. • Give students the main idea of a paragraph from an accessible text and have them find the details that support it. • Pair up students and have them use part of their instructional reading materials to infer main ideas using the prompts on page 224.

Assessing Students' Understanding of Identifying the Main Idea

1. Have students complete one or both reproducibles: Finding Sentences That State the Main Ideas (pages 226–227) and Key Details and Inferring Main Ideas (page 228).

2. Use students' writing about main ideas in their smart notebooks.

Supporting English Language Learners

◗ Model the steps on page 229 for identifying explicitly stated main ideas, then have students practice.

◗ Continue having students practice until they can work independently.

◗ Have students complete the reproducible Finding Sentences That State the Main Ideas (pages 226–227).

Reproducibles

Finding Sentences That State the Main Ideas (pages 226–227)

Key Details and Inferring Main Ideas (page 228)

Finding Sentences That State the Main Ideas

Name _____ Date _____

Title _____ Author _____

Directions:

1. Read an article or section of informational text.

2. For each paragraph find a main idea sentence. Is it the first or topic sentence? The last sentence?

3. Complete the organizers below, filling out one for each paragraph of your text. Write the main idea sentence and its location in the paragraph. Use as many boxes as you need to jot details that support the main idea.

Main Idea:
Details:

(Continued)

Main Idea:

Details:

Main Idea:

Details:

Key Details and Inferring Main Ideas

Name _____ Date _____

Title _____ Author _____

Directions: Use the questions below to help you find key details in all the paragraphs under a heading for a section of text. Jot them down and answer the question at the bottom of the page. Use the back of this page if you need more room to write.

1. What do you learn about the topic from the title or heading?

_____

_____

_____

_____

2. What do the details in a paragraph or section tell you about the topic?

_____

_____

_____

_____

3. Choose three to six details that are important to the topic and jot them down on the lines below.

_____

_____

_____

_____

Reread your answers to the questions above. What is the main idea you figured out using the important details? Write the main idea below.

_____

_____

_____

_____

Teaching Explicitly Stated Main Ideas

"Who Climbs Everest?" (Excerpt From *Tales From the Top of the World*) by Sandra Athans

Finding main ideas in the first or last sentence of a paragraph or section of a text is concrete and should precede having students infer to find main ideas.

Before teaching main ideas, preview texts you plan to use to ensure they'll work for finding explicitly stated or inferred main ideas. Partner talk is an effective way for students to discuss and identify explicitly stated or inferred main ideas. A whole-class discussion provides a great way to wrap up a main idea lesson. Ask students to share their main ideas for paragraphs and then identify the main idea for the entire selection.

Materials

Excerpt from *Tales From the Top of the World*; smart notebooks

Lesson Guidelines

| Preparing Students to Find Explicit Main Ideas *(15–20 minutes)* | Day 1 |

▶ Review the six steps for finding main ideas. NOTE: Since the main idea is explicitly stated in this piece, students will not need to infer in Step 5.

1. Read the paragraph.

2. List the key details.

3. Use the details to figure out the general topic.

4. What is most important about the topic?

5. Is the main idea in the topic sentence? In the last sentence? If not, use details to infer the main idea.

6. Write the main idea.

▶ Read aloud paragraph 1 from the excerpt and think aloud to review that the first sentence can be the main idea. Say something like:

Here's how I use the six steps to find that the main idea is in the first sentence. The key details are that people who climb Everest have climbed other peaks in the Himalayas and other high mountains. The general topic is "who can scale Everest." What's most important is that it's not for beginners but for experienced climbers. The main idea is in the first sentence: "Everest is not a mountain for beginners."

▶ Read aloud paragraph 5 from the excerpt and think aloud to show the main idea can be the last sentence. Say something like:

Using the six steps helps me find the main idea in the last sentence. The key details discuss altitude or height above sea level and that there's less and less oxygen the higher above sea level you climb. The general topic is what happens to the amount of oxygen in the air from sea level to high altitudes. The most important idea is that higher altitudes

(Continued)

229

(Continued)

have less oxygen. The main idea is in the last sentence: "We say the air at high altitudes is 'thin' because it has less oxygen."

❯ Encourage students to ask questions.

Day 2

Guided Practice Using the Six Steps *(30–40 minutes)*

❯ Post and review the six steps for finding main ideas from Day 1.

❯ Organize students into pairs.

❯ Read aloud or have students read the excerpt from *Tales From the Top of the World* for the gist.

❯ Have students partner talk to discuss the gist (5–6 minutes).

❯ Reread out loud or have students reread the excerpt.

❯ Ask students to partner talk to find the main idea of each numbered paragraph (except 1 and 5) using the six steps and write the main ideas in their smart notebooks (20 minutes).

❯ Organize a whole-class discussion and have students share their main ideas; post them. Then invite students to read all the main ideas and suggest one for the entire piece. Here's what a seventh-grade student suggested:

Only experienced, healthy climbers should tackle the challenges of climbing Everest.

Notes to Yourself About Teaching the Lesson

_____

_____

_____

_____

_____

_____

_____

_____

_____

Teaching How to Infer Main Ideas

"Defying Gravity: Mae Jemison"
by Anina Robb

MODEL
LESSON
7.5B

Finding main ideas in the first or last sentence of a paragraph or section of a text is concrete and should precede having students infer to find main ideas.

Before teaching main ideas, preview texts you plan to use to ensure they'll work for finding explicitly stated or inferred main ideas. Partner talk is an effective way for students to discuss and identify explicitly stated or inferred main ideas. A whole-class discussion provides a great way to wrap up a main idea lesson. Ask students to share their main ideas for paragraphs and then identify the main idea for the entire selection.

Materials

"Defying Gravity: Mae Jemison"; smart notebooks

Lesson Guidelines

Preparing Students to Infer the Main Idea *(20–30 minutes)*

Day 1

▶ Review the steps for identifying main ideas. NOTE: In this text, the main idea is not stated in a topic sentence or the last sentence, so students must infer it from details.

1. Read the paragraph.

2. List the details.

3. Use the details to figure out the general topic.

4. What is most important about the topic?

5. Is the main idea in the topic sentence? In the last sentence? If not, use details to infer the main idea.

6. Write the main idea.

▶ Read aloud the first paragraph. Think aloud using the six steps to show how you infer a main idea. Say something like:

> *Here are important details: Mae wondered if she should study science or become a professional dancer. The topic is what Mae should do to realize her dream of studying science and becoming an astronaut. The key details that relate to the topic are that Mae Jemison became a dancer and a scientist and showed that dancing supported space travel and becoming an astronaut. I review this information and infer the main idea: Mae Jemison used what she loved most, dance and science, to become the first African American astronaut.*

▶ Read aloud the second paragraph.

▶ Have students use partner talk and the six steps to find the main idea (10 minutes). Here's what fifth graders said:

> *Even when Mae was in kindergarten, her goal was to be a scientist.*

(Continued)

(Continued)

Day 2

Guided Practice for Inferring Main Ideas *(25–30 minutes)*

▶ Read aloud or have students read the rest of the biography once for the gist and a second time to infer main ideas.

▶ Invite students to use the six steps from Day 1 and partner talk to infer a main idea for each paragraph and jot it in their smart notebooks (15 minutes).

▶ Have a whole-class discussion to discuss main ideas, and then find a main idea for the entire piece. Here's what fifth-grade students suggested:

Doing what you love can help you reach your dream or goal.

Notes to Yourself About Teaching the Lesson

_____

_____

_____

_____

_____

_____

_____

_____

_____

_____

_____

_____

_____

CHAPTER 8

Reflecting on the Process of Read, Talk, Write

B y bringing rich and meaningful talk into your classroom, you give students daily opportunities to clarify what they do and don't understand about a lesson or text. Equally important are the energy and intensity for exchanging ideas that occur during literary conversations as, together, students journey toward deeper understandings of texts they read and view.

Four Key Skills

In addition to helping students develop independence in learning as well as analytical and critical thinking, literary conversations boost students' thinking fluency—their ability to evaluate and analyze fiction and nonfiction using guiding and/or interpretive questions. As students engage in meaningful conversations about literature, they also develop four skills they'll use in college, in their career, and while living a productive and fulfilling life in the 21st century and beyond.

Skill 1: Taking Risks

Holding regular literary conversations and valuing students' voices in talk and writing creates an environment in which students feel comfortable making mistakes. Students who can take risks without fear of criticism from their teacher and peers can become better problem solvers and creative thinkers. In a comfortable and safe space, they can learn from their mistakes.

Skill 2: Creativity

When students engage in a variety of literary conversations, they think about and create ideas in their own unique way. Students who think creatively have multiple ways to interpret a story, painting, video, or movie.

Skill 3: Empathy

Through literary conversations, students can step into the shoes of literary characters and persons, understand life as they do, empathize with their problems, and share their joys. Literary conversations about fiction and nonfiction as well as watching videos and movies about other cultures and ways of life other than their own develop and expand students' ability to empathize with peers and adults. Literary conversations in culturally diverse classrooms lead to empathy—understanding and respecting cultural differences and developing social responsibility.

Skill 4: The Ability to Negotiate

Engaging in literary conversations fosters independence in learning as students and teachers become co-decision makers for setting deadline dates, suggesting projects, writing topics, developing test questions, and deciding on the amount of assigned homework.

Keep in mind that it's the wrestling with controversy—different ideas—that unlocks creative thinking and respect for diverse but valid interpretations. And all the time, students move back and forth between talk and writing in their smart notebooks about what they know, ideas they challenge and disagree with, and questions that challenge them to rethink and revise positions.

Writing Is Knowing

Writing is equivalent to understanding and knowing, and it reveals learners' level of comprehension because they can write (and visualize) only what they truly understand (Atwell, 2014, Murray, 1984). Writing invites students to transform literary conversations—oral texts—into written texts so they can see what they think and know. Literary conversations combined with writing in smart notebooks are students' forays into a world of ideas and information they can sort, refine, adjust, and ultimately come to know what they think and believe.

So let's get started and consider how to integrate literary conversations and writing in smart notebooks into your present curriculum.

Making the Changeover

Red flags wave in teachers' minds and anxiety develops at the thought of adding more to an already packed curriculum. I'm not asking you to do that—talking and brief writing about reading can be easily integrated into your daily lesson plans. What I am asking you to do is shift your teaching emphasis to a student-centered approach that reaches all learners. I recommend that you slowly reduce the amount of writing in workbooks and completing novel unit packets that students do in favor of the authentic writing that occurs in smart notebooks and on the reproducibles in this book. So let's have a go.

Take the First Steps

Begin with what you can try quickly and easily.

- Use turn-and-talk, a 2- to 3-minute discussion between students, during and after daily read-alouds and mini-lessons.
- After they turn-and-talk, invite students to jot ideas in smart notebooks once during a read-aloud and once after a lesson. Experience will quickly let you know when the writing is beneficial and when it's fine to skip it.

Climb That First Hill

When your students are comfortable with turn-and-talk and short writing forays, become a facilitator of student-led literary discussions.

▶ Continue using turn-and-talk, and introduce whole-class discussions during which students will learn about the give-and-take of ideas, experience that it's okay to revise and refine responses, and practice being active listeners.

▶ Practice developing guiding questions that start whole-class discussions; teach students how to create them as well.

▶ Practice summarizing key points halfway through a whole-class discussion and to close it.

▶ After a whole-class discussion, invite students to jot key ideas discussed in their smart notebooks, reactions to the discussion, lingering questions, and so on.

Start Slowly Down the Hill

Build on your momentum by engaging students in two to four whole-class discussions. As soon as students can lead and participate productively in these discussions, introduce partner talk.

▶ Explain that partner talk can take 5–15 minutes and provides students with the time they need to have in-depth discussions.

▶ Use partner talk when you want to make sure all students participate, as it's easier to risk sharing ideas with one person.

Continue Moving Along the Path

Introduce students to in-the-head conversations.

▶ Show students the benefits and importance of in-the-head conversations.

▶ Use bookmarks to monitor what students think about as they read.

▶ Review students' bookmarks so you can support their application of specific strategies and help them always think and question while reading.

Picture Your Destination

Now that you're confident of your students' abilities to participate in high-level literary conversations independently, it's time to introduce small-group discussions. Since membership in small groups changes throughout the school year, students can develop relationships with classmates they might not interact with by choice. Differentiation can be a part of small-group discussions when students read materials they can learn from at their instructional reading levels. In small groups, students can become careful listeners and develop social skills as they contribute their ideas and evaluate and comment on the ideas of peers.

▶ Start with the fishbowl technique so students both experience and observe what happens in small-group, student-led discussions.

▶ Accept that you cannot monitor four to five groups, so settle for listening to two different groups each time they meet.

▶ Use the Teacher's Checklist for Assessing Small-Group Discussions (page 48) to monitor groups you don't observe.

Make a Teaching Investment With Student Paybacks

Sometimes the pressure we teachers feel to improve test scores by using premade test-prep practice and worksheet packets can reduce students' engagement with tasks and their motivation to work hard to achieve. Literary conversations and writing about reading are authentic tasks that research has shown improves learning in all subjects.

Remember the research on fourth-grade teachers that Allington, Johnston, and Pollack Day (2002) conducted, concluding that it's the teacher who makes the difference in students' learning and achievement. You are the key to developing highly literate students! And when you make learning meaningful for students with literary conversations and writing about reading, you keep students at the center of instruction, inspiring them to read, think, talk, and write—and continually improve their reading and writing expertise!

List of Top-Notch Books for Instruction and Class Libraries

Books by Priscilla Cummings

A Face First, New York, NY: Puffin, 2003

Blindsided, New York, NY: Puffin, 2011

Cheating for the Chicken Man, New York, NY: Dutton, 2015

Journey Back, New York, NY: Puffin, 2013

Red Kayak, New York, NY: Puffin, 2006

Books by Kathleen Krull

Albert Einstein (Giants of Science), New York, NY: Puffin, 2009

Charles Darwin (Giants of Science), New York, NY: Puffin, 2010

Isaac Newton (Giants of Science), New York, NY: Puffin, 2008

Leonardo DaVinci (Giants of Science), New York, NY: Puffin, 2005

Lives of Extraordinary Women: Rulers, Rebels (and What the Neighbors Thought), Boston, MA: HMH Books for Young Children, 2013

Lives of the Explorers: Discoveries, Disasters (and What the Neighbors Thought), Boston, MA: HMH Books for Young Readers, 2014

Lives of the Presidents: Fame, Shame (and What the Neighbors Thought), Boston, MA: HMH Books for Young Readers, 2011

Lives of the Scientists: Experiments, Explosions (and What the Neighbors Thought), Boston, MA: HMH Books for Young Readers, 2013

Marie Curie (Giants of Science), New York, NY: Puffin, 2009

Wilma Unlimited: How Wilma Rudolph Became the Fastest Woman in the World, Scholastic, 2000

Books by Seymour Simon

Bones: Our Skeletal System, HarperCollins, 2000

Earthquakes, Smithsonian, 2011

Coral Reefs, HarperCollins, 2013

Global Warming, HarperCollins, 2013

Hurricanes, HarperCollins, 2007

Lightning, HarperCollins, 2006

Our Solar System, HarperCollins, 2014

The Brain: All About Our Nervous System and More!, HarperCollins, 2006

The Heart: All About Our Circulatory System and More!, Harper Collins, 2006

The Moon, Simon and Schuster, 2003

Bibliography of Professional Materials

Adler, M., & Rougle, E. (2005). *Guilding literacy through classroom discussion*. New York, NY: Scholastic.

Allington, R. L. (n.d.). The six t's of effective elementary literacy instruction. Retrieved from http://www.readingrockets.org/article/six-ts-effective-elementary-literacy-instruction

Allington, R. L., Johnston, P. H., & Pollack Day, J. (2002). Exemplary fourth-grade teachers. *Language Arts, 79,* 462–466.

Anderson, R. C., Pichert, J. W., & Shirey, L. L. (1983). Effects of the reader's schema at different points in time. *Journal of Educational Psychology, 75,* 271–279.

Applebee, A. N., & Langer, J. A. (2011a). *The national study of writing instruction: Methods and procedures*. Albany, NY: CELA.

Applebee, A. N., & Langer, J. A. (2011b). A snapshot of writing instruction in middle schools and high school. *English Journal, 100*(6), 14–27. Retrieved from http://www.english.illinois.edu/-people-/faculty/debaron/402/402readings/hswriting.pdf

Applebee, A. N., Langer, J. A., Nystrand, M., & Gamoran, A. (2003). Discussion-based approaches to developing understanding: Classroom instruction and student performance in middle and high school English. *American Educational Research Journal, 40,* 685–730.

Atwell, N. (2014). In the middle: A lifetime of learning about writing, reading, and adolescents (3rd ed.). Portsmouth, NH: Heinemann.

Baca, J. S., & Lent, R. C. (2010). *Adolescents on the edge: Stories and lessons to transform learning*. Portsmouth, NH: Heinemann.

Cazden, C. B. (2001). *Classroom discourse: The language of teaching and learning*. Portsmouth, NH: Heinemann.

Coles, R. (1990). *The call of stories: Teaching and the moral imagination*. Boston, MA: Houghton Mifflin.

Daniels, H. (1994). *Literature circles: Voice and choice in the student-centered classroom*. York, ME: Stenhouse.

Daniels, H. (2002). *Literature circles: Voice and choice in book clubs and reading groups* (2nd ed.). Portland, ME: Stenhouse.

Daniels, H. (2006). What's the next big thing with literature circles? *Voices From the Middle, 13*(4), 10–15.

Davis, B. H., Resta, V., Davis, L. L., & Comacho, A. (2001). Novice teachers learn about literature circles through action research. *Journal of Reading Education, 26,* 1–6.

Dewitz, P., & Graves, M. F. (2014). Teaching for transfer in the Common Core era. *The Reading Teacher, 68*(2), 149–158.

Duke, N., Caughlan, S., Juzwik, M., & Martin, N. (2011). *Reading and writing genre with a purpose in K–8 classrooms*. Portsmouth, NH: Heinemann.

Duke, N., & Purcell-Gates, V. (2003). Genres at home and at school: Bridging the known to the new. *The Reading Teacher, 57*(1), 30–37.

Fassler, J. (2016, March 1). Can writing be both true and beautiful? *The Atlantic*. Retrieved from http://www.theatlantic.com

Fisher, D., Brozo, W. G., Frey, N., & Ivey, G. (2007). *50 content area strategies for adolescent literacy*. Upper Saddle River, NJ: Merrill/Prentice Hall.

Fletcher, R. (2015). *Making nonfiction from scratch*. Portland, ME: Stenhouse.

Gillespie, A., & Graham, S. (2011, Winter). Evidence-based practices for teaching writing. *Better: Evidence-Based Education*. Retrieved from http://education.jhu.edu/PD/newhorizons/Better

Goodman, Y. (2014). Value students' voices, open your classroom doors, and speak up! *Council Chronicle, 24*(1), 18–20.

Graham, S., & Harris, K. R. (2016). A path to better writing: Evidence-based practices in the classroom. *The Reading Teacher, 69,* 359–365.

Graham, S., Harris, K. R., & Santangelo, T. (2015). Research-based writing practices and the Common Core: Meta-analysis and meta-synthesis. *Elementary School Journal, 115,* 498–522.

Graham, S., & Hebert, M. (2010). *Writing to read: Evidence for how writing can improve reading.* New York, NY: Carnegie Corporation and Alliance for Excellent Education.

Greene, R. (2013). 5 key strategies for ELL instruction. Retrieved from https://www.teaching channel.org/blog/2013/10/25/strategies-for-ell-instruction

Hall, L. A. (2012). Moving out of silence: Helping struggling readers find their voices in text-based discussions. *Reading & Writing Quarterly, 28,* 307–332.

Harre, R., & Gillett, G. (1994). *The discursive mind.* Thousand Oaks, CA: SAGE.

Heitin, L. (2015). NAEP score drop spurs speculation. *Education Week, 35*(11), 1, 12.

Hoch, M. L. (2015). *Talking to learn: A formative experiment on constructing meaning through collaborative classroom interactions* (Doctoral dissertation). Retrieved from http://digital-commons.nl.edu

Johnston, P. H. (2004). *Choice words.* Portland, ME: Stenhouse.

Johnston, P. (2012). *Opening minds: Using language to change lives.* Portland, ME: Stenhouse.

Johnston, P., Ivey, G., & Faulkner, A. (2011). Talking in class: Remembering what is important about classroom talk. *The Reading Teacher, 65,* 232–237.

Kucan, L., & Palincsar, A. S. (2013). *Comprehension instruction through text-based discussion.* Newark, DE: International Reading Association.

Langer, J. A., & Close, E. (2001). *Improving literary understanding through classroom conversation.* Albany, NY: National Research Center on English Learning & Achievement.

Lent, R. C. (2007). *Literacy learning communities: A guide for creating sustainable change in secondary schools.* Portsmouth, NH: Heinemann.

Maloch, B. (2002). Scaffolding student talk: One teacher's role in literature discussion groups. *Reading Research Quarterly, 37,* 94–112.

McTighe, J., & Wiggins, G. (2013). *Essential questions: Opening doors to student understanding.* Alexandria, VA: Association for Supervision and Curriculum Development.

Murray, D. (1984). *Write to learn.* New York, NY: Holt, Rinehart and Winston.

Newkirk, T. (2014). *Minds made for stories: How we really read and write informational and persuasive texts.* Portsmouth, NH: Heinemann.

Nichols, M. (2006). *Comprehension through conversation: The power of purposeful talk in the reading workshop.* Portsmouth, NH: Heinemann.

Paterson, K. (1989). *The spying heart: More thoughts on reading and writing books for children.* New York, NY: Lodestar Books.

Paterson, K. (2010. May). The power of story. *Sojourners.* Available from https://sojo.net/magazine

Pearson, P. D. Roehler, L. R., Dole, J. A., & Duffy, G. G. (1992). Developing expertise in reading comprehension. In S. H. Samuels & A. Farstrup (Eds.), *What research has to say about reading instruction* (2nd ed., pp. 145–199). Newark, DE: International Reading Association.

Probst, R. E. (2007). Tom Sawyer, teaching, and talking. In K. Beers, R. E. Probst, & L. Rief (Eds.), *Adolescent literacy: Turning promise into practice* (pp. 43–60). Portsmouth, NH: Heinemann.

Robb, L. (2010). *Teaching reading in middle school.* New York, NY: Scholastic.

Robb, L. (2013). *Unlocking complex texts: A systematic framework for building adolescents' comprehension.* New York, NY: Scholastic.

Robb, L. (2016). *The reading intervention toolkit.* Huntington Beach, CA: Shell Education.

Rosenblatt, L. (1978). *The reader, the text, the poem: The transactional theory of the literary work.* Carbondale: Southern Illinois University Press.

Rothstein, D., & Santana, L. (2011). Teaching students to ask their own questions. *Harvard Education Letter, 27*(5), 1–2.

Superville, D. R. (2015). Students take too many redundant tests, study finds. *Education Week, 35*(10), 1, 9.

Tyler, R. W. (2013). *Basic principles of curriculum and instruction.* Chicago, IL: Chicago University Press.

Vygotsky, L. S. (1978). *Mind in society* (M. Cole, V. John-Steiner, S. Scribner, & U. E. Souberman, Eds. & Trans.). Cambridge, MA: Harvard University Press.

Wiggins, G. (2007, November 15). What is an essential question? *Big Ideas*. Retrieved from http://www.authenticeducation.org/ae_bigideas

Wiggins, G. (2012, March 13). Everything you know about curriculum may be wrong. Really. Retrieved from https://grantwiggins.wordpress.com/2012/03/13/everything-you-know-about-curriculum-may-be-wrong-really

Wilhelm, J. (2007). *Engaging readers and writers with inquiry*. New York, NY: Scholastic.

Wilhelm, J. (2012). *Improving comprehension with think-aloud strategies: Modeling what good readers do* (Rev. ed.). New York, NY: Scholastic.

Wozniak, C. L. (2010). Reading and talking about books: A critical foundation for intervention. *Voices From the Middle, 19*(2), 17–21.

Zimmerman, S., & Keene, E. O. (2007). *Mosaic of thought*. Portsmouth, NH: Heinemann.

Zinsser, W. (1993). *Writing to learn*. New York, NY: Harper & Row.

Zwiers, J., & Crawford, M. (2011). *Academic conversations: Classroom talk that fosters critical thinking and content understanding*. Portland, ME: Stenhouse.

Children's Literature Cited

Anonymous. (1803). Lord Randall. Retrieved from http://poetry.about.com/od/poemsbytitlel/l/bllordrandall.htm

Athans, S. (2013). *Tales from the top of the world: Climbing Mount Everest with Pete Athans*. Minneapolis, MN: Millbrook Press.

Athans, S. K. (2014). *Secrets of the sky caves: Danger and discovery on Nepal's Mustang Cliffs*. Minneapolis, MN: Millbrook Press.

Bartoletti, S. C. (2015). *Terrible typhoid Mary: A true story of the deadliest cook in America*. Boston, MA: HMH Books for Young Readers.

Bauer, J. (2008). *Peeled*. New York, NY: Penguin Books for Young Readers.

Bridges, R. (1999). *Through my eyes*. New York, NY: Scholastic.

Brown, D. (2015). *Drowned city: Hurricane Katrina and New Orleans*. Boston, MA: HMH Books for Young Readers.

Coolidge, O. (1997). Phaethon, son of Apollo. In *Greek Myths*. Boston, MA: Houghton Mifflin.

Cummings, P. (2006). *Red kayak*. New York, NY: Penguin.

Cummings, P. (2016). Snow day. In L. Robb, *Read, talk, write: 35 lessons that teach students to analyze fiction and nonfiction*. Thousand Oaks, CA: Corwin.

Curtis, C. P. (1999). *Bud, not buddy*. Austin, TX: Holt, Rinehart and Winston.

D'Aulaire, I., & D'Aulaire, E. P. (1992). *D'Aulaires' book of Greek myths*. New York, NY: Delacorte Press.

Homer. (1998). *The iliad*. New York, NY: Penguin Classics.

Homer. (2006). *The odyssey*. New York, NY: Penguin Classics.

Jackson, S. (1948). *The lottery*. Retrieved from https://sites.middlebury.edu/individualandthesociety/files/2010/09/jackson_lottery.pdf

Krull, K. (2016). How Ada Lovelace leaped into history. In L. Robb, *Read, talk, write: 35 lessons that teach students to analyze fiction and nonfiction*. Thousand Oaks, CA: Corwin.

Krull, K. (2016). Isaac Newton and the day he discovered the rainbow. In L. Robb, *Read, talk, write: 35 lessons that teach students to analyze fiction and nonfiction*. Thousand Oaks, CA: Corwin.

Lowry, L. (1993). *The giver*. Boston, MA: Houghton Mifflin.

Muñoz Ryan, P. (1998). *Riding freedom*. New York, NY: Scholastic.

Muñoz Ryan, P. (2012). *Esperanza rising*. New York, NY: Scholastic.

Paterson, K. (2004). *Lyddie*. New York, NY: Puffin.

Reynolds, P. N. (2000). *Shiloh*. New York, NY: Simon & Schuster.

Robb A. C. (2016). Coming clean. In L. Robb, *Read, talk, write: 35 lessons that teach students to analyze fiction and nonfiction*. Thousand Oaks, CA: Corwin.

Robb, A. C. (2016). Defying gravity: Mae Jemison. In L. Robb, *Read, talk, write: 35 lessons that teach students to analyze fiction and nonfiction*. Thousand Oaks, CA: Corwin.

Robb, A. C. (2016). Hoops tryouts. In L. Robb, *Read, talk, write: 35 lessons that teach students to analyze fiction and nonfiction*. Thousand Oaks, CA: Corwin.

Rowling, J. K. (1997–2007). *The Harry Potter series.* New York, NY: Scholastic.

Ryan, P. M. (1999). *Riding freedom.* New York, NY: Scholastic.

Ryan, P. M. (2002). *Esperanza rising.* New York, NY: Scholastic.

Simon, S. (2016). New horizons in space. In L. Robb, *Read, talk, write: 35 lessons that teach students to analyze fiction and nonfiction.* Thousand Oaks, CA: Corwin.

Southey, R. (1837). God's judgment on a wicked bishop. Retrieved from https://tspace.library.utoronto.ca/html/1807/4350/poem1956.html

Index

Notes

Notes

Notes

Notes

CORWIN LITERACY | BECAUSE ALL TEACHERS ARE LEADERS

Laura Robb
On helping students tackle the biggest barrier of complex texts

Nancy Akhavan
On top-notch nonfiction lessons and texts for maximizing students' content-area understanding

Douglas Fisher, Nancy Frey, & John Hattie
On identifying the instructional routines that have the biggest impact on student learning

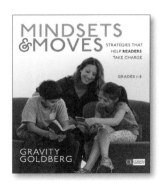

Gravity Goldberg
On the ownership crisis, and how teachers can step back so readers can step forward

Leslie Blauman
On writing about reading in a clear, concrete process in fiction and nonfiction

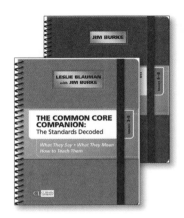

Leslie Blauman & Jim Burke
On what the standards really say, really mean, and how to put them into action, Grades 3–5 & 6–8

Bring Laura Robb to your school or district!

Areas of Expertise

- Vocabulary building
- Teacher motivation
- Reading-writing connection
- Productive talk about reading
- Assessment and feedback

Laura can help you

- Uncover how children learn words and the relationship of reading and writing to word learning
- Teach students to talk about reading in ways that enable them to write about a text with depth
- Help students identify main ideas and themes and infer with fiction and informational texts
- Support students' comprehension, recall, and the ability to connect ideas among texts
- Teach students steps that allow them to pinpoint themes and main ideas

About the Consultant

Laura Robb taught for more than 40 years in Grades 4–8. She presently coaches teachers in vocabulary, productive talk about reading, deep reading and writing, and teacher motivation. Laura has written more than 25 books for teachers; her books for Corwin Literacy include *Vocabulary Is Comprehension* (2014) and *Read, Talk, Write* (October 2016). Laura has been recently named as NCTE's recipient of the 2016 Richard W. Halle Award for Outstanding Middle Level Educator.

WHAT YOUR COLLEAGUES SAY

"Teachers welcome her because she respects where they are and is always positive when she's working on change that benefits students."

—Kip Tuttle, Assistant Principal
Johnson Williams Middle School, Berryville, VA

"Laura gave all the teachers in the room a new approach to looking at their teaching and how it affects student learning. Teachers went away feeling empowered to improve the reading comprehension of their students. Laura is truly a master teacher with a passion for teaching that is contagious."

—Wanda Killips, Achievement Initiatives
Literacy Coordinator
Washtenaw Intermediate School District, Ann Arbor, MI

"Laura is a 'teacher's consultant,' sharing real experiences—including trials that confront teachers every day. She demonstrates authentic strategies that she has used directly with students in classroom settings almost daily throughout her years of consulting. Laura knows what works with struggling readers and writers because of her commitment to 'always remain a teacher.'"

—Sarah Armstrong
Assistant Superintendent of Instruction
Staunton City School, Staunton, VA

To bring Laura Robb to your school,
call 800-831-6640

N169H3

CORWIN HAS ONE MISSION: to enhance education through intentional professional learning.

We build long-term relationships with our authors, educators, clients, and associations who partner with us to develop and continuously improve the best evidence-based practices that establish and support lifelong learning.